English in Action

4

Barbara H. Foley

Elizabeth R. Neblett

THOMSON

HEINLE

Australia • Canada • Mexico • Singapore • Spain • United Kingdom • United States

THOMSON

HEINLE

English in Action 4
by Barbara H. Foley and Elizabeth R. Neblett

Publisher, Adult and Academic ESL: *James W. Brown*
Senior Acquisitions Editor: *Sherrise Roehr*
Director of Development: *Anita Raducanu*
Developmental Editor: *Sarah Barnicle*
Editorial Assistant: *Audra Longert*
Marketing Manager: *Eric Bredenberg*
Director, Global ESL Training & Development: *Evelyn Nelson*
Senior Production Editor: *Maryellen Killeen*
Senior Print Buyer: *Mary Beth Hennebury*
Project Manager: *Tünde A. Dewey*
Compositor: *Pre-Press Co., Inc.*

Text Printer/Binder: *C&C Offset Printing CO., Ltd.*
Text Designer: *Sue Gerould*
Cover Designer: *Gina Petti/Rotunda Design House*
Cover Art: *Zita Asbaghi*
Unit Opener Art: *Zita Asbaghi*
Photo Researcher: *Jill Engebretson*
Photography Manager: *Sheri Blaney*
Illustrators: *Scott MacNeill; Ray Medici; Glen Giron, Roger Acaya, Ibarra Cristostomo, Leo Cultura of Raketshop Design Studio, Philippines*

Printed in China
7 8 9 10   09 08 07

For more information contact Heinle, 25 Thomson Place, Boston, Massachusetts 02210 USA, or you can visit our Internet site at http://www.heinle.com

For permission to use material from this text or product contact us:
Tel: 1-800-730-2214
Fax: 1-800-730-2215
Web: www.thomsonrights.com

Library of Congress Cataloging-in-Publication Data

Foley, Barbara H.
    English in action I / Barbara H. Foley, Elizabeth R. Neblett.
        p. cm.
    The new grammar in action. ©1998.
    ISBN-13:978-0-8384-2830-6
    ISBN-10:0-8384-2830-4
        1. English language—Textbooks for foreign speakers.
    2. English language—Grammar—Problems, exercises, etc. I. Neblett, Elizabeth R. II. Foley, Barbara H. New grammar in action. III. Title.

    PE1128 .F559 2002
    428.2'4—dc21   2002017281

International Division List

United States
Thomson Heinle
25 Thomson Place
Boston, MA 02210-1202
United States
Tel: 617-289-7700
Fax: 617-289-7844

Asia
Thomson Learning
(A division of Thomson Asia Pte Ltd)
Tel: 65-6410-1200
Fax: 65-6410-1208

Australia / New Zealand
Nelson / Thomson Learning
Tel: 61-(0)3-9685-4111
Fax: 61-(0)3-9685-4199

Brazil
Thomson Learning Ltda.
Tel: (5511) 36659931
Fax: (55 11) 36659901

Canada
Nelson / Thomson Learning
Tel: 416-752-9448
Fax: 416-750-8102

Japan
Thomson Learning
(A division of Thomson Corporation K.K.)
Tel: 81-3-3511-4390
Fax: 81-3-3511-4391

Korea
Thomson Learning
Tel: 82-2-322-4926
Fax: 82-2-322-4927

Latin America
Thomson Learning
Tel: (52 55) 1500-6000
Fax: (52 55) 1500-6019
Toll Free: 01-800-800-3768

Spain / Portugal
Paraninfo / Thomson Learning
Tel: 34-(0)91-446-3350
Fax: 34-(0)91-466-6218

Taiwan
Thomson Learning
Tel: 886-2-2558-0569
Fax: 866-2-2558-0360

UK / Europe / Middle East / Africa
Thomson Learning
Tel: 44-20-7067-2500
Fax: 44-20-7067-2600

Acknowledgments

We would like to acknowledge the many individuals who helped, encouraged, and supported us during the writing and production of this series. In keeping with an open-ended format, we would like to offer a matching exercise. Please be advised, there is more than one correct "match" for each person. Thank you all!

Jim Brown

Eric Bredenberg

Sherrise Roehr

Maryellen Killeen

Audra Longert

Sarah Barnicle

Tünde A. Dewey

All the Heinle sales reps

The students at Union County College

The faculty and staff at UCC

Our families

- for your creative eye for art and design.
- for your enthusiasm and support.
- for your support, patience, and humor while guiding this project.
- for your faith in the authors.
- for your smiles and your stories.
- for your encouragement, comments, and suggestions.
- for putting up with us!
- for your understanding of the needs of teachers and programs.
- for your keeping us all on schedule.
- for your help with research.

The authors and publisher would like to thank the following reviewers and consultants:

Linda Boice
Elk Grove Unified School District, Sacramento, CA

Rocio Castiblanco
Seminole Community College, Sanford, FL

Jared Erfle
Antelope Valley High School, Lancaster, CA

Rob Kustusch
Triton Community College, River Grove, IL

Patricia Long
Old Marshall Adult School, Sacramento, CA

Kathleen Newton
New York City Board of Education, Bronx, NY

Alberto Panizo
Miami-Dade Community College, Miami, FL

Eric Rosenbaum
Bronx Community College, Bronx, NY

Michaela Safadi
South Gate Community, South Gate, CA

Armando Valdez
Huantes Learning and Leadership Development Center, San Antonio, TX

Contents

Contents

To the Teacher

Many years ago, I attended an ESL workshop in which the presenter asked a full audience, "How many of you read the **To the Teacher** at the front of the text?" Two participants raised their hands. Since that time, I have begged my publishers to release me from this responsibility, but have always been overruled.

As a teacher, you can form a clear first impression of this book. Flip through the pages. Will the format appeal to your students? Look carefully through the table of contents. Are most of the structures and contexts that your program has established included in the text? Thumb slowly through a few units. Will the activities and exercises, the support, the pace be appropriate for your students? If you wish, you can even read the rest of **To the Teacher** below.

English in Action is a four-level core language series for ESL/EFL students. It is a comprehensive revision and expansion of *The New Grammar in Action*. The popularity of the original edition delighted us, but we heard the same requests over and over: "Please include more readings and pronunciation," and "Could you add a workbook?" In planning the revision, our publisher threw budgetary concerns to the wind and decided to produce a four color, redesigned version. The revision also allowed us, the authors, an opportunity to refine the text. We are writers, but we are also teachers. We wrote a unit, then immediately tried it out in the classroom. Activities, tasks, and exercises were added, deleted, and changed in an ongoing process. Students provided daily and helpful feedback.

This fourth book is designed for high-intermediate level students. Students at this level already have good control of the basic tenses and structures of English, and can apply them in meaningful communication. The units in this text gradually expand the students ability to use more complex language to discuss high-interest, universal topics.

Units are completely contextualized and gradually build around topics such as leisure activities, sports, job performance, business and industry, and country music. Throughout each unit, there is support in the form of clearly illustrated situations, vocabulary boxes, grammar notes, and examples. As students move through the unit, they engage in situations and activities in which they can see, hear, and practice English. Listening is a key component of the unit. Initially, students are asked to listen for the structures in individual sentences. As the unit develops, the structure is incorporated into dialogues and longer narratives. The pronunciation section additionally reinforces the structure, providing practice with elements such as contractions and tense contrast.

Active Grammar

Each unit opens with an illustration or photo and discussion questions to introduce the topic and to draw the students into the unit. The following six to seven pages of exercises integrate the context and the new grammar. As students progress through this section, they will find a wide variety of both controlled and open-ended activities. There are pictures to discuss, opportunities to interview their teachers and their classmates, conversations to develop, stories to enjoy, dictations for students to present to a partner, and even a few traditional fill-in-the-blank exercises to complete. We encourage you to try them all.

The directions are clear and there are examples for each exercise. Artwork and photos illustrate the context clearly. For many of the exercises, the entire class will be working together with your direction and explanations. Other exercises show a pairwork icon 🔵🔵 —students can try these with a partner or in a small group. You should walk around the classroom, listening to students and answering questions. With this variety of activities, this book should appeal to every learning style.

Pronunciation

Within the **Active Grammar** section is an exercise that focuses on pronunciation. These are specific pronunciation points that complement the grammar or vocabulary of the lesson, such as contractions, syllable stress, reductions, and linking.

The Big Picture

This is our favorite section, integrating listening, vocabulary, and structure. A large, lively picture shows a particular setting or situation, such as obtaining a driver's license, speaking to a school counselor, or gossiping about friends. After listening to a short narrative or conversation, students answer questions, fill in information, review structures, or complete conversations.

Reading

In the fourth book, the reading feature has been significantly expanded and is now a two-page spread. Each reading is longer and is directly related to the context of the unit. There are new vocabulary words and structures that have never been introduced. Teachers can help ESL readers learn that understanding meaning is primary. It is not necessary to master or look up every new word. Each reading is followed by exercises that help to develop reading skills, such as scanning for information, reading for details, taking a multiple choice test, understanding vocabulary in context, and understanding the pros and cons of a topic.

Writing Our Stories

The writing section has also grown into a two-page format. The first page provides a writing model and some form of brainstorming, such as a checklist, discussion questions, fill-in sentences, or a chart. The writing tasks usually ask students to write about their lives or opinions. For variety, other units may direct student to describe a process, write street directions, or write an opinion letter. Each section also practices or develops one writing point, such as using transition words, using quotation marks, or organizing ideas before writing. Several teachers have told us about the creative ways they share student writing, including publishing student magazines, designing a class Web page, and displaying stories and photos taken by their students. Included at the end of the writing page is a new feature entitled *Looking at the Internet*. If your school has a computer lab or students have Internet access at home, these short suggestions will provide a starting point for follow-up activities on the Internet.

Practicing on Your Own

Some teachers ask students to do the exercises in class. Another suggestion for homework is the audio component. Ask students to listen to it three or four more times, reviewing the vocabulary and the exercises they did in class. Our students tell us that they often write the story from the Big Picture as a dictation activity.

Grammar Summary

Some teachers wanted this summary at the beginning of the unit; others were pleased to see it at the end. Use this section if and when you wish. Some students like to see the grammar up front, having a clear map of the developing grammar. We have found, though, that many of our students at the intermediate level are confused with long grammar explanations at the beginning of a unit. There are small grammar charts as needed throughout the unit. The ending summary brings them together.

I am sure we will be revising the text again in three or four years. We will be gathering your input during that time. You can always e-mail us at www.heinle.com with your comments, complaints, and suggestions.

Liz and I both work at Union County College in Elizabeth, New Jersey. We teach at the Institute for Intensive English, a large English as a Second Language program. Students from over 70 different countries study in our classes. Between us, Liz and I have been teaching at the college for over 40 years! When Liz isn't writing, she spends her time traveling, taking pictures, and watching her favorite baseball team, the New York Mets. Liz took many of the pictures in the texts, for which our students eagerly posed. In the warm weather, I can't start my day without a 15- or 20-mile bicycle ride. My idea of a good time always involves the outdoors: hiking, kayaking, or simply working in my garden.

Barbara H. Foley
Elizabeth R. Neblett

Photo Credits

This page constitutes an extension of the copyright page. We have made every effort to trace the ownership of all copyrighted material and to secure permission from copyright holders. In the event of any question arising as to the use of any material, we will be pleased to make the necessary corrections in future printings. Thanks are due to the following authors, publishers, and agents for permission to use the material indicated.

All photos courtesy of Elizabeth R. Neblett with the following exceptions:

p. 2, top left: Phil Borden/Photo Edit
p. 2, top right: Liba Taylor/CORBIS
p. 2, bottom left: Table Mesa Prod./Index Stock Imagery
p. 2, bottom right: Jan Halaska/Index Stock Imagery
p. 4, bottom left: Phil Cantor/Index Stock Imagery
p. 4, bottom right: Tom Carter/Index Stock Imagery
p. 30, left: Roman Soumar/CORBIS
p. 30, right: Kevin Fleming/CORBIS
p. 36, top: Bill Lai/Index Stock Imagery
p. 36, bottom: IT STOCK INT'L/Index Stock Imagery
p. 62: Grant Heilman Photography/Index Stock Imagery
p. 63: Patricia Barry Levy/Index Stock Imagery
p. 75: Table Mesa Prod./Index Stock Imagery
p. 76, top right: Stephen Umahtete/Index Stock Imagery
p. 76, center left: Bud Freund/Index Stock Imagery
p. 76, center middle: Martin Fox/Index Stock Imagery
p. 76, center right: Raenne Rubenstein/Index Stock Imagery
p. 76, bottom left: Antonio Mendoza/Index Stock Imagery
p. 76, bottom middle: Yvette Cardoza/Index Stock Imagery
p. 76, bottom right: PhotoDisc/Getty Images
p. 88: Joe Bator/CORBIS
p. 107, top left: Sam Greenwood/IPN/AURORA
p. 107, top right: Duomo/CORBIS
p. 107, bottom left: Reuters NewMedia Inc./CORBIS
p. 107, bottom right: Reuters NewMedia Inc./CORBIS
p. 110: AFP/CORBIS
p. 116: Owen Franken/CORBIS
p. 127, center: Frank Siteman/Index Stock Imagery
p. 127, bottom: Ellen Skye/Index Stock Imagery
p. 128: Christian Peacock/Index Stock Imagery
p. 132, top left: Royalty-Free/CORBIS
p. 132, top right: Stephen Derr/Getty Images
p. 132, bottom left: Orion Press/Index Stock Imagery
p. 132, bottom right: Morton Beebe/CORBIS
p. 138: Kareem Black/Stone
p. 142: Digital Vision/Getty Images
p. 158, top: Andy Sacks/Stone
p. 158, center: Ted Wilcox/Index Stock Imagery

p. 158, bottom: Rob Lewine/CORBIS
p. 190: Dennis Brack/IPN/AURORA
p. 192, top: Myrleen Cate/Index Stock Imagery
p. 192, bottom: PhotoDisc/Getty Images
p. 206, top: Royalty-Free/CORBIS
p. 212, top left: PhotoDisc Green/Getty Images
p. 212, top second from left: John Luke/Index Stock Imagery
p. 212, top second from right: photolibrary.com/Index Stock Imagery
p. 212, top right: GOLDBERG DIEGO/CORBIS SYGMA
p. 212, center left: Spencer Grant/Photo Edit
p. 212, center second from left: Eyewire/ Getty Images
p. 212, center second from right: Allen Fredrickson/Index Stock Imagery
p. 212, center right: PhotoDisc/Getty Images
p. 212, bottom left: Randy Lorentzen/Index Stock Imagery
p. 212, bottom second from left: PhotoDisc/Getty Images
p. 212, bottom second from right: Ryan McVay/PhotoDisc/Getty Images
p. 212, bottom right: Courtesy of Dieceland
p. 214: Bettmann/CORBIS
p. 228, top left: Jeff Albertson/CORBIS
p. 228, top middle: AP Photo/Hussein Malla
p. 228, top right: Reuters NewMedia Inc./CORBIS
p. 228, center left: AFP/CORBIS
p. 228, center middle: AP Photo/Reed Saxon
p. 228, center right: Manuel Zambrana/ CORBIS
p. 228, bottom left: Reuters NewMedia Inc./ CORBIS
p. 228, bottom middle: AFP/CORBIS
p. 228, bottom right: Abilio Lope/CORBIS
p. 230: Reuters NewMedia Inc./CORBIS
p. 233, top: Reuters NewMedia Inc./CORBIS
p. 233, bottom: Reuters NewMedia Inc./CORBIS
p. 236, top left: AP Photo/John Russell
p. 236, top right: David McNew/Getty Images
p. 236, bottom: AP Photo/Mark Humphrey
p. 238, top: Evan Agostini/Liaison/Getty Images
p. 238, bottom: AP Photo/Luca Bruno

Education

A. High school. Which picture best describes a high school classroom in your native country?

1.

2.

3.

4.

B. Schools are different from country to country. Answer or complete the following statements about high school in your native country. Then, compare your answers with a group of classmates.

1. The school year begins in _____ and ends in _____.
   (month)   (month)

2. The school day begins at ___:___ and ends at ___:___.
   (time)   (time)

3. School **meets / does not meet** on Saturdays.

4. High school students **choose / do not choose** some of their own courses.

5. Students **type / do not type** their papers for their classes.

6. All students **study / do not study** the same subjects in school.

7. Students **study / do not study** with students of the same ability.

8. The teacher **changes / does not change** classrooms.

9. The teacher **gives / does not give** oral tests.

10. Most students **work / do not work** after school.

11. Families **pay / do not pay** for books.

12. Students **wear / do not wear** uniforms.

13. There **are / are not** after-school clubs for the students.

14. What kind of tests do high school students take in your native country? Circle all correct answers.

    a. multiple-choice

    b. true / false statements

    c. essay (write compositions)

    d. oral tests

    e. other _____

15. High school students are required to study the following subjects. Circle all correct answers.

    biology   foreign languages

    physics   literature

    chemistry   typing

    psychology   secretarial skills

    sociology   physical education

    cooking   woodworking

    art   sewing

    music theory   mathematics

    musical instruments   Latin or Greek

    drama   geography

    history   government

A. Look at the pictures. In your notebook, write as many sentences as you can in ten minutes. Compare your sentences with a partner.

A student *is talking* on the telephone.

Be Statements		
I	am am not	
He She	is is not	studying.
We You They	are are not	

1.

2.

3.

4.

B. *Yes/No questions.* Answer the questions about the photos in Exercise A.

Photo 1

1. Are the students taking a test?

2. Are they working together?

3. Are they listening to a tape?

Yes/No Questions		
Am	I	
Is	he she	studying?
Are	we you they the students	

Photo 2

4. Are some students working on computers?

5. Are they working in the library?

6. Are they using the printer right now?

Photo 3

7. Is the young woman concentrating on her work?

8. Is the student behind her talking?

9. Are the students taking a test?

Photo 4

10. Are the students playing soccer?

11. Is everyone wearing a uniform?

12. Are they playing in bad weather?

Write two more questions about the photos. Ask a classmate your questions.

13. _____?

14. _____?

C. Your classroom. Look around your classroom and answer the following questions. Write your answers on the blanks.

Present Continuous Tense: *Who**		
Who	is	studying English? reading a novel? writing an essay? talking to you?
Who takes the *singular* verb form.		

Present Continuous Tense: *Wh-* Questions			
What Where Why	am	I	studying? reading? writing? doing?
	is	he she	
	are	we you they the students	

1. Who is sitting next to the door? _____

2. Who is talking to the teacher? _____

3. What are the students doing? _____

4. Where is the teacher standing? _____

5. Who is wearing a suit? _____

6. What are you wearing? _____

7. Where are you sitting? _____

8. What language are the students speaking? _____

A. Your school. Complete the sentences about your school. Use the verbs in parentheses.

I We You They	study do not study don't study	English.
He She	studies does not study doesn't study	

1. I _____ (study) in the morning.

2. Students _____ (pay) tuition for classes.

3. A typical student _____ (go) to classes every day.

4. Students _____ (live) in dormitories.

5. I _____ (call) my teachers by their first names.

6. Our school _____ (have) good computer facilities.

7. There _____ (be) a library in my school building.

8. The school _____ (offer) after-school activities for the students.

9. Teachers _____ (give) many tests during the semester.

10. My classmates and I _____ (take) class trips.

B. Adverbs of frequency. Talk about your teacher, using adverbs of frequency.

> speak loudly
> My teacher *almost always* **speaks** loudly.

1. speak softly

2. (be) on time

3. give quizzes

4. use a tape recorder

5. write on the chalkboard

6. give spelling tests

7. show videos

8. use red ink to correct our papers

9. give homework on the weekends

10. _____

> Place adverbs of frequency **after** the verb *to be* and **before** all other verbs.
>
> He **is** *never* on time.
> He *always* **comes** to school late.
>
> | always | 100% |
> | usually | 90% |
> | frequently
often | 70–80% |
> | sometimes | 50% |
> | rarely
seldom | 10–20% |
> | almost never | 5% |
> | never | 0% |

C. Study habits. How do you study? Read each statement and check (✓) *always*, *sometimes*, or *never* about your own study habits. Then, listen to your partner describe his or her study habits.

	Me			My partner		
	always	sometimes	never	always	sometimes	never
1. I do my homework.						
2. My homework is neat.						
3. I ask questions in class.						
4. I read a newspaper in English.						
5. I try to speak English outside of class.						
6. I ask for extra help when I need it.						
7. I speak English in class.						
8. I study in a quiet place.						
9. I study an hour or more a day.						
10. I get to class on time.						

Complete these sentences about you and your partner. Use the adverbs in parentheses.

1. My partner _____. (always)

2. I _____. (always)

3. My partner _____. (never)

4. I _____. (sometimes)

5. My partner _____. (sometimes)

6. My partner and I _____. (always)

7. My partner and I _____. (sometimes)

8. My partner and I _____. (never)

A. Roommates. Sophie and Lizzy are college roommates, but they have very different schedules, habits, and interests. Listen to the two roommates, complete the questions with "Do" or "Does," and then, answer the questions.

Yes/No Questions

Do you work?	Yes, I **do**.	No, I **don't**.
Does she work?	Yes, she **does**.	No, she **doesn't**.

1. ___Does___ Sophie take all of her courses in the morning? ___Yes, she does___.
2. _____ you take your English class in the morning? _____.
3. _____ Sophie keep her side of the room neat? _____.
4. _____ Sophie get up early? _____.
5. _____ you get up early? _____.
6. _____ Sophie study in the room? _____.
7. _____ you study in your bedroom? _____.
8. _____ Lizzy take all of her courses in the afternoon? _____.
9. _____ Lizzy keep her side of the room neat? _____.
10. _____ you keep your home neat? _____.
11. _____ Lizzy hand in her papers on time? _____.
12. _____ you hand in your homework on time? _____.

Are you more like Sophie or Lizzy? Explain.

B. **Wh- questions.** Work with a small group of students. Interview each other about your daily schedules and habits.

Wh- Questions			
What Where Why How	do	I we you they	study English? work?
How much	does	he she	eat?

Question	You	Partner 1	Partner 2
1. What time do you get up?			
2. What do you eat for breakfast?			
3. What time do you leave your home?			
4. Where do you eat lunch?			
5. How do you get to school?			
6. How long does it take?			
7. What hours do you work?			
Write three more questions to ask your partners.			
8.			
9.			
10.			

C. Pronunciation: Linking: /do you/. Listen and repeat each question.

1. What do you do?
2. Where do you work?
3. When do you get up?
4. How do you get home?
5. Where do you live?

6. Why do you study here?
7. What do you do on weekends?
8. When do you do your homework?
9. What time do you leave for school?
10. Where do you shop for food?

Practice asking and answering the questions with a partner.

D. Who questions. Answer these *who* questions about students in your class.

1. Who always arrives on time?
2. Who wears a baseball cap to class?
3. Who often arrives late?
4. Who always has a pencil sharpener?
5. Who goes to work after class?

Who- Questions		
Who	studies goes lives	English? to work? close to school?

Write three more Who questions.

Active Grammar: Nonaction Verbs

The following verbs usually take the simple present form.

appear	have	like	own	sound
believe	hear	look	prefer	taste
feel	hope	love	see	understand
hate	know	need	smell	want

A. Ask and answer the questions with a partner. Use the simple present form.

Do you believe in UFOs?
No, I don't.

1.
you / believe in

2.
you / like

3.
which / you / prefer

4.
your teacher / have
(bird/turtle/cat)

5.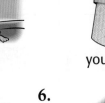
you / own

6.
FRANCE
your teacher /
know how to speak

7.
what kind of /
your teacher / have

8.
you / want to / take

B. The Student Center.

Use the cues to write sentences about the students in the picture on page 10. Many of the verbs are nonaction verbs. Write the sentences in your notebook.

1. Students / like / to meet / student center
2. They / need to relax / between classes
3. Two students / play / video games
4. Some students / study / together
5. Some music / play / in the background
6. Students / hope to pass / their exams
7. They / (not) hear / the noise
8. Lana and her boyfriend / watch / TV
9. Bill / look / bored
10. He / (not) like / daytime dramas
11. Two students / buy / pizza
12. The pizza / smell / good

C. The chess players. Read this story about the two chess players in the picture. Fill in the correct form of the verbs in parentheses. Use the present continuous or the simple present form.

Lee and Jamal are juniors in the computer science department. They (always / study) _____always study_____ hard, but every afternoon, they (take) _____ a break to play their favorite game — chess. Lee and Jamal both (belong) _____ to their school's chess team, and they (be) _____ two of the best players on the team. They (prefer) _____ the chess team to any of the other teams at the school. Lee and Jamal (play) _____ chess almost every afternoon at 3:00 in the Student Center. It's 4:00 now, and as usual, they (play) _____ a game. Right now, Lee (think) _____ about his next move, and Jamal (smile) _____ because he (know) _____ that he is about to win this game. Even though the Student Center is noisy, and students (talk) _____, music (play) _____, and the TV (be) _____ on, Lee and Jamal (hear / not) _____ the noise. They (concentrate) _____ on their game. Lee (want) _____ to win because Jamal has won their last two games.

Write a paragraph in your notebook about another student or students in the picture. Use the simple present and the present continuous forms.

The Big Picture: The University of Texas at San Antonio

A. Listen to the description of this university. As you listen, complete and (circle) the correct information.

1. Location: urban   suburban   rural

2. Degrees: two-year   four-year

3. Type of university: public   private

4. Number of full-time students: _____ Part-time students: _____

   Graduate students: _____

5. Number of faculty: _____

6. Application fee: $ _____ Online application available: Yes   No

7. Recommendations for high school applicants:

   _____ years of English   _____ years of a social science

   _____ years of a foreign language   _____ years of a lab science

   _____ years of math   _____ years of fine arts

8. Minimum SAT score required: _____

9. Three possible majors: _____ _____ _____

10. Number of computers on campus: _____

11. Services available for students:

    a. _____ for students who need extra help

    b. Examples of student activities: _____

    c. Programs for freshman students: _____

B. True or False. Read each statement. Then, (circle) T for *True*, or F for *False*.

1. The University of Texas at San Antonio is a four-year university.   T   F
2. U.T.S.A. is a private university.   T   F
3. The main campus is in downtown San Antonio.   T   F
4. The university has two campuses.   T   F
5. U.T.S.A. has a graduate school.   T   F
6. U.T.S.A. employs about eight hundred faculty.   T   F
7. Students pay $15 for the application fee.   T   F
8. The university recommends two years of a foreign language.   T   F
9. The university recommends a lab science.   T   F
10. Most future students take the SAT.   T   F

C. Listen and write short answers to the questions about the university.

Yes, it is.	Yes, there is.	Yes, it does.	Yes, they do.	Yes, there are.
No, it isn't.	No, there isn't.	No, it doesn't.	No, they don't.	No, there aren't.

1. _____   6. _____
2. _____   7. _____
3. _____   8. _____
4. _____   9. _____
5. _____   10. _____

D. University life. Fill in the correct present tense form of the verbs in parentheses.

1. The University of Texas at San Antonio _____has_____ (have) many campuses.
2. About 9,400 students _____ (study) at U.T.S.A.
3. Future students _____ (pay) an application fee.
4. Students _____ (take) standardized tests before they go to U.T.S.A.
5. U.T.S.A. _____ (have) a learning center with tutors and counselors for the students.
6. The university _____ (give) the students free career counseling.
7. Students _____ (go) to the employment service when they _____ (need) to find jobs.

A. Before You Read. Scan the reading to find the answers to the following questions.

1. Where is the school located?
2. Does N.J.I.T. have a graduate school?
3. How much is the application fee?
4. What is the minimum SAT score?
5. What is the minimum grade average that N.J.I.T. accepts?
6. Does the school offer evening classes?

New Jersey Institute of Technology, or ① N.J.I.T., is located in Newark, New Jersey, ten miles from New York City. It is a four-year public university and technical college. The college offers bachelor's degrees in science, engineering, computer science, architecture, management, technology, and many other fields. N.J.I.T. also has graduate programs in many subjects, in addition to programs for educators. Ninety percent of the students come from New Jersey and 70 percent commute between home and school. The average age of entering students is eighteen.

In addition to an application, students who are interested in applying to N.J.I.T. need to prepare the following materials for admission:

- the application fee; in 2002, the fee was $35
- an official high school transcript of grades
- official SAT (Scholastic Aptitude Test) scores; the recommended score is 1000 total or above
- for non-U.S. citizens, students must send a photocopy of visas or permanent resident cards

The college requires all interested students to have a strong math and science background. Students must have a B average, four years of high school English and two years of science, including one of a laboratory science. Different majors, such as management, require three years of high school mathematics.

N.J.I.T. has a comprehensive program available for students who prefer distance learning, or learning on their computers. N.J.I.T. offers bachelor and master degree programs and graduate certificates online. Students who want to take a course or two without getting a degree or certificate can take noncredit courses online. Online courses are designed for students who need flexibility. Maybe they have demanding jobs that require overtime during the week, so they cannot take classes during the week. Maybe they have an odd work shift. Some students may have disabilities, which do not permit them to go to classes in person. Distance-learning courses may be right for these types of students who want to study from home.

In addition to day classes and online classes, N.J.I.T. offers many evening and early morning classes. It also has a summer session. Students who need extra preparation get special instruction, English as a second language classes, or tutoring. Like many other colleges today, a computer is a necessary requirement for N.J.I.T.'s students, so N.J.I.T. gives each student a personal computer for use until graduation. The students can purchase computers at graduation.

On campus, there are dormitories for the students who prefer to live on campus or who live too far away to commute. There is also fraternity housing for students who are members of one of the fraternities. For fun, students can participate in the many clubs and organizations that N.J.I.T. offers. For example, there are organizations for the variety of ethnic groups such as the Korean Student Association, the Polish Student Association, and the Caribbean Student Organization. For students interested in media, there is a theater group, a radio station, and a newspaper. Finally, there are many organizations for students in different majors.

If you think you might be interested in this college, look at its Web site on the Internet for more information.

B. Reading for details. Number and <u>underline</u> the answers to the following questions.

1. Where is N.J.I.T. located?

2. What percent of the students commute to the campus?

3. What is the average age of entering students?

4. What is the minimum SAT score for applicants?

5. Does the college accept foreign students?

6. Do all majors require three years of high school mathematics?

7. What is *distance learning*?

8. Who takes online courses?

9. Why do students like online courses?

10. What type of services are available for students who need more preparation?

11. What kinds of clubs and organizations can students join?

Writing Our Stories: My Schedule

A. Read.

I am a student at N.J.I.T. This is my freshman year, and my major is computer engineering. I have a very full schedule.

I'm taking six courses this semester. On Mondays, Wednesdays, and Fridays I have Introduction to Computer Science from 9:00 to 9:50. Then, I go to English class until 10:50. We read literature and write papers. At 11:00, I go to Calculus II. (I took calculus in high school, so I received credit for Calculus I.) At 12:00, I have a physical education class. I play soccer in that class. Finally, I have a lunch break at 1:00. After lunch I have my freshman seminar. This course helps freshman students adjust to their first year in college. We talk about how to take notes and how to arrange our time so that we can do all of our work. We also talk about social life on campus. Tuesdays and Thursdays are my light days. I only have one class—history—at 10:00. Then, I'm free for the rest of the day, so I have time to work part-time at my uncle's store. I work from 12:00 to 6:00, and I also work on weekends. I do my homework in the evening.

Tarsem

B. In your notebook, describe your weekly school schedule and your classes. Try to answer the following questions in your description:

- What school do you attend?
- Are your classes difficult, easy, or just right?
- What's your favorite class? Why?
- When and where do you study? How many hours do you study a week?
- What kind of tests do you have?
- Do you like your school? Why or why not?

C. Such as. Complete each sentence with appropriate examples.

> *Such as* introduces examples. When you write a paragraph, it is important to include examples. Give two or three examples after *such as.*
>
> The university offers many fine arts majors *such as* art history and studio art.
> Some colleges *such as* junior colleges and community colleges offer two year programs.

1. My classmates come from different countries such as

   _____, _____,

   and _____.

2. In our English class, we are studying many things such as

   _____ and _____.

3. Computers are useful for many things such as _____

   and _____.

4. A medical student has to study subjects such as _____

   and _____.

5. Languages such as _____ and

   _____ are difficult to learn.

D. Edit. There is one <u>underlined</u> mistake in each sentence. Correct each mistake.

1. The Division of Physical Education <u>offer</u> many recreational programs.

2. N.J.I.T. <u>is develop</u> many programs to attract women and minority students to engineering and the sciences.

3. U.T.S.A.'s campuses <u>provides</u> opportunities for many students.

4. Some students <u>are preferring</u> to study from their own homes, using computers.

5. What kind of exams <u>students usually take</u>?

6. The students <u>leave rarely</u> their classes without a homework assignment.

 Looking at the Internet

Most colleges and universities have Web sites that describe their programs, activities, and admission procedures. Their URLs (Internet addresses) end in **.edu**, which stands for education. Here are two examples: New York University's URL is www.nyu.edu. The University of Texas at San Antonio's URL is www.utsa.edu. Click on **Search** and enter the name of a college or university that interests you.

A. Complete this story. Use the simple present or the present continuous tense.

Joe is the manager of the student center, and this is his twentieth year
working there. Joe _____ (know) the names of almost
all of the students who _____ (visit) the center every
day. He _____ (like) to talk to the students, and he
_____ (miss) them during vacations.

Today is the beginning of final exams, so the student center _____
(negative–be) as busy as usual. A few students _____
(talk) in a corner, soft music _____ (play), and a group
of students _____ (discuss) a final project. Many
students _____ (study) in the library this week and
_____ (type) their papers in the computer centers.
Today, Joe _____ (prepare) some special treats for the
students because he _____ (understand) that exam
time is very stressful. The students _____ (negative–have)
a lot of free time during exam weeks, and they _____
(miss–often) their meals at the dining hall. It's 11:30 P.M., and Joe
_____ (make) some cookies, and pizzas _____
(bake) in the ovens. The center _____ (smell) wonderful.
Students _____ (look) up from their books and
_____ (get) ready to take a study break.

B. In your notebook, write 10 questions about the story.

Does Joe know the names of almost all of the students?   Yes, he does.
Are some students talking?   Yes, they are.

Grammar Summary

▶ **1. Present continuous tense**

   a. Use the present continuous to talk about an action that is happening now.

   b. Time expressions such as *now, right now, at the moment,* and *at this moment* are often used with the present continuous.

Are you **using** the computer?	No, I**'m not.** I**'m talking** on the phone.
Is she **buying** her books?	Yes, she **is.**
What **are** you **doing**?	I **am studying.**
Who **is drinking** a cup of coffee?	The students **are.**
Where **are** they **studying**?	They **are studying** in the library.
Why **is** he **talking** to the counselor?	He **is talking** to the counselor about a course.

▶ **2. Simple present tense**

   a. Use the simple present tense to describe a routine, a schedule, or a repeated action.

   b. These time expressions are often used with the simple present tense:

every day	**on the weekends**	**in the summer**
every year	**on Mondays**	**in the fall**

Do you **study** in the morning?	Yes, I **do.**	No, I **do not.**
Do the students **speak** English in class?	Yes, they **do.**	No, they **do not.**
Does she **work** part-time?	Yes, she **does.**	No, she **does not.**
Does he **take** any science courses?	Yes, he **does.**	No, he **does not.**
Where **do** you **study**?	I **study** in the library.	
How often **do** they **speak** English?	They **always speak** English.	
When **does** she **work**?	She **works** three evenings a week.	
How much **does** it **cost**?	It **costs** $250 per course.	

▶ **3.** *Who* **questions**   *Who* takes a singular verb form.

Who **speaks** English in class?	I do.
Who **arrives** on time?	All of the students do.
Who **has** an extra pencil?	She does.

▶ **4. Adverbs of frequency**

Place adverbs of frequency **after** the verb *to be,* but **before** all other verbs.

They **are always** on time.	He **always arrives** late.

▶ **5. Nonaction verbs**   Nonaction verbs usually take the present tense form.

This class is easy. I **know** all the answers.

She's studying hard because she **wants** to do well on the exam.

The students **like** the class because it is interesting and fun.

Colonial Times
(1607–1776)

A. Colonial America. Look at the map of colonial America and answer the questions.

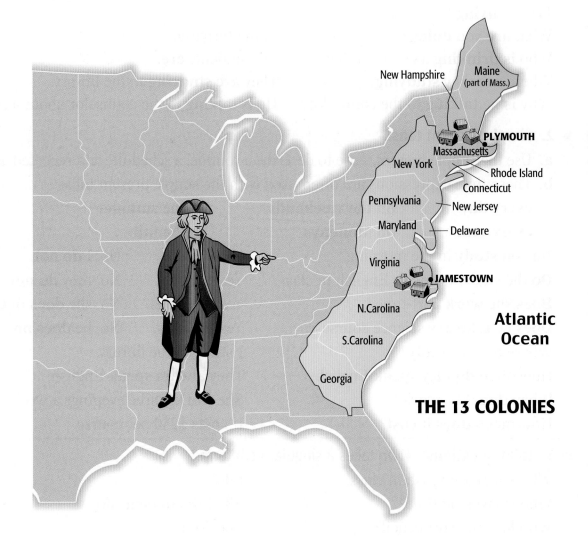

THE 13 COLONIES

1. What is a colony?
2. Who is a colonist?
3. How many original colonies were there in the United States?
4. What country were the colonists from?
5. Which colony was the farthest south?
6. What ocean bordered the colonies to the east?
7. Where was the colony of Jamestown?
8. Where was the colony of Plymouth?

Active Grammar: Past Tense

A. Read about the first English settlements in the United States.

The colonial period in the United States **lasted** from 1607 to 1776. Most early colonists **were** men and women from England who **decided** to start a new life in the United States. The colonists **settled** along the eastern coast of what is now the United States, from Georgia to New Hampshire. Many people **made** the difficult trip across the Atlantic Ocean to find religious freedom. Other people **came** for political freedom. The new country **offered** other families the opportunity to own land and to earn a living in farming, trade, or fishing.

The first settlements **were** small and life **was** very difficult. In 1607, three shiploads with 105 settlers **arrived** in what is now Virginia and **started** the colony of Jamestown. Life **was** difficult in the new land and over half the settlers **died** in the first two years from the cold, disease, and lack of food. The colonists **learned** about tobacco and smoking from Native Americans and **discovered** that tobacco **grew** well in Virginia. The tobacco crop finally **gave** the colonists a way to earn money as pipe smoking **became** popular in Europe.

In 1620, another settlement **began** in Plymouth, in the state that is now Massachusetts. In England, everyone **had** to practice the same religion. The Pilgrims **wanted** religious freedom. More than 100 men, women, and children **made** the long trip across the Atlantic Ocean on the *Mayflower*. Unfortunately, they **landed** in America in late November and **did not have** time to plant crops. The Wampanoag Indians **helped** them through the winter. Even though the Indians **showed** them how to hunt and fish, half the settlers **died** that first winter. In the spring, the Indians **gave** them seeds of native plants and **showed** the Pilgrims how to plant corn, beans, and squash. The Pilgrim settlement **survived** and **grew** slowly.

B. Answer these questions using the past tense.

1. When was the colonial period in the history of the United States?
2. What country were most early colonists from?
3. Why did people come to the new land?
4. What part of the United States did the first colonists settle in?
5. Why was life so difficult in the colonies?
6. Were the colonists the first people in the United States?
7. How did the people in Jamestown finally earn a living?
8. Where did the Pilgrims land?
9. Why did they come to the new land?
10. Who helped them through the first winter?
11. How did they help them?
12. About 100 men, women, and children landed in Plymouth. How many were alive one year later?

☀ Colonial Life

A. Look at the pairs of pictures and listen to the comparison between life in colonial times and life today.

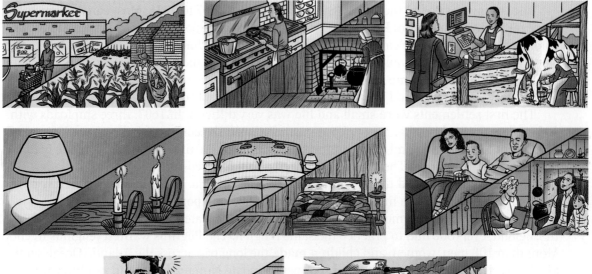

B. Look at each picture. Describe life in colonial America.

C. Write the past tense forms of these verbs.

Regular verbs

call	_____	talk	_____
cook	_____	travel	_____
milk	_____	use	_____
play	_____	watch	_____

Irregular verbs*

buy	_____	make	_____
drive	_____	read	_____
go	_____	sleep	_____
grow	_____	write	_____

***Note**: See the chart of irregular verbs on page 273.

D. Complete these sentences about life in Colonial America. Write a past tense verb from Exercise C.

1. People _____didn't go_____ to supermarkets.
2. They _____ their own food.
3. People _____ over open fires.
4. They _____ stoves.
5. People _____ their own cows.
6. They _____ milk at the supermarket.
7. Families _____ candles for light.
8. People _____ on mattresses.
9. At night, families _____ TV.
10. They _____ and _____ games.
11. People _____ one another on the telephone.
12. They _____ letters to one another.
13. People _____ by horse and wagon.
14. They _____ cars.

E. Ask and answer these questions about your first year in the United States.

1. When did you arrive in the United States?
2. How did you travel here?
3. Why did you come to the United States?
4. What did you bring with you?
5. Who did you live with at first?
6. Did you speak any English?
7. When did you begin to study at this school?
8. Where was your first job?
9. How did you find your first job?
10. Was your first year in the United States difficult?

F. What's wrong with this picture? There are 16 things wrong with this picture. In a group of two or three students, see how many you can find. Check your answers on page 35.

> Children **didn't play** with toy trucks.
> House **didn't have** air conditioners.

 Past Tense: *Be*

I He/She It	was	difficult.
You We They	were	young.

There	was	no kitchen.
There	were	few schools.

A. Was/Were. Complete these sentences with *was* or *were*.

1. Life _____ very difficult for the first settlers in the New World.

2. The first homes _____ small buildings made of wood and mud.

3. There _____ no kitchen in the house.

4. There _____ no bathroom, either. There _____ a small outhouse in the back.

5. Windows _____ small because no glass _____ available.

6. The first settlers _____ (negative) farmers or hunters, so they _____ often hungry.

7. At first, there _____ few schools in the colonies.

8. Many girls _____ married by the age of 16.

9. The newspaper _____ an important source of information.

10. By 1776 the population of the colonies _____ over three million.

B. Now and then The sentences in the first column tell about life today. Use the information in the second column to talk about life in the late 1700s.

The president is _____ .
The first president was George Washington.

Today

1. The president is _____ .
2. The president's salary is $400,000 a year.
3. The capital is in Washington, D.C.
4. There are fifty states.
5. The largest state is Alaska.
6. The population is about 280 million.
7. The average family size is three people.
8. Life expectancy is about 77.
9. Cars are the main form of transportation.
10. The largest city is New York.

1790

1. George Washington
2. $25,000
3. New York
4. thirteen states
5. Virginia
6. about four million
7. eight people
8. 32
9. horses and wagons
10. Philadelphia

Used to

 **A. Pronunciation: *Used to*.** Listen and repeat.

1. Today, people drive cars. In colonial times, they used to drive horses and wagons.
2. Today, people cook on stoves. They used to cook over open fires.
3. Today, people buy food in supermarkets. They used to grow their own food.
4. Today, people take medicine when they are sick. In colonial times, they used to take herbs.
5. Today, people write e-mails to their friends. They used to write letters.

B. Talk about life in colonial times using *used to*. Read each sentence about life today. Use the vocabulary box to talk about life in colonial America. Be careful of your pronunciation.

wooden mugs	candlelight	one-room schoolhouses
read to each other	cloaks	spoons and their fingers
long dresses	almost everyone	leather boots

1. Today, girls wear jeans or dresses or skirts.
   In colonial times, girls used to wear long dresses.
2. Today, people wear coats in the winter.
3. Today, people eat with forks, knives, and spoons.
4. Today, people drink from glasses.
5. Today, most children study in large public schools.
6. Today, most families watch TV at night.
7. Today, children wear sneakers.
8. Today, people read by electric lights.
9. Today, some people go to church every Sunday, but others never go.

cloak

wooden mug

C. Complete these sentences about life in your country. Then, read your sentences to a partner.

1. When I lived in _____, I used to _____.
2. My family and I used to _____ every summer.
3. My friends and I used to _____ on Saturday nights.
4. I used to _____ TV _____ hours a day.
5. I _____ typical foods such as _____ and _____.
6. I never used to _____.

☀ Past Tense Questions

Where When	did	I you she he we they	work? live? play?

🔊 **A. Interview.** Listen to Eric speak about his childhood in Peru. Complete the questions. Then, ask and answer the questions with a partner.

1. Where _did he grow up_ ? (grow up)

2. How many brothers and sisters _____? (have)

3. Where _____? (live)

4. What _____ his family _____? (own)

5. How _____ to school? (get)

6. What _____ after school? (do)

7. What _____ in the summer? (do)

8. _____ on vacation? (go)

9. Where _____ sometimes _____ in the summer? (go)

10. What _____ his grandmother always _____? (make)

👥 **B. Ask your partner about his/her childhood. Use these cues.**

1. Where / grow up?

2. have a big family?

3. How many brothers and sisters / have?

4. live / in the city?

5. How / get to school?

6. like school?

7. What / do / after school?

8. spend time / grandparents?

9. go on vacation?

10. study English in school?

11. play a sport?

12. work when you were in high school?

The Big Picture: Benjamin Franklin

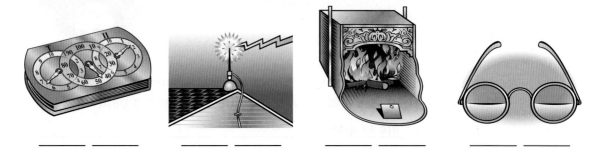

A. Listen. Which invention is each sentence describing? Write the number of the correct sentence under each invention.

_____ _____   _____ _____   _____ _____   _____ _____

B. Note taking. Listen and complete this outline about the life of Benjamin Franklin.

A. Early life

1. Born in _____ on _____

2. Attended school for _____ years

3. Trained to become a _____

4. Moved to _____

5. Opened a _____

B. Franklin helped to improve life in the city of Philadelphia.

1. Started the first _____

2. Helped to organize the first _____

3. Served as _____ and set up _____

4. Convinced city officials to pave the _____

C. Four inventions

1. _____

2. _____

3. _____

4. _____

D. Contributions as a leader

1. Signed the Declaration of _____ and the Constitution.

2. Served as minister to _____

E. Death

1. Died on _____

C. Look at your outline and answer these questions.

1. Where was Benjamin Franklin born?
2. How long did he attend school?
3. What trade did he learn?
4. What city did he move to?
5. What business did he open?
6. What service did Franklin help to start?
7. How else did he help the city of Philadelphia?
8. What did he invent to measure distance?
9. What important documents did he sign?
10. When did he die?

D. Complete. Write the questions to the answers.

1. When _____?
   He was born in 1706.

2. _____ from high school?
   No, he didn't graduate from high school.

3. How many languages _____?
   He spoke five languages.

4. What _____ when he was postmaster?
   He set up the mail routes for the city.

5. What _____ with?
   He experimented with electricity.

E. Proverbs. Listen and complete these famous sayings of Ben Franklin. Then, discuss their meanings.

1. A penny _____ is a penny _____.
2. Time is _____.
3. Early to _____, early to rise, makes a man
   _____, _____, and wise.
4. Fish and _____ smell in three days.
5. An _____ a day keeps the _____
   away.
6. Well done is _____ than well said.
7. There was never a good _____ or a bad
   _____.

A. Before You Read.

This house is a reproduction of a pilgrim home from 1627.

Notice the clothing of the woman. She is a museum staff member dressed as a colonial woman from 1627.

Name one historic area in your country. Why is it famous?

Match each vocabulary word with its definition.

_____ **1.** archaeologist   **a.** an item or piece of item from the past. It is often dug from the ground.

_____ **2.** artifact   **b.** a copy or reproduction of an original item

_____ **3.** replica   **c.** a person who studies artifacts to learn about the past

Plymouth, Massachusetts, about forty-five miles south of Boston, is a popular tourist attraction. Plymouth was the site of the second colony in America. On November 11, 1620, a small ship of English settlers landed there and started a colony, looking for a better life and religious freedom.

One of the most popular attractions in Plymouth is Plimouth Plantation. Plimouth Plantation was the dream of Henry Hornblower II. When he was a boy, Hornblower read and heard stories about the pilgrims who lived in Plymouth. When he was older, he worked with archaeologists in Plymouth for many years. They found more than 350,000 artifacts from the time of the colonists. At the same time, historians studied pilgrims' journals and writings to learn about the lives of the early colonists. In 1945, Henry Hornblower's father gave $20,00 to the Pilgrim Society, allowing it to begin the reconstruction of Plimouth Plantation. The Society made reproductions of the clothes, tools, furniture, and houses of the 1620s. The museum opened in 1947, with just one reproduction of a colonial home.

Today, Plimouth Plantation brings to life the original settlement of 1627. It is a living museum of more than twenty homes, shops, and gardens. Visitors can walk through the colonial town where each house on the main street looks exactly like a house of the 1620s. The village is not just a collection of exhibits to look at. The museum staff are the "colonists," and they dress, talk, and carry out the activities of colonial America. They wear the same kinds of clothes that the Plymouth colonists used to wear. The women cook in open fireplaces and follow colonial recipes. The men raise the same vegetables and care for the same kinds of animals that were present in colonial times. Everyone uses the same kinds of tools that the pilgrims used almost four hundred years ago. When visitors talk to the "colonists," the "colonists" answer with the same English and the same accent that the colonists had.

Over the years, Plimouth Plantation has expanded. Today, it is also possible to visit a replica of the Mayflower II, the ship the pilgrims sailed from England to Plymouth. There is also a reproduction of a Wampanoag homesite, which introduces visitors to the life of the Indian tribe who helped the colonists survive their first years in their new country. A trip to Plimouth Plantation is a trip back in history.

B. Check your comprehension.

1. When did the pilgrims come to America?

2. Was Plymouth, Massachusetts, the first colony?

3. Why did the pilgrims leave England?

4. How did Henry Hornblower find out about the pilgrims at Plymouth?

5. What did archaeologists find at the site?

6. How did historians reproduce the plantation?

7. Why is Plimouth Plantation a living museum?

8. What do the "colonists" wear?

9. What do the "colonists" do?

10. What language do the "colonists" speak?

11. What else can visitors at Plimouth Plantation see?

C. Place these events in chronological order.

_____ **a.** Reconstruction of the settlement began.

_____ **b.** The museum expanded to include the larger settlement.

_____ **c.** Henry Hornblower I donated money to begin the reconstruction of Plymouth

_____ **d.** Visitors can now see a replica of the *Mayflower II* and an Indian homesite.

_____ **e.** The museum with just one building opened to the public.

__1__ **f.** Archaeologists and historians began to study Plymouth.

Writing Our Stories: Growing Up in Bangladesh

A. Read Mahmuda's story about growing up in Bangladesh.

I grew up in Dhaka, the capital of Bangladesh. I was the second oldest of five children. We lived in a small house in a busy area of the city. I smile as I remember growing up in my country.

I started school when I was five years old. In elementary school, I used to walk to school with my brothers and sisters. The classes at our school were large, usually with 50 to 70 students. Boys and girls attended the same classes; however, boys sat on one side of the room and girls sat on the other. The girls wore a blue and white uniform to school. My pants were white and over them I wore a large, comfortable blue shirt called a *camis*. The girls covered their hair with white head scarves.

In high school, I took public transportation to school. Girls attended classes in the morning, from 8:00 to 12:00, and boys attended classes in the afternoon from 12:30 to 4:30. We studied Bengali, our language, and English, Arabic, history, science, geography, and math. Our teachers were very strict. If we talked in class or didn't do our homework, they hit our hands or shoulders with a stick.

The school year began in January and ended in December. We also had a few weeks off in the summer. At that time, my family visited my grandparents, who lived in a small village. They had a large rice paddy. We played, swam in the pond, and ran after the cows and chickens.

After school, we had to be creative in order to entertain ourselves. Like most families, we didn't have a telephone. Until I was in eighth grade, we didn't have a television, either. In the afternoon, I did my homework, helped my mother, took care of my younger brothers and sisters, and played with my girlfriends. We told stories, sewed, jumped rope, and, like students all over the world, gossiped about our teachers and the other students in our class.

Mahmuda

B. Brainstorming.

Before writing, it is helpful to think about your topic. Many writers brainstorm for five or ten minutes, writing down all ideas that come to mind. They don't write sentences, just words and phrases. They then choose several of these ideas to include in their stories.

Before writing, Mahmuda brainstormed for ten minutes. Which of her ideas did she use in her story?

Elementary School	High School	Vacation	Ramadan	After School
walked	tuition	school: Jan to Dec.	Feb. or March	no telephone
50–70 students	bus	summer	celebration	no TV
uniform	girls—a.m.	grandparents	special food	homework
head scarves	boy—p.m.	rice paddy	gifts	help at home
	teachers—strict	play		girlfriends
	sports			

C. My childhood
Brainstorm about your childhood for ten minutes, writing down all ideas that come into your mind. Choose two or three of your ideas and write a composition about growing up.

D. Edit. Find and correct the mistakes.

1. I not live with my parents. I lived with my grandparents.
2. I use to play with my friends after school.
3. Before I went to school, I milk the cow.
4. We didn't had a telephone.
5. When I am eight years old, we moved to the city.
6. What you did after school?
7. After I came home from school, I play soccer with my friends.
8. How old you were when you started school?
9. Did you work when you are in high school?
10. How many brothers and sisters you had?

Looking at the Internet

Historical Sites. Click on **Search.** Enter the name of your state and the phrase "historical sites." You will find the names of several parks, forts, museums, churches, early houses, and other sites in your state with historical significance. Read about one of these places. Tell your class the name of the historical site and show its location on a map of your state. Give the following information.

1. What can you see and do at this site?
2. When is it open?
3. How much is the admission?

Practicing on Your Own

A. Jamestown: The first English settlement. Write the past tense form of the verbs in parentheses.

In January 1607, three small ships _____ (leave) England for America. Four months later, they _____ (arrive) in America. Several of the men on the ship _____ (negative—survive) the long, stormy journey. The men _____ (choose) an area on the James River that is now in the state of Virginia. They _____ (begin) to build a fort. The men _____ (be) "gentlemen" and _____ (negative—be) used to working with their hands. Their purpose in America _____ (be) to hunt for gold and to start a small colony for England.

But there _____ (negative—be) any gold. The winter _____ (come) and there _____ (negative—be) enough food. Many men _____ (get) sick. By the end of the first winter, only forty men _____ (be) still alive.

Over the next three years, more settlers _____ (arrive), but they _____ (negative—be) farmers, so the first few years of the colony _____ (be) very difficult. Disease, starvation, and Native Americans _____ (kill) most of the settlers. Eventually, the colonists _____ (learn) more about farming and the weather. They _____ (make) peace with the Indians. Tobacco, not gold, _____ (produce) the real wealth of the new colony. As the years _____ (go) by, more and more settlers _____ (arrive), and many small towns _____ (grow) along the river.

B. Past questions. Complete these questions about life in colonial times.

1. What _____? Vegetables.
2. Where _____? In wooden houses.
3. What _____? Long dresses.
4. How _____? By horse and wagon.
5. Where _____? On feather beds.
6. What _____ in the winter? Bread and meat.
7. How _____? They read to one another.

Grammar Summary

► **1. Past tense**

We use the simple past tense to talk about actions that happened in the past time.

Regular past verbs end in **-ed**.

The chart of irregular past verbs is on page 273.

► **2. Past time expressions**

yesterday	a few minutes ago	last night	in 1750
the day before yesterday	a few days ago	last week	in 1995
	a few weeks ago	last year	

► **3. Past tense: *be***

Jamestown **was** the first English settlement.

Many settlers **were** very religious.

Was the voyage long and difficult? Yes, it **was**.

Were the settlers farmers? No, they **weren't**.

Where **was** the first settlement? It **was** in Jamestown.

► **4. Past tense verb forms**

Regular verbs	**Irregular verbs**
Colonial people **worked** hard.	Colonial women **wore** long dresses.
They **lived** on farms.	Colonial families **had** gardens.
Families **didn't live** in cities.	Houses **didn't have** bathrooms.
Did children **attend** school?	**Did** children **wear** sneakers?
Yes, they **did**.	No, they **didn't**.
Where **did** colonial people **live**?	When **did** the first colonies **begin**?
They **lived** on farms.	They **began** in the 1600s.

► **5. *Used to*** **Used to** shows habitual or repeated actions in the past.
The action was true in the past, but not any longer.

People **used to milk** their own cows. (Now people buy milk in the supermarket.)

I **used to live** near the beach. (Now I live in the city.)

Answers for Exercise F on page 24.

Note: You should have the same idea, but your sentences may be different.

1. Children didn't play with toy trucks.
2. Houses didn't have air conditioners.
3. People didn't fly helicopters.
4. People didn't smoke cigarettes.
5. Girls didn't wear short skirts.
6. People didn't wear sneakers.
7. Wagons didn't have rubber tires.
8. Farmers didn't use tractors.
9. Streets didn't have traffic lights.
10. Towns didn't have paved streets.
11. Women didn't cook on barbecue grills.
12. People didn't have electricity.
13. There were no TVs.
14. People didn't have portable tape players.
15. People didn't wear wristwatches.
16. Houses didn't have doorbells.

3 Family Matters

A. Marriage and divorce statistics. Read this information about marriage and divorce in the United States. Then, discuss the questions.

- Over two million couples are married each year in the United States.
- The average age at marriage is rising. Currently, the average age at marriage is 26 for women and 29 for men.
- Forty-three percent of first marriages end in divorce within 15 years.
- The older a woman is at marriage, the longer the marriage will last. Teenagers who marry are more likely to get divorced than couples who are older.
- Massachusetts has the lowest divorce rate in the United States. Nevada has the highest divorce rate.
- The divorce process takes about one year.
- Over 75% of women and 80% of men who get divorced remarry within five years.
- Second marriages have a greater chance of failure than first marriages.

1. Were you surprised by any of these statistics?

2. How does this information compare with marriage and divorce in your native country?

Active Grammar: Future Tense

A. The divorce. Read Tom's account of his marriage and divorce. Underline all future tense verbs.

Amy and I got married twelve years ago. At first, we were really happy together, but after a few years, we began to have problems. I don't really know what happened. We went to marriage counselors, we made promises, and then we broke them. We argued about everything. Even though we tried to work things out, we couldn't. Finally, we decided to get a divorce. I'm not worried about Amy or myself because we're adults, but I'm worried about the kids. We have two children, Carly and Jason. Carly is seven; Jason is ten. Amy and I have agreed on joint custody of the children. I'm packing now because I'm going to move to an apartment in the next town. Amy is going to stay here in the house. The children will live with her during the week, and they will live with me on the weekends. They will still go to the same school and be with all their friends. In the summer, they will live with me in July and with Amy in August. That way we can plan vacations and time with the kids.

Amy and I are working on the arrangements with our lawyers. I'm going to pay child support and I'm going to pay alimony for three years. Amy was a homemaker and she stayed home with the children for ten years. She's going to need a job now. Before we got married, she finished one year of college. She'll go back to school part-time and study accounting.

Life is going to be very different for all of us.

Future: *Be + going to* + verb			
Amy Tom	is isn't	going to	find a job.
I	am am not		move.
You We They	are aren't		get a divorce.

Future: *Will*		
I She He We You They	will	find a job. get married. go to school.

B. Answer these questions about Tom and Amy. Try not to look back at the story.

1. How long were Tom and Amy married?
2. How did they try to work out their problems?
3. When is Tom going to leave?
4. Where is he going to live?
5. Who will the children live with?
6. What is joint custody?
7. Where are the children going to live in the summer?
8. How long is Tom going to pay alimony?
9. Does Amy have a job?
10. What is she going to study?
11. How will life be different for this family?

C. **Amy's plans.** Complete these sentences about Amy's plans using the future tense. Some of the sentences are negative.

hire	join	study	be	stay	get
attend	register	cover	✓look	help	start

1. Amy _____is going to look_____ for a job.

2. Amy _____ for college next semester.

3. Amy _____ school part-time.

4. She _____ accounting.

5. She _____ home all day anymore.

6. When the children come home from school, Amy

   _____ at work.

7. Amy _____ a babysitter for the children

   in the afternoon.

8. Amy's mother _____ her when the children are sick

   and when they have a day off from school.

9. Amy _____ medical benefits from Tom's employer

   for one year. After that, his company _____ only

   the children.

10. Amy _____ a group for single parents.

11. She _____ dating if she meets someone special.

D. **Tom's plans.** Tom is going to move this weekend. Use the cues to describe his future plans in the present continuous tense.

Present Continuous: Future Meaning

If a specific time in the future is stated or understood, the present continuous tense can show future meaning.

Tom **is moving** tomorrow.

1. pack / tonight

2. rent a van / this weekend

3. move / Sunday

4. his brother / help him move

5. sign a lease / for a year

6. take / his stereo system

7. keep / the computer

8. buy / new furniture / next week

9. telephone company / install his phone / Monday

10. see / his lawyer / next week

E. My plans. What are your plans after class? What are your plans for tomorrow? Using the present continuous, write your plans on the lines.

_____

_____

_____

_____

F. Find someone who . . . Walk around the room and ask your classmates these questions about their future plans. Use *be + going to* or *will*. Try to find someone who answers *Yes* to an item. Write that student's name on the line.

Are you going to change jobs? No, I'm not. (Continue to ask other students.)

Are you going to change jobs? Yes, I am. (Write that student's name on the line.)

1. get married? _____

2. move? _____

3. visit your native country? _____

4. buy a house? _____

5. see a lawyer? _____

6. attend a wedding? _____

7. change jobs? _____

8. take a vacation? _____

9. start a business? _____

10. graduate from college? _____

Active Grammar: Will—Promises and Predictions

A. Offers to help. You are a helpful person. Offer to help each person. Use the expressions in the box to help you. You will need to use one of the expressions two times.

> Who will take my children to school if it's raining?
> Don't worry. I'll drive them.

introduce you
give you directions
help you
✓ drive them
help you find them
show you how
translate it
check it
change it
give you a ride

1. I don't understand this homework.
2. My car broke down and I don't have a ride to school.
3. I can't find my keys.
4. I don't know how to use my new DVD player.
5. I just moved in and I don't know anyone around here.
6. How do you get to the mall?
7. I wrote this report, but I need someone to read it over for me.
8. I received a letter in English, but I don't understand it.
9. My car has a flat tire.
10. My income taxes are due, but I don't know how to fill out the form.

B. Predictions. Sit in a group and read these predictions about the future of family life in the next 20 years. Check (✓) *Agree* or *Disagree*. Explain the reason for you choice.

	Agree	Disagree
1. Families will have more children.		
2. The number of divorces will increase.		
3. There will be more single mothers.		
4. More women will stay home and take care of their children.		
5. More people will work from home offices.		
6. More men will stay home with their children.		
7. Men will help more with household chores.		
8. Women will receive the same pay as men.		
9. More companies will offer day-care facilities.		
10. More grandparents will live with their children.		

C. Changes. How will life change for each of these people? Make four predictions about each person or couple.

1.

2.

3.

4.

5.

6.

What is one change that will take place in your life in the next year or two?

Active Grammar: Future Time Clauses

A. Future plans. Sonia, a young college student, is dreaming about her future. Match these sentences that tell about her plans.

> **Future Time Clauses**
>
> **a.** If I study hard, I'll graduate in two years.   **b.** I'll graduate in two years if I study hard.
>   (time clause)   (main clause)   (main clause)   (time clause)
>
> The main clause and the time clause can be reversed. If the time clause is at the beginning of the sentence, use a comma **after** the time clause. No comma is necessary if the time clause is at the end of the sentence.

_____ 1. If she works hard,   **a.** she'll buy a new car.

_____ 2. When she takes a vacation,   **b.** she'll get a promotion.

_____ 3. After she saves some money,   **c.** she'll accept the best offer.

_____ 4. If she meets the right person,   **d.** she'll travel around Europe.

_____ 5. After she interviews for several jobs,   **e.** she'll get married.

Now, use your imagination and continue to write about Sonia's future. Each sentence has a time clause. The main clause takes the future tense.

1. Before Sonia gets married, _____.

2. _____ when she has children.

3. If she decides to become a full-time mother, _____.

4. _____ after her children are grown.

5. If Sonia decides to change careers, _____.

6. When Sonia has enough money, _____.

7. _____ when she retires.

B. Pronunciation: *Stress*. Listen and repeat these sentences.
1. I'm going to BUY a comPUTer when I GET a RAISE.
2. He's going to TAKE his vaCAtion when his SON gets MARried.
3. She's going to STUDY SPANish before she GOES to MEXico.
4. I'm going to REgister for SCHOOL after I reTURN from vaCAtion.

5. After he reTIRES, he's going to MOVE to FLOrida.
6. We're going to RENT a CAR when we LAND in ChiCAgo.

Practice these sentences with a partner.

C. Maybe tomorrow. Ask and answer these *When* questions with a sentence containing a future time clause. Use *before*, *after*, *if*, or *when*.

> When are you going to get married?
> I'm going to get married when I find the perfect man/woman.

1. When are you going to get married?
2. When are you going to graduate?
3. When are you going to do your homework?
4. When are you going to call your parents?
5. When are you going to pay the telephone bill?
6. When are you going to travel out of the country?
7. When are you going to take a day off?
8. When are you going to give a party?
9. When are you going to open a savings account?
10. When are you going to get a credit card?

D. A happy life. George is 20 years old. Talk together and put these events in his life in order from 1 to 8. Make sentences about his life using *before*, *after*, or *when*.

> Before George finds a job, he's going to graduate from college.
> He's going to get married when he meets a wonderful woman.

find a job

buy a house

get married

graduate from college

have a daughter

have a son

meet a wonderful woman

save a lot of money

The Big Picture: The Divorce Agreement

A. Before You Listen. Read and discuss.

Tom and Amy are working with a mediator. She is trying to help them come to an agreement about their divorce.

In mediation, a professional mediator works with a couple who is getting a divorce. The mediator does not represent the man or the woman. The mediator meets with the man and woman several times, both separately and as a couple. Together, the mediator helps the couple to develop an acceptable divorce agreement, including how to divide their possessions, child support, alimony, visitation rights, and any other matters related to the divorce. The agreement is a legal document and both people must follow it.

B. Listen for numbers. Listen as the mediator meets with Tom and Amy and reviews their assets. Complete the information below.

Tom's and Amy's Assets

Tom's salary:	$_____ a year
Overtime:	$_____ a month
Savings account:	$_____
House:	
Original price:	$_____
Value today:	$_____
Mortgage and taxes:	$_____ a month
Cars:	
Minivan:	paid off
New car:	$_____ a month for _____ more year(s)
Retirement account:	$_____
Other assets:	_____

C. Tom's and Amy's assets. Answer these questions.

1. Does Tom always earn overtime?
2. How much money does Amy earn?
3. When did they buy their house?
4. Do they have any loans?
5. What other assets do they own?

D. Listen as the mediator reviews the agreement between Tom and Amy. Complete the information about the agreement.

Divorce Agreement

House: _____ will live in the house for _____ more years.

Tom will pay $_____ a month.

Amy will pay $_____ a month and _____.

When they sell the house, _____ the sale price will go to each person.

Savings: Tom: $_____   Amy: $_____

Retirement: Tom: $_____   Amy: $_____

Cars: New car: Tom   Amy   Minivan: Tom   Amy

Insurance on cars: _____

Furniture: Tom   Amy

Electronic equipment: Tom   Amy

Children: During the week: Tom   Amy

                  On weekends: Tom   Amy

                  July: Tom   Amy   August: Tom   Amy

Child support: $_____ a month

Alimony: $_____ a month for _____ years

Dog: Tom   Amy

E. Discuss the answers to these questions.

1. How much will each person pay of the mortgage and taxes? Why do you think that Tom is going to continue to pay part of this expense?
2. Who will pay the insurance for Amy's car?
3. When Tom works overtime, who will receive his overtime pay?
4. Why does Amy need alimony?
5. Is this custody agreement good for the children?
6. Is this agreement fair for both Tom and Amy?
7. How is this agreement similar to or different from divorce agreements in your country?

Culture Note

Child support is a legal obligation. If a parent does not pay child support, the court will arrest him/her.

Reading: Dating

A. Before You Read.

1. Are you married or do you have a boyfriend/girlfriend? How did you meet?

2. What do you know about Internet dating services?

3. Do you know anyone who has met this way?

Luisa and Tim

Working long hours and being tired in the evenings, Jim E. had little opportunity to meet someone special. One Friday night, he entered a computer chat room for Florida singles. He found himself **attracted to** one of the participants, so they left the public chat room and continued to a private computer chat room for the next three hours. Jim explained, "We were communicating so well, finding ourselves interested in the same things and sharing the same views, that we took a giant step and decided to share phone numbers that same night." They spoke on the phone the rest of the night. Two days later, they met in person at a nearby diner. "We **clicked** immediately." Jim and Luisa have been married for four years and their son, Jacob, is eight weeks old.

Joanne W., 30 years old, was not as lucky. After subscribing to an Internet dating service, she read the bios (information) of dozens of men and then wrote information about herself. Bob L. e-mailed her the next week. They chatted on the computer, then by phone, and met a few weeks later. After dating for two months, she discovered that Bob was married and the father of three children. She was upset, but she says, "The same thing can happen when you meet someone at a club."

Internet chat rooms and dating services are the new **matchmakers**. Chat rooms are the easiest places to meet someone on the computer. Some chat rooms are for singles only. Other chat rooms **target** specific interests, such as music, tennis, or French cooking. If two people take a special interest in one another, they can enter a private chat room.

Internet dating services provide a more detailed search for long-term relationships. Members send a photo and enter information about themselves and the person they would like to meet. Members usually describe their personalities and are sometimes asked to complete sentences, such as "I would love to take a vacation to _____" or "When I have free time, I like to _____." By providing this information, members hope to meet a **compatible** person.

Members pay for the service by the month. They enter the dating site and can **browse** for hours through the hundreds of photos, bios, and other information. No personal names are used. Each person has a username, or handle, such as *LuckyLady* or *Niceguy2*. If one member is interested in another member, he or she clicks on the e-mail button and sends a message. Will this member respond? Will they "click" online? Will they meet in person and continue their relationship?

B. Choose the best title for this story.

1. How to Meet Your True Love

2. Internet Dating

3. Beware of Internet Dating

C. Vocabulary in context. (Circle) a word or phrase that is similar in meaning.

1. He found himself **attracted** to one of the participants.
   a. close to   b. interested in   c. talking to

2. We **clicked** immediately.
   a. talked to   b. liked each other   c. met

3. Internet chat rooms and dating services are the new **matchmakers**.
   a. people who arrange marriages   b. people who like each other
   c. computer programmers

4. Other chat rooms **target** specific interests, such as music, tennis, or French cooking.
   a. present   b. contain pictures of   c. concentrate on

5. By providing this information, members hope to meet a **compatible** person.
   a. athletic   b. like-minded   c. beautiful

6. They enter the dating site and can **browse** for hours through the hundreds of photos, bios, and other information.
   a. look   b. sleep   c. talk

D. Sit in a group and discuss Internet dating. Check (✓) *do* or *don't* for each idea based on what you would or would not do.

	Do	Don't
1. Send an up-to-date photo.	___	___
2. Give personal information, like your salary.	___	___
3. Get involved emotionally on the Internet.	___	___
4. Meet in a public place, like a restaurant or museum.	___	___
5. Describe yourself honestly.	___	___
6. Give out your address.	___	___
7. If you think you might like someone, try to meet them soon.	___	___
8. Believe everything you read in a chat room.	___	___

E. Give your opinion.

1. Would you ever try Internet dating? Why or why not?

2. Do you think that people who use an Internet dating service might be better matched than people meeting at a party or a club?

3. What are some of the positive aspects of using an Internet dating service?

4. What are some problems that might occur when using an Internet dating service?

Writing Our Stories: More about Me

A. Read this information about an Internet dating service member.

My Bio

Age: 27

Location: Massachusetts, Boston area

Hair: Brown   Eyes: Brown

Height: 6' (182.88cm)

Body Type: Athletic

Language: English, Spanish

Ethnicity: Hispanic

Occupation: Electrician

Education: Some college

Income: I'll tell you later

Married: Never married   Children: None

More about me . . .

I never thought I would use an Internet dating service, but here I am. I'm a friendly, fun-loving person. My friends say that I'm easy to talk to, happy, and helpful. If a friend needs a ride or help with moving, I'm the one they call. I like to keep in shape, so I work out at the gym three or four times a week. When I have a free day, you can find me walking in the park, watching a baseball game, or lying on the beach. A perfect evening is a romantic dinner in a fine restaurant, talking about things we enjoy. I want to begin a relationship with an interesting, active woman. Let's start out as friends and see what develops.

B. Circle the adjectives that describe you.

friendly	hardworking	athletic	intelligent
romantic	shy	outgoing	supportive
happy	helpful	competitive	dependable
funny	sensitive	serious	artistic
generous	energetic	fun-loving	honest

C. Verbs after *like, love, enjoy,* and *go.* Complete the sentences with the gerund or infinitive form of the verbs in parentheses.

> We often use a verb after **like, love, enjoy,** and **go.** After these verbs, use the gerund form (simple verb + *-ing*).
> I **enjoy** <u>eating</u> at ethnic restaurants.
> I **like** <u>walking</u> in the park.
> I **go** <u>dancing</u> on the weekends.
> After **like** and **love,** we can also use the infinitive (*to* + simple verb).
> I **like** <u>to walk</u> in the park.

1. I enjoy (listen) ____<u>listening</u>____ to music and (dance) ____<u>dancing</u>____.

2. I like (watch) _____ romantic movies.

3. On the weekends, I often go (camp) _____.

4. When I have free time, I like (read) _____ or (visit) _____ an interesting museum.

5. Family is very important to me. I enjoy (spend) _____ time with them.

6. My passion is sports. I love (play) _____ baseball, (practice) _____ kung fu, or (ride) _____ my bicycle.

7. You'll find me serious and sensitive. I enjoy (talk) _____ about politics and world events.

D. You have decided to use an Internet dating service to attract that special someone. Write a short paragraph describing your personality and the things you enjoy in life.

> **More about me . . .**
>
>
>
>
>
>
>

 Looking at the Internet

The U.S. Census Web site is filled with interesting facts and statistics about life in the United States. Enter www.uscensus.gov and browse the site. Copy one interesting fact about life in the United States.

Practicing on Your Own

A. Complete these conversations with an offer to help or a promise. Use _will_.

1. **Child:** Dad, I'm sorry. I broke the window when I was playing baseball.
   Father: _Don't worry. I'll fix it._

2. **Wife:** I'm tired tonight. I don't feel like making dinner.
   Husband: _____

3. **Mother:** Your bedroom looks like a disaster area!
   Daughter: _____

4. **Father:** You can use the car, but don't bring it back with an empty tank.
   Son: _____

5. **Daughter:** I have to be at school tomorrow morning at 7:00 for band practice.
   Mother: _____

6. **Son:** Mom, my uniform is dirty and we have a baseball game tomorrow.
   Mother: _____

7. **Son:** Dad, my driving test is next week. Can you take me out to practice?
   Father: _____

B. Sentence combining. The students in one ESL class gave these "hints" for a happy marriage. Combine their sentences using the words in parentheses and a future time clause.

1. I'm going to get married. I'm going to meet the right person. (when)
   I'm going to get married when I meet the right person.

2. We're going to get married. My husband and I are going to have separate bank accounts. (after)

3. My husband is going to cook dinner. I'm going to feel tired. (when)

4. I'm going to be busy. My wife is going to cut the lawn. (when)

5. We are going to have an argument. The whole family isn't going to know about it. (when)

6. My mother will come for a visit. She will only stay for a week. (when)

7. My husband is going to tell me something in confidence. I'm going to keep it to myself. (when)

8. I'm still going to laugh. My husband is going to tell the same joke twice. (if)

9. We are going to go to bed each night. I'm going to tell my husband I love him. (before)

10. We are going to have a son. We are going to name him after my husband. (when)

Grammar Summary

▶ **1. The future tense**

We use the future tense to talk about actions in the future time, such as tomorrow, next week, next year, etc. There are two forms of the future: **be + going to** and **will**.

Both future forms talk about future actions and plans.

In addition, **will** expresses promises or predictions.

▶ **2. Present continuous tense: Future meaning**

If a specific time in the future is stated or understood, the present continuous tense can show future meaning.

Tom is **leaving** this weekend.

He**'s taking** the children on vacation in July.

▶ **3. Future time expressions**

tomorrow	next week	in a few minutes	soon
the day after tomorrow	next month	in an hour	later
	next year	in a little while	

▶ **4. Future**

be + going to	*will + verb*
I**'m going to move** next month.	I **will move** next month.
She**'s going to get** a divorce.	She **will get** a divorce.
Are you **going to move**?	**Will** you **move**?
Is Tom **going to pay** alimony?	**Will** Tom **pay** alimony?
When **are** you **going to move**?	When **will** you **move**?
Where **is** Tom **going to live**?	Where **will** Tom **live**?

▶ **5. Future time clauses**

A time clause begins with words such as *if, when, before, after,* and *as soon as.*

A time clause has a subject and a verb, but it is not a complete sentence by itself.

A time clause may come at the beginning or at the end of a sentence. With a future time clause, the verb in the main clause is in the **future tense**. The verb in the time clause is in the **present tense**.

I'll get married **when I meet the right person**.

　(main clause)　　　　　(time clause)

When I meet the right person, I'll get married.

　　　(time clause)　　　　　(main clause)

Note: When a time clause comes at the beginning of a sentence, use a comma to separate it from the main clause.

Comparisons—

A. Find the countries listed in the box and label them on the map.

Brazil	South Korea	Russia	United States	India	Egypt
Japan	Turkey	Canada	Mexico	Thailand	China

Global and Local

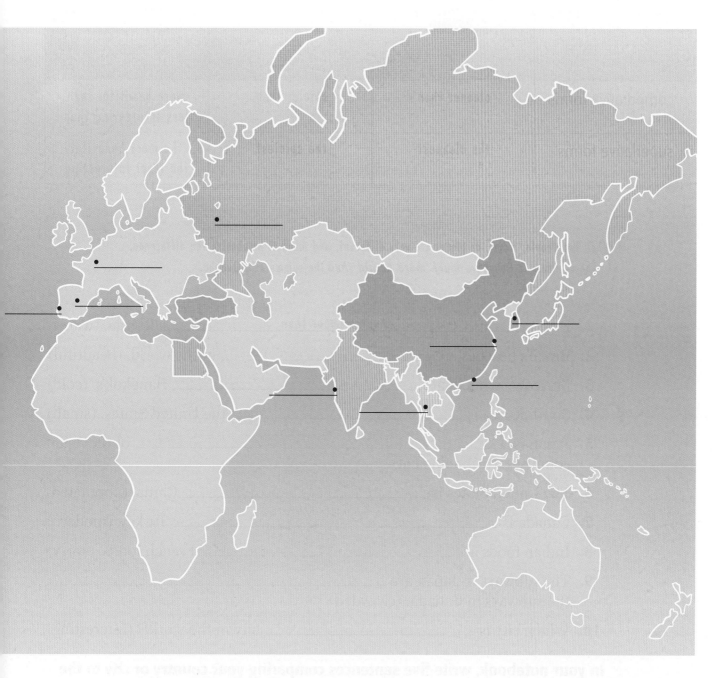

B. **Locate each city listed in the box. Then, write the name of each city on the line on the map.**

Hong Kong	Madrid	Bombay	Lisbon	Shanghai	New York City
Paris	Seoul	Bangkok	Moscow	Quebec	Acapulco

Active Grammar: Comparative and Superlative Adjective Forms

A. Complete the sentences with the correct form of the adjectives in parentheses.

	One-syllable adjectives	Two-syllable adjectives, ending with -y	Two or more syllables, not ending with -y
comparative forms	cleaner than	spicier than	more beautiful than less interesting than
superlative forms	the cleanest	the spiciest	the most beautiful the least interesting

When two people, items, or places are very different, add *much* to emphasize the difference.
The summers in Seoul are ***much more humid than*** the summers in Quebec.

1. Egypt is _____much warmer than_____ Russia. (warm)

2. Brazil's beaches are _____ in the world. (beautiful)

3. Moscow's winters are _____ Bangkok's. (cold)

4. South Korea is _____ the United States. (small)

5. Japan is _____ of the Asian countries. (technological)

6. The United States is _____ China. (populated)

7. Canada is _____ Turkey. (modern)

8. Indian foods are _____ French foods. (spicy)

9. The subways in Japan are _____ the subways in Canada. (crowded)

10. Which city is _____ city in the world? (interesting)

In your notebook, write five sentences comparing your country or city to the countries and cities labeled on the map on pages 52–53.

A. Look at the picture of an English class. Read the facts about the class. Write sentences comparing and contrasting the class.

More and *fewer*	Examples
more + noun + than	There are **more women than** men in this class. There are **many more students** with dark hair than with light hair.
fewer + noun + than	There are **fewer men than women** in this class.

Facts about the class

__4__ men	__1__ European	__6__ students over 5'4" tall
__11__ women	__10__ South Americans	__9__ students under 5'4" tall
__5__ single women	__2__ Carribeans	__6__ students with short hair
__3__ single men	__2__ Asians	__9__ students with long hair
__6__ married women		
__1__ married man		

1. There are _fewer men than women in this class._

2. _____

3. _____

4. _____

5. _____

6. _____

7. _____

B. Now, with a group of students, make a list of facts about your class. Then, in your notebook, write eight sentences comparing the students in your class.

As . . . as shows that two items, people, or places are the same.
The negative *not as . . . as* shows that two items, people, or
places are not the same.

France has **as many telephones as** it has televisions.
Meaning: the number is the same.

Brazil doesn't have **as many cell phones as** France does.
Meaning: The numbers aren't the same.

A. Read the information in the chart about telecommunications.

Country	Telephones (million)	Cell phones (million)	Televisions (million)	Internet users (million)
Brazil	17	4.4	36.5	8.65
France	34.8	11	34.8	9
India	27.7	2.9	63	4.5
Japan	60.4	63.9	86.5	27
Russia	30	2.5	60.5	9.2
United States	194	69.2	219	148

Source: World Factbook 2001 at www.cia.gov

 Listen and complete the comparisons. Use *as many . . . as*.

1. Brazil doesn't have _____ Russia does.

2. France has _____ it has televisions.

3. India doesn't have _____ it has telephones.

4. Japan doesn't have _____ the United States does.

5. Russia doesn't have _____ the other countries do.

6. Brazil has _____ France does.

7. Russia has _____ India does.

B. Pronunciation: *as . . . as* versus *not as . . . as*. Listen to each statement. (Circle) *same* if you hear *as . . . as*. (Circle) *different* if you hear *not as . . . as*.

1. same   different   3. same   different   5. same   different
2. same   different   4. same   different   6. same   different

C. Practice reading the sentences to a partner. (Circle) the affirmative or the negative verb form. Your partner will listen and say "same" or "different."

1. My city **is** / **isn't** as populated as this city.
2. The transportation here **is** / **isn't** as cheap as in my city.
3. The food here **is** / **isn't** as delicious as it is in my country.
4. The gasoline prices here **are** / **aren't** as expensive as those in my city.
5. My city **is** / **isn't** as diverse as this city.
6. The cars here **are** / **aren't** as small as those in my city.

D. Read the information in the bar graph. Then, (circle) *True* or *False*.

1. Bombay is more populated than Bangkok.   True   False
2. Seoul is less populated than Bangkok.   True   False
3. Shanghai is almost as populated as Bombay.   True   False
4. Tokyo is more populated than Seoul.   True   False
5. Bangkok is the least populated of the group.   True   False

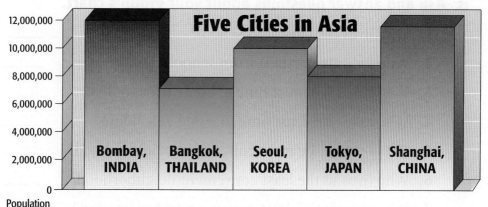

Five Cities in Asia

Bombay, INDIA | Bangkok, THAILAND | Seoul, KOREA | Tokyo, JAPAN | Shanghai, CHINA

Population

E. Ask and answer these questions with a partner.

1. Is Bombay as populated as Bangkok?
2. Is Seoul more populated than Bangkok?
3. Is Tokyo less populated than Seoul?
4. Is Bangkok the least populated of the group?
5. Is Tokyo as populated as Shanghai?

Active Grammar: Superlative Adjectives

A. Compare modes of transportation. With a group of three or four students, fill in the information in the chart.

Student Name	Minutes to school	Miles/km to school	Daily cost of transportation	Convenient		Public Transportation		
				Yes	No	Bus	Train	Subway

B. Ask and answer questions about your group's chart.

1. Who lives the closest to school? _____
2. Who lives the farthest from school? _____
3. Who takes the most time to come to school? _____
4. Who takes the least time to come to school? _____
5. Who lives in the most convenient neighborhood? _____
6. Who lives in the least convenient neighborhood? _____
7. Who spends the most money on transportation? _____
8. Who spends the least money on transportation? _____
9. Who spends the most time on public transportation? _____
10. Who spends the least time on public transportation? _____

C. Complete the sentences about your group's chart. Use the correct adjective form: comparative, superlative, or *as . . . as.*

1. _____ travels _____.
   (student name)   (adjective form)

2. _____'s neighborhood is _____.
   (student name)   (adjective form)

3. _____'s transportation is as _____ as _____'s.
   (student name)   (adjective form)   (student name)

4. _____'s neighborhood is as _____ as _____'s.
   (student name)   (adjective form)   (student name)

5. _____'s costs are _____ _____'s.
   (student name)   (adjective form)   (student name)

6. _____ has _____ transportation.
   (student name)   (adjective form)

D. Student to student dictation.

Student A: Turn to page 244.

Student B: Look at the pictures. Listen to Student A. In the chart below, circle the number of the family that matches the description. When you finish, change pages.

Family 1   **Family 2**   **Family 3**

1. Family	1 2 3	4. Family	1 2 3
2. Family	1 2 3	5. Family	1 2 3
3. Family	1 2 3	6. Family	1 2 3

Student B: Turn to page 244.

Student A: Look at the pictures. Listen to Student B. In the chart above, circle the number of the family that matches the description.

A. Look at the picture and describe this town as it looked 25 years ago.

B. Listen and take notes about the changes in the town. What is different about the town today?

1. _____more housing_____   6. _____
2. _____new people_____   7. _____
3. ___2 new elementary schools___   8. _____
4. _____   9. _____
5. _____   10. _____

C. Read each statement about the town today. (Circle) the correct answers.

1. There are **more / fewer** residents.

2. Neighbors live **closer to / farther from** each other.

3. Traffic is **lighter than / heavier than** it used to be.

4. There are **fewer students / more students** than there used to be.

5. There are **fewer places / more places** to shop than there used to be.

6. The town has **many more jobs / fewer jobs** than it used to have.

7. The buildings are **as tall as / much taller than** they used to be.

D. Complete the sentences with the correct comparative or superlative form. Use the expressions from the box below and the words in parentheses.

(much) more . . . than	*as + adjective + as*	*as many + noun + as*
(much) adjective + er than	*not as + adjective + as*	*not as many + noun + as*
fewer . . . than		

1. Twenty-five years ago, the town was _____ not as populated as _____
   it is today. (populated)

2. Twenty-five years ago, there were _____
   for children as there are today. (schools)

3. Twenty-five years ago, downtown was _____
   it is today. (crowded)

4. Today, traffic is _____ it used to be. (heavy)

5. Twenty-five years ago, the movie theater showed
   _____ the new cineplex does today. (movies)

6. The waitresses at Millie's Luncheonette are _____
   they were twenty-five years ago. (friendly)

E. *Which* questions. Ask and answer questions about the old town *and* the new town. Use the adjectives and nouns below.

Adjectives
populated
diverse
busy
large
industrial

Which town is busier, the old town or the new town?

The new town is.

Which town has more parking, the old town or the new town?

The new town does.

Nouns
parking
shopping
farms
children
job opportunities

Reading: Suburban Sprawl

A. Before You Read.

1. What is the difference between rural, suburban, and urban areas?

2. In which type of area do you live? In which type of area would you like to live? Why?

3. Put the following words or phrases in the correct categories. Some words or phrases may fit into more than one category.

larger houses and yards	farms	high crime rates
traffic jams	many trees	tall apartment buildings
parking lots	pollution	wildlife
taxis	shopping malls	many open spaces

Urban	Suburban	Rural
traffic jams	larger houses and yards	larger houses and yards

As the population in the United States grows, many people move from the cities, and the services that they need, such as shopping centers and stores, move with them. The suburban areas outside of the cities become more crowded, and more housing is needed. Then, the suburbs begin to extend into the rural areas. The new residents need services; therefore, developers build more shopping centers, restaurants, and housing on the land in the rural areas. The rural areas begin to shrink. As a result, there is less open space in the rural areas. This effect is called suburban sprawl. According to the organization Sprawl City, by the year 2050, the United States will have 110 million fewer acres of rural countryside.

Why do people leave the urban areas? They want large houses and yards, lower crime rates, and better schools. They are looking for a better quality of life.

Sprawl is becoming an increasing problem, and environmentalists are protesting the growth into the rural areas. Community organizations are also fighting the development. They say that sprawl contributes to the decline of natural habitats for wildlife. As cities spread, suburban development may damage the water quality when chemicals go into the water. Wildlife, such as birds, disappears from the area.

Besides environmental changes, sprawl also brings changes to rural communities. For example, a rural community might have one movie theater that shows two movies. It has one hardware store that has everything that a household needs. There is one grocery store, and the employees live in the community and know everyone who shops at the store. When the nearby suburb begins to expand, large chain store companies open stores closer to the expanding suburb, and gradually other stores, restaurants, and a large twelve-screen movie theater move into the area. The rural store owners become worried. They provide friendly, personal service to the town residents, but they cannot compete with the prices and services offered at the chain stores. When the rural residents begin to shop at the chain stores, and the residents go to movies at the new movie theater, the rural center begins to die.

People who support the chain stores say that there will be more tax revenues for the town, lower prices for residents, and new jobs. The people who are against the stores argue that there will be more traffic, only minimum-wage jobs, and the small town will have less of a small-town feeling. Is your area experiencing sprawl?

B. Reread the first paragraph. On the lines below, explain the process of sprawl.

1. People leave the cities and move to the suburbs. _____

2. _____

3. _____

4. _____

C. Listing paragraphs. The reading contains several listing paragraphs. These paragraphs describe more than one reason/cause/effect/characteristic, etc. Find and underline this information in the reading.

1. Find three reasons that people leave urban areas.

2. Find three negative effects of sprawl.

3. Find two effects of sprawl on rural communities.

4. Find three positive effects of building chain stores in rural areas.

5. Find three negative effects of building chain stores in rural areas.

Writing Our Stories: Three Cities

A. Read.

I have lived in three cities: Seattle, Miami, and Boston. Boston is a much better city for college students; there are many more excellent colleges and universities there than in the other two cities. For weather, I prefer Miami because the winters are much warmer. I can go to the beach all year long. Seattle and Boston are much colder in the winter. Boston is a much older and more historical city, so it has the most museums and historical sites to visit. Miami is like Boston. Both cities have many fun places to go for entertainment, and there are many theaters, clubs, and shops. Seattle is the best place if you like the outdoors. You can visit beautiful Mount Rainier. It's the best place for hiking. I don't know which city is my favorite. I like all three.

Andres

B. *Like, alike.* Complete the sentences with *like, alike, not like,* or *not alike.*

> The weather in Miami is **like** the weather in my country.
> Meaning: The weather is similar.
> The weather in Miami and the weather in my country are **alike.**
> Meaning: The weather is similar. Use *alike* at the end of a sentence.
>
> The weather in Miami is **not like** the weather in New York.
> The weather in Miami and the weather in my country are **not alike.**

1. The buses in this city and in my native city are _____.

2. The winters in this city and the winters in my native city are _____.

3. My home in this city is _____ my home in my native country.

4. This city is _____ my hometown.

5. The gasoline prices in this city are _____ the prices in my native city.

6. The cost for clothing in this country and the cost for clothing in my native country are _____.

C. Comparing cities. Choose three cities in your area to compare and contrast. Use the information in the chart to organize your composition.

Location	Transportation	Downtown	Entertainment
near school	bus	busy	excellent
near my job	train	crowded	good
near my relatives	subway	quiet	average
near downtown	near airport		poor

Job Opportunities	Population	
excellent average few	_____ (City #1)	_____ (Population)
	_____ (City #2)	_____ (Population)
	_____ (City #3)	_____ (Population)

In your notebook, write a composition comparing three cities.

D. Edit. There is one <u>underlined</u> mistake in each sentence. Correct the mistakes.

1. There are <u>less</u> soccer players in the United States than basketball players.

2. Russia is <u>one of the large</u> countries in the world.

3. The subways in Paris are <u>as convenient</u> the subways in Montreal.

4. The <u>most long</u> river in China is the Yangtze River.

5. Spanish is not <u>difficulter</u> as English.

6. Indian food is <u>much spicier then</u> Japanese food.

7. The United States is not <u>as bigger as</u> Canada.

8. China is <u>most populated</u> country in the world.

www Looking at the Internet

There are many Web sites that can help you find facts about different countries and cities. Search the Internet for the U.S. Census to find facts about the United States. For international facts, search for an almanac or *The World Factbook.* Share one interesting fact about the United States and one interesting international fact that you found with the class.

A. Complete each sentence with the correct adjective form.

1. Seoul is one of _____ (humid) cities in the summer.

2. Shanghai's port is _____ (busy) in Asia.

3. Paris is _____ (fashionable) Moscow.

4. Istanbul is _____ (modern) Quebec.

5. China is _____ (populated) country.

6. Acapulco has some of _____ (beautiful) beaches.

7. New York City is _____ (diverse) Madrid.

8. Summers in Shanghai are _____ (hot) those in Seoul.

9. People in Madrid eat dinner _____ (late) people in Tokyo.

10. Mexico is not _____ (rainy) France.

B. Complete the sentences with the correct adjective form. Use the information in the chart. You can use *more . . . than*, *as many . . . as*, or *fewer . . . than*.

FRANCE: 75,500,000
ITALY: 41,200,000
CHINA: 31,200,000
MEXICO: 20,600,000
CANADA: 20,400,000

Top Tourist Spots

Source: World Tourism Organization

1. France has _____ visitors per year.

2. China has _____ both Italy and France.

3. _____ visitors go to Italy _____ to France.

4. _____ visitors go to France _____ to China.

5. Canada has almost _____ visitors _____ Mexico.

6. Canada has _____ visitors of the group.

7. France has _____ visitors _____ China.

Grammar Summary

▶ 1. Comparative adjectives

    a. Use the comparative form of an adjective to compare two people or things.

        New York City is **larger than** Boston.

        New York City is **more diverse than** Boston.

        Canada is **less populated than** China.

    b. When two items, people, or places are very different, add *much* to emphasize the difference.

        Canada is **much less populated than** China.

One-syllable adjectives	Two-syllable adjectives, ending with -*y*	Two or more syllables, not ending with -*y*
larger than	*busier than*	*more populated than*

▶ 2. Superlative adjectives

    a. Use the superlative form of an adjective to compare three or more people, places, or things.

        Brazil is **the largest** country in South America.

    b. Use the superlative form of an adjective to compare one person, place, or thing to a larger group.

        China is **the most populated** country in the world.

One-syllable adjectives	Two-syllable adjectives, ending with **-*y***	Two or more syllables, not ending with **-*y***
the largest	*the busiest*	*the most populated*

▶ 3. Comparing nouns

    a. Use *more* + **noun** + *than* or *fewer* + **noun** + *than* to compare count nouns.

        There are **more women than** men in our class.

        There are **fewer men than** women in our class.

    b. Use *more* + **noun** + *than* or *less* + **noun** + *than* to compare non-count nouns.

        There is **more traffic** in Mexico City **than** in Montreal.

        There is **less pollution** in my hometown **than** in this city.

▶ 4. *as* + adjective + *as* / *not as* + adjective + *as*

    a. Use *as* + **adjective** + *as* to show that two items, people, or places are the same.

        Moscow's winters are **as cold as** St. Petersburg's winters.

    b. Use *not as* + **adjective** + *as* to show that two items, people, or places are not the same.

        Japan is **not as large as** India.

▶ 5. *as many* + noun + *as* / *not as many* + noun + *as* / *as much* + non-count noun + *as*

    a. Use *as many* + **noun** + *as* to show that two people, places, or things are the same.

        France has **as many telephones as** it has televisions.

    b. Use *not as many* + **noun** + *as* to show that two people, places, or things are not the same.

        Brazil **doesn't** have **as many telephones as** it has televisions.

    c. Use *as much* + **noun** + *as* to compare non-count nouns.

        Rural areas don't have **as much traffic as** urban areas do.

Label the hobbies and leisure activities. Which do you like to do?

1. _____dominoes_____

2. _____cricket_____

3. _____mah-jongg_____

4. _____

5. _____

6. _____

7. _____

8. _____

9. _____

10. _____

11. _____

12. _____

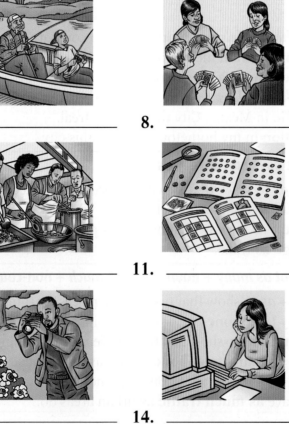

13. _____

14. _____

15. _____

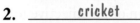

Active Grammar: *Yes/No Questions*

A. **Complete the questions in each category. If you need more help in writing the questions, look at the Grammar Summary on page 83.**

1. Are you going to _____ *go fishing* _____ this weekend?

2. Will you _____ next month?

3. Are you going to _____ next month?

4. Will you _____ by 2010?

5. Were you _____ *at a club* _____ last weekend?

6. Were you _____ yesterday?

7. Were you _____ last month?

8. Do you _____ *take photographs* _____?

9. Do you _____ every day?

10. Do you _____ every weekend?

11. Did you _____ *play a sport in your country* _____?

12. Did you _____ yesterday?

13. Did you _____ back in your native country?

14. Are you _____ *playing a card game* _____ now?

15. Are you _____ right now?

16. Are you _____ right now?

B. **Ask and answer the questions in Exercise A with a partner.**

| Yes, I am. | Yes, I do. | Yes, I was. |
| No, I'm not. | No, I don't. | No, I wasn't. |

| Yes, I did. | Yes, I will. |
| No, I didn't. | No, I won't. |

Wh-Questions

A. *Who/Whom/Whose.* Listen to these people talk about how they spend their free time. Take notes.

Gina   Roberto   Yelena

B. Circle the correct question word. Then, answer the questions with the name of the correct speaker.

Whose	umbrella is under the chair?	Whose refers to possession.
Who	likes sports?	Who refers to the subject.
Whom	are you going to go to the movies with?	Whom and who can both refer to
Who	did you call last night?	the object. Whom is more formal.

1. **Who / Whom / Whose** likes to go dancing?   _____ does.

2. **Who / Whom / Whose** father taught her chess?   _____'s did.

3. **Who / Whom / Whose** has many books about his hobby?   _____ does.

4. **Who / Whom / Whose** does Gina go dancing with?   _____.

5. **Who / Whom / Whose** friends often meet at dance clubs?   _____'s do.

6. **Who / Whom / Whose** does Roberto meet once a month?   _____.

7. **Who / Whom / Whose** worries about water chemistry?   _____ does.

8. **Who / Whom / Whose** has more free time now?   _____ does.

9. **Who / Whom / Whose** is Yelena going to teach chess to?   _____.

C. Sit with a small group of students. Write the correct question word: *Who, Whom,* or *Whose.* Ask and answer the questions.

1. _____ has a hobby?
2. _____ often goes to a park?
3. _____ music do you like?
4. _____ is planning a vacation?

5. _____ works full time?
6. _____ has a pet at home?
7. _____ do you spend time with?
8. _____ lives close to school?

D. Look at the pictures. Then, read the questions and match each question with the appropriate answer. Finally, label the people in the pictures.

Ryan and April

_____   _____   _____   Ryan and April

___f___	**1.** Who is nervous about his match?	**a.** Kazuki does.
_____	**2.** Who had a match a few minutes ago?	**b.** Eric does.
_____	**3.** Who collects comic books?	**c.** Ryan and April do.
_____	**4.** Who is planning a trip?	**d.** Eric will.
_____	**5.** Who plays a sport well?	**e.** Irina did.
_____	**6.** Who will probably add to a collection?	**f.** Kazuki is.
_____	**7.** Who wants to win?	**g.** Ryan and April are.
_____	**8.** Who likes to spend time outdoors?	**h.** Irina does.

E. Each student in your class should take a personal possession, such as a watch, notebook, keys, sunglasses, or pen, and put it on a desk in the middle of the classroom. Then, take turns asking *Whose* questions to find the owner of each item.

Whose book is that?

It's Jaime's.

F. *How* questions. Complete these questions with the correct *How* expression. Then, ask and answer the questions.

How **often** do you come to school?	Once a week.	Every day.
How **much** money do you have?	Five dollars.	A little.
How **many** tickets do you have?	Six.	Just one.
How **long** did you wait?	Six months.	Thirty minutes.
How do you get to work?	By bus.	I drive.
How **far** is it to your home?	Five miles.	Twenty minutes.

1. ___How often___ do you visit your native country?

2. _____ siblings do you have?

3. _____ do you spend on transportation to school?

4. _____ are you going to live in this country?

5. _____ hours do you sleep a night?

6. _____ do you live from your job?

7. _____ did you find out about this school?

8. _____ do you go to the movies?

9. _____ did it take you to get to class today?

10. _____ is it from your home to school?

G. Mixed questions. Form questions with these cues. Then, take turns asking your teacher each question.

1. Where / you / grow up?

2. How many sibilings / you / have?

3. What / you / want to be / when you were a child?

4. you / speak / another language?

5. How many languages / you / speak?

6. When / you / start to teach at this school?

7. What kind of music / you / like?

8. Who / your favorite musician?

9. you / take / a vacation / next summer?

Are you a pet owner?
What **is** your address?
When **does** class begin?
Where **did** you **buy** that CD?
What kind of car **do** you **have**?

Write two more questions for your teacher.

H. Student to student dictation: How Faye became interested in cooking.

Student A: Turn to page 245.

Student B: Listen to Student A and write the questions in the correct space. When you finish, change pages.

1. _____?

   My father did.

2. _____?

   My father did, and I taught myself from cookbooks.

3. _____?

   Yes, I regularly watch cooking shows on public television.

4. _____?

   No, but we remodeled it a few years ago to make it better for cooking.

5. _____?

   I took Indian cooking, candy-making, and afternoon tea, to name a few.

Student B: Turn to page 245 and read questions 6–10.

Student A: Listen to Student B and write the questions in the correct space.

6. _____?

   Sometimes. He took a couple of classes with me.

7. _____?

   We took a Valentine's Day class and a Mexican cooking class.

8. _____?

   I cooked oatmeal, but it was terrible!

9. _____?

   He likes everything that I cook.

10. _____?

   Because my old job wasn't fun anymore, and I love to cook.

Practice asking and answering the questions above.

I. Interview: A collector. Laurence collects items of a popular cartoon character. Listen to the interview. As you listen, take notes.

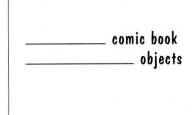

Note Taking

_____ comic book
_____ objects

J. Complete these questions and answers about Laurence's collection.

1. What _____?

   His sister bought him a _____.

2. Where _____?

   She found it at a _____.

3. How many objects _____?

   He has _____ objects in his collection.

4. Where _____ his collection?

   He keeps it in _____.

5. Where _____?

   He finds them at yard sales, _____,

   and _____.

6. What _____?

   He's looking for a _____.

Active Grammar: Tag Questions

A. Pronunciation: Tag questions. Listen and draw an arrow showing the correct intonation. <u>Underline</u> the main verbs.

> Example 1: They <u>are having</u> a nice time, **aren't they?** ↘
> (The speaker expects a "yes" answer.)
>
> Example 2: You <u>don't like</u> to fish, **do you?** ↗
> (The speaker isn't sure of the answer.)

1. They like to fish, don't they? ↘
2. Fishing isn't expensive, is it? ↗
3. There aren't a lot of boats in the lake, are there?
4. They don't fish every day, do they?
5. They're fishing in a lake, aren't they?
6. It's not a hot day, is it?
7. Fishing isn't tiring, is it?
8. They hope to catch a lot of fish, don't they?

B. Fill in the correct tag.

1. You are studying English, ____aren't you____?
2. You will be in class tomorrow, _____?
3. Our teacher is from the United States, _____?
4. This classroom isn't small, _____?
5. You're thirsty, _____?
6. We're not from Canada, _____?
7. We don't have English class on weekends, _____?
8. It wasn't snowing yesterday morning, _____?
9. You didn't come to class late today, _____?
10. I can't leave class early today, _____?

C. Ask and answer the questions in Exercise B with a partner. Use rising or falling intonation according to the answers you expect.

The Big Picture: My Hobby

A. What is Robert's hobby? Look at the pictures below. Label the pictures.

one-time-use camera	photography club	portrait
scanning a photo	camera lenses	wedding photo
darkroom	an SLR camera	black-and-white photo

1._____

2. _____

3. _____

4._____

5. _____

6. _____

7._____

8. _____

9. _____

B. Listen and retell the story.

76   UNIT 5

C. Listen and write the questions. Then, circle the answers.

1. _____?

    a. At a film store.   **b.** At a hardware store.   **c.** In the morning.

2. _____?

    a. Every day.   **b.** Six days a week.   **c.** Weekends only.

3. _____?

    a. To get married.   **b.** To open a hardware store.   **c.** To be a photographer.

4. _____?

    a. A Polaroid® camera.   **b.** An SLR camera.   **c.** A one-time-use camera.

5. _____?

    a. From classes.   **b.** A few years ago.   **c.** From a friend.

6. _____?

    a. At a birthday party.   **b.** At a family event.   **c.** Take photos.

7. _____?

    a. A color photo course.   **b.** A career course.   **c.** A computer course.

D. Complete each question with the correct word from the list below. Then, ask and answer the questions with a partner.

Is	Was	Were	Does	Did

1. ___Does___ Robert work for his father?

2. _____ working at the store his dream?

3. _____ his first camera expensive?

4. _____ his father teach him how to use the camera?

5. _____ he take pictures of his friends?

6. _____ his photos better after he took a course?

7. _____ he a member of a photography club?

8. _____ he know how to scan photos?

9. _____ he going to put a darkroom in his father's store?

10. _____ he want to become a professional photographer?

A. Before You Read.

1. Do you have a collection at home?

2. Do you notice the stamps on your letters?

3. Do you keep stamps that are particularly interesting or beautiful?

4. Look at the stamps in the reading. What countries do they come from?

B. Vocabulary. Scan the reading to find the definitions of the following vocabulary. Then, write the definitions.

1. greeting cards: _____

2. philatelic: _____

3. auctions: _____

4. a fresh stamp: _____

5. a cancellation mark: _____

   Collecting is one of many popular hobbies. Popular items to collect include dolls of all kinds, coins, records, cars, dishes, furniture, and more.

   The United States Postal Service (U.S.P.S.) delivers more than two hundred billion pieces of mail a year, and 46 percent of the world's letters and **greeting cards,** such as birthday and anniversary cards, are delivered by the U.S.P.S. Each of those cards and letters cannot be delivered without a stamp. Stamp collecting has been a leisure activity for many years.

   Every country's postal service sells stamps that reflect its history, people, arts, and culture. Stamp collectors can buy stamps of animals, flowers, historical events, and so forth. Most countries have clubs or societies that serious stamp collectors can join to share information. In addition, there are societies or clubs for collectors who specialize in particular categories of stamps. For example, collectors can join a Christmas **Philatelic** Club, whose members collect Christmas-related stamps.

One famous stamp collector was President Franklin D. Roosevelt. He was so interested in stamps that he designed several stamps. His stamp designs reflected what was happening in the country at the time. It was Roosevelt's design that was used for the first Mother's Day stamp. A woman wrote the President a letter giving him the idea. The stamp was first available on May 2, 1934.

Stamp collectors add to their collections by checking letter envelopes and postcards, and by attending stamp collecting societies and **auctions** – public sales where people compete to buy a valuable stamp. The Internet is another place where collectors can buy and sell valuable stamps and exchange information with others about hard-to-find stamps.

Many factors determine the value of a stamp. **A fresh stamp** is new and not used. The black circular mark that you usually see on a stamp on your mail is called a **cancellation mark.** This mark tells the date and place where the letter was mailed. If only part of the stamp is covered by the mark, the stamp is considered partially cancelled.

An example of how valuable a stamp can become is the story of the "Inverted Jenny" stamp. The "Inverted Jenny" is one of a group of stamps that have printing errors. This stamp was sold at the end of World War I in 1918. A "Jenny" was an old airplane and, by mistake, the post office printed the plane flying upside down. The exact story is not clear, but one story is that a stamp collector went to a post office and asked for one hundred airmail stamps. He noticed the mistake on the stamps, and later, he sold the stamps to another collector for $15,000, who sold them to another collector for $20,000. In 2002, one single "Inverted Jenny" sold at auction for $135,000.

There are also stamps that raise awareness of social or medical problems and may even earn money for an organization. On July 29, 1998, the U.S.P.S. issued the "Breast Cancer Awareness" stamp, which was the first U.S. stamp to earn money for a cause. Two hundred million stamps were originally printed, but the stamp was so popular that eighty million more stamps were printed. The stamp was valued at 33 cents, but it cost 40 cents to purchase. The profits from sales raised 27.2 million dollars for breast cancer research. The next time you receive a letter, pay attention to the stamp. Will it become part of a collection?

C. Reading for details. Read each statement. Circle *T* for *true* or *F* for *false*.

1. The U.S. Postal Service delivers more than half of the world's mail.   T   F

2. Each country has stamps that show its culture.   T   F

3. Some collectors collect particular types of stamps.   T   F

4. President Roosevelt's mother suggested the Mother's Day stamp.   T   F

5. Stamp collectors sometimes compete to buy a stamp.   T   F

6. A fresh stamp has a cancellation mark.   T   F

7. The "Inverted Jenny" was valuable because it was a new stamp.   T   F

8. Some stamps can raise money for social causes.   T   F

D. Look at your letters at home. Bring in letters that have interesting stamps. Look for examples of cancellation marks. Share them with your classmates.

A. Read.

Pineapple is a very popular fruit in my country and in other Carribean, South American, and Southest Asian countries. Some people do not know how to cut a pineapple properly, so they waste the fruit.

First, put the pineapple upside down on a table for a few minutes so that the most delicious juice can drip into the rest of the pineapple. Second, twist the green top off. Then, with a sharp knife, cut the pineapple in half lengthwise. Then, cut the halves in half. Take one quarter of the pineapple, and slice off the tough inner core. Some people like to eat this part, so don't throw it away. Finally, slice the pineapple off the tough skin, and slice it into smaller pieces. It's ready to serve.

B. A process. Read the following sentences about how to prepare stamps for a collection. Put the steps in order from 1 to 10. Then, rewrite the sentences in paragraph form in your notebook. Use the transition words in Exercise A.

_____ **a.** Flatten the dry stamps in a heavy book for a few days.

_____ **b.** Rinse the stamps in the clean water.

_____ **c.** First, find a few envelopes with interesting stamps and cut them off the envelope.

_____ **d.** Put the stamps in the small bowl, picture side up.

___1___ **e.** It is easy to start a stamp collection.

___6___ **f.** Get a second bowl of clean water.

_____ **g.** Wet the stamps until they easily slide off the envelope paper.

_____ **h.** Fill a small bowl with lukewarm water.

_____ **i.** Finally, put the stamps in a stamp album.

_____ **j.** Place the stamps on dry newspaper and let them dry.

C. Transition words. You can use the following transition words to describe a process. Look at the reading on page 80 and (circle) the transition words.

- First,
- Second, Third,
- Next,
- After that,
- Then,
- Finally,

D. In your notebook, write directions on how to do something related to one of your hobbies or interests. Use transition words in your paragraph. Here are some examples of topics.

- How to play dominoes
- How to take care of an aquarium
- How to take care of a pet
- How to buy a bicycle

E. Edit. Find and correct the mistakes.

1. What you doing?

2. Why does she has so many pets?

3. Where did you found these stamps?

4. How long will they plays this game?

5. You going to work in your garden?

6. Who did play a sport last weekend?

7. Whom are they play tennis with?

www Looking at the Internet

There are many Web sites that have information about hobbies and leisure activities. Click on **Search** and enter the name of a hobby or activity that you find interesting. For example, search "coin collecting," "bowling," or "salsa dancing."

A. Write questions with these cues. Then, write the answers.

1. who / your teacher?

   _____

   _____

2. who / immigrate / to this country with you?

   _____

   _____

3. where / you / live /?

   _____

   _____

4. when / you / come / to this country?

   _____

   _____

5. how / you / feel / today?

   _____

   _____

6. what / you / do / right now?

   _____

   _____

7. what kind of books / you / like?

   _____

   _____

8. whom / you / usually / speak English with?

   _____

   _____

9. how many people / in your family?

   _____

   _____

10. why / you / take / this class?

   _____

   _____

Grammar Summary

▶ **1.** *Yes/No questions*

You are a student.	**Are you** a student?
She is jogging.	**Is she** jogging?
They were tired.	**Were they** tired?
We are going to watch TV.	**Are we** going to watch TV?
We study English.	**Do you study** English?
I had a test yesterday.	**Did you have** a test yesterday?
She will get married soon.	**Will she** get married soon?

▶ **2.** *Who questions*   *Who* takes a singular verb form.

Who is a student?	I am.
Who is jogging?	They are.
Who is going to play soccer?	Those girls are.
Who studies every day?	We do.
Who had a test yesterday?	I did.

▶ **3.** *Whom/who*   *Whom* and *who* can both refer to the object in a sentence. Both are used in speaking and in writing, but *whom* is considered more formal. *Whom* is often used with a preposition.

Jamie sends e-mails to **his cousins**.	**Whom** does he send e-mails to?
	To whom does he send e-mails?
	Who does he send e-mails to?

▶ **4.** *Whose questions*   *Whose* refers to possession. A singular or plural noun can follow *whose.*

Whose photo is that?	That is my photo.
Whose CDs did you borrow?	I borrowed my cousin's CDs.

▶ **5.** *Wh-questions*

Where were you yesterday?	**Why** do you collect stamps?
What do you do in your free time?	**How much** is your collection worth?
When are you going to take a trip?	**How many** stamps do you have?
How did you learn how to do that?	**How long** does it take to get there?

▶ **6. Tag questions**   Tag questions have rising or falling intonation. Falling intonation shows that the speaker expects a "yes" answer. Rising intonation shows that the speaker isn't sure of the answer. The tag depends on the main verb.

You like football, **don't you?**	It isn't expensive, **is it?**
Your favorite music is classical, **isn't it?**	You won't be free tomorrow, **will you?**
They didn't drive, **did they?**	We're having a good time, **aren't we?**

Driving

Read each traffic sign. Match each sign with the correct traffic rule.

a. You must not ride bikes here.

b. Trucks must not use this road.

c. You must not turn left.

d. You must stop for pedestrians.

e. You must not park here or you will be towed.

f. You must stay to the right.

g. You must look out for deer.

h. You must slow down. This is a school zone.

i. You must not park here.

j. You must slow down. The road is slippery when wet.

k. You must slow down and be prepared to stop. Construction ahead.

l. You must turn right. One-way street.

1. _____

2. _____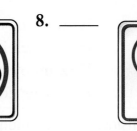

3. _____

4. _____ NO PARKING

5. _____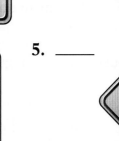

6. _____

7. _____

8. _____ P TOW AWAY ZONE

9. _____

10. _____ ONE WAY

11. _____

12. _____

Active Grammar: Modals—Must/Must not

Must shows rules, obligation, or necessity. You **must** stop at a stop sign.

Must not shows that an action is against the law or rules, or is not permitted. Drivers **must not drive** through a red light.

I He Drivers	must	stop at a red light. drive at the speed limit.
	must not mustn't	drive without a license.

A. Use each sentence to state the traffic law. Use *must* or *must not*.

1. Stop at a stop sign.   *You **must stop** at a stop sign.*
2. Pass cars on the right.   *You **must not pass** on the right.*
3. Pay traffic fines.
4. Drink and drive.
5. Register your car.
6. Drive over the speed limit.
7. Leave the scene of an accident.
8. Wear your seat belt.
9. Stop for a school bus with flashing lights.
10. Drive without a license.

B. Rules at school. Read each rule. Check (✓) *Yes* or *No* about your school.

Rules	Yes	No
1. We must arrive on time.		
2. We must pay for this class.		
3. We must call our teacher if we are absent.		
4. We must wear uniforms.		
5. We must speak English.		
6. We must buy our books.		

Write three more rules about your school.

1. We must _____
2. We must _____
3. We must not _____

☀ Have to/Doesn't have to/Don't have to

Have to shows *obligation* or *necessity*. **Have to** can be used in most situations instead of **must**. I **have to get** car insurance. You **have to do** your homework. She **has to babysit** her niece.	I You We They She He	**have to** **has to**	stop at a red light. drive at the speed limit. drive with a license.

A. Complete the sentences with *have to* or *has to*. Use the verbs in parentheses.

1. She ____has to move____ her car to another area. (move)

2. She _____ for the ticket. (pay)

3. She _____ the fine to City Hall in a few days. (mail)

4. He _____ the tires. (change)

5. He _____ for help. (call)

6. He _____ new tires. (buy)

7. They _____ their sports car. (sell)

8. They _____ a bigger car. (buy)

9. They _____ a car seat. (get)

B. Restate each sentence. Use *doesn't have to* or *don't have to*.

Doesn't have to / Don't have to shows that something is *not* necessary. You **don't have to own** a car.	I You We They She He	**do not have to** **don't have to** **does not have to** **doesn't have to**	buy a new car. work today. go to school today.

1. It's not necessary for a new driver to buy a new car.

   *A new driver **doesn't have to** buy a new car.*

2. It's not necessary for you to have a radio in your car.

3. It's not necessary for new drivers to have jobs.

4. It's not necessary for a new learner to go to a private driving school.

5. It's not necessary for drivers to have cell phones.

6. It's not necessary for a new driver to have a high school diploma.

7. It's not necessary for drivers to wash their cars every week.

C. Listen to Rebecca talk about her schedule. Check (✓) the tasks that she has completed.

Task	To Do (✓)
buy stamps	
mail her bills	
do the laundry	
go to the supermarket	
make a bank deposit	
visit her parents	
make a dentist appointment	
put gas in her car	

Ask and answer questions about Rebecca's to-do list. Use the information in her list in Exercise C.

Does Rebecca have to buy stamps?

No, she doesn't. She bought some yesterday.

D. Tell a partner the things that you had to do or didn't have to do before you came to this country and when you first arrived in this country.

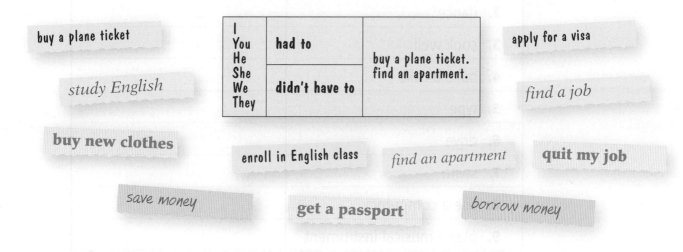

buy a plane ticket

study English

buy new clothes

I You He She We They	had to	buy a plane ticket. find an apartment.
	didn't have to	

apply for a visa

find a job

enroll in English class

find an apartment

quit my job

save money

get a passport

borrow money

Can/Can't

> **Can** shows ability or possibility.
> I **can** drive a truck.
>
> **Can** also shows that an action is permitted.
> **Can't/Cannot** shows inability or an action that is *not* permitted.
> I **can drive** at night by myself.
> You **can't drive** through red lights.

I You She	can	drive.
He We They	can't	park in this area.

A. Pronunciation: *Can* versus *can't*. Listen to Marcus talk about his driving experience. Complete the sentences with *can* or *can't*.

1. He ____can't____ drive very well.

2. He _____ drive only with a licensed driver in the car.

3. He _____ back up.

4. He _____ parallel park.

5. He _____ drive on a busy highway.

6. He _____ drive at night alone.

7. He _____ drive with the radio on.

B. Find someone who . . . Walk around the room. Ask your classmates what they can do. If someone answers, "Yes, I can," write the name in the space. If someone answers, "No, I can't," ask another person.

Can	I you he she we they	drive a truck? swim? speak French?

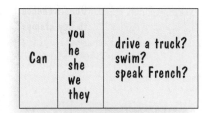

Question	Name
1. speak another language	
2. dance	
3. cook well	
4. bake a cake	
5. type	
6. drive	
7. swim	
8. use a computer	
9. play a musical instrument	

C. Can you identify the car parts? Label the pictures.

I can identify **all** / **most** / **some** / **none** of the car parts.

accelerator	hood	stick shift
brake	horn	tires
bumper	signal	trunk
clutch	steering wheel	windshield
		windshield wipers

D. Interview: An accident. Listen to Emily talk about her car accident.

1. When was the accident?
2. Was Emily hurt?
3. Where did the accident happen?
4. Who were the drivers in the accident?
5. Who caused the accident?
6. What did Emily have to do after the accident happened?
7. Did Emily have to call the police?
8. What does she have to do now?

☀ *Should/Shouldn't*

A. Look at the grammar explanation. Then, read each statement. Check (✓) your opinion. Then, discuss your reasons with a small group of classmates.

Should expresses an opinion or advice.
I should buy a smaller car.
Reason: Small cars get good gas mileage.

Shouldn't/Should not shows that something is *not* a good idea.
You **shouldn't put** your packages in the back seat.
Reason: Someone will see them.
You **should put** them in your trunk.

I You She He We They	should / shouldn't	drive at night. buy that car.

Opinion	Agree	Disagree
1. Drivers should drive more carefully near elementary schools.		
2. Teenagers are too young to drive cars.		
3. Small children should always ride in the back seat of a car.		
4. People over 80 years old should not drive.		
5. Drivers should not eat and drive at the same time.		
6. The highway speed limit is too low.		
7. All drivers should have car insurance.		

B. Give advice in each situation. Use *should* or *shouldn't*. Discuss your answers with a classmate.

1. A family of five children is shopping for a new car. What kind of car should the family buy?

2. Chen wants to learn how to drive. Who should teach him—his grandfather, his mother, or a private teacher?

3. Valeria is 16 years old. In her state, teenagers can drive at 16 years of age. Should she try to get her driver's license now, or should she wait until she is out of high school?

4. Pierre is a new immigrant to the United States. Everyone at his job speaks his native language. He doesn't speak any English. What should he do?

5. Rafael and Marcello are classmates in English class. They are from different countries. They need conversation practice. What should they do?

6. Andrea is new in town. She's living with her aunt and uncle, but she doesn't know anyone her own age. How should she meet some people her own age?

Had better/Had better not

Had better expresses a strong warning.
Had better is stronger than **should.**

You**'d better check** your tire.
(Or you'll have a flat tire.)

I**'d better not miss** another class.
(Or I'll fail the class.)

I You She He We They	had better 'd better	wear your seat belt. use a car seat.
	had better not 'd better not	drive without a license. forget to fill the gas tank.

 A. Pronunciation: 'd better / 'd better not. Listen and complete the sentences.

1. ___I'd better stay_____ home. I don't feel well.

2. _____ the baby in the car seat.

3. _____ the police and report the accident.

4. _____ the party inside. It's beginning to rain.

5. _____ another piece of cake. He'll get sick.

6. _____ a dog. Your landlord won't allow it.

7. _____ down. The roads are icy.

8. _____ that. I can't afford it.

Listen again and repeat the sentences to a partner.

B. Give a warning in each situation. Use *'d better* or *'d better not.*

A. Jennifer is 17 years old and very excited. Listen to Joanne talk about getting her driver's license. Complete the chart. What does she have to do to get her license?

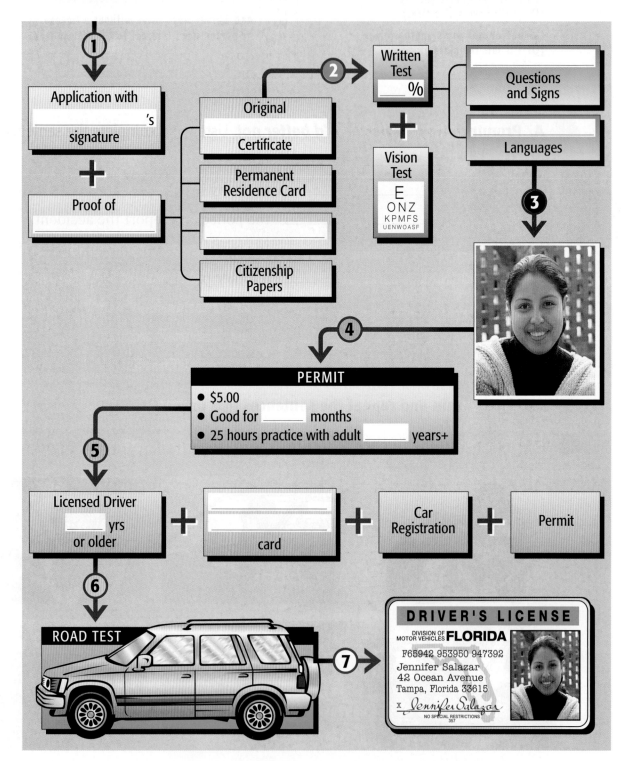

B. Getting the facts. Read each sentence about the process of getting a driver's license. (Circle) *T* for *true* or *F* for *false*. If the answer is false, tell the correct information.

1. Jennifer must take two tests before she gets her permit.   T   F

2. Jennifer has to show her birth certificate for proof of age.   T   F

3. Jennifer can take the written test in her native language.   T   F

4. Jennifer has to get 90 percent correct to pass the written test.   T   F

5. She can practice six months with her permit.   T   F

6. Jennifer's sister can teach her how to drive.   T   F

7. Eighteen-year-olds must drive with someone 21 or older.   T   F

8. Jennifer has to show an auto insurance card to take the road test.   T   F

9. Jennifer must go to the road test with a licensed driver.   T   F

Talk about getting a driver's license in your state. How is the process the same or different from Jennifer's state? Has anyone in the class gotten a license recently?

C. Ask and answer questions about getting a driver's license.

Does Jennifer have to get 100% correct to pass the written test?

No, she doesn't. She has to get 80% correct to pass.

show proof of age

practice for six months

practice with an adult

take a vision test

have the registration for her car

buy a car

show her citizenship papers

buy auto insurance

have a parent's signature

A. Before You Read.

1. Do you have a driver's license?
2. If so, did you take the written test in English?
3. What was the minimum passing score?

B. Read each sample question of a driving test. Fill in the circle next to the correct answer.

●   ⊗   ☑   ◖

Yes   **No**   **No**   **No**

1. A driver approaching a flashing red traffic signal must . . .
   - ○ **a.** drive carefully without stopping.
   - ○ **b.** stop first, and then, pass through the intersection.
   - ○ **c.** go through the light slowly.
   - ○ **d.** slow down at the intersection.

2. You must stop your vehicle . . .
   - ○ **a.** at an intersection with a stop sign.
   - ○ **b.** where there is a red light.
   - ○ **c.** when a traffic officer orders you to stop.
   - ○ **d.** all of the above.

3. You must turn on your headlights . . .
   - ○ **a.** when you turn on your wipers.
   - ○ **b.** in the evening.
   - ○ **c.** one half hour before sunset.
   - ○ **d.** all of the above.

4. If you are driving behind a school bus, and it shows a flashing red light, you must . . .
   - ○ **a.** slow down.
   - ○ **b.** slow down and pass on the left.
   - ○ **c.** stop at least 25 feet away.
   - ○ **d.** all of the above.

5. You are driving on a highway with a 65 mph limit. Most of the other vehicles are driving 70 mph or faster. You may legally drive . . .
   - ○ **a.** 70 mph or faster.
   - ○ **b.** no faster than 65 mph.
   - ○ **c.** between 65 and 70.
   - ○ **d.** as fast as you like.

6. You have a green light, but the traffic is blocking the intersection. You must . . .
   ○ **a.** pass the traffic on the left.
   ○ **b.** honk your horn.
   ○ **c.** wait until the traffic clears. Then, go.
   ○ **d.** pass the traffic on the right.

7. You must obey instructions of school crossing guards . . .
   ○ **a.** at all times.
   ○ **b.** when school is closed.
   ○ **c.** in the morning.
   ○ **d.** when it is raining.

8. If you pass your exit on a highway, you should . . .
   ○ **a.** go to the next exit.
   ○ **b.** turn around on the highway and return to your exit.
   ○ **c.** cross to the other side of the highway and make a U-turn.
   ○ **d.** back up slowly to the exit that you want.

9. What does the sign mean?
   ○ **a.** Three-way intersection.
   ○ **b.** Stop.
   ○ **c.** Railroad crossing ahead.
   ○ **d.** No turns.

10. What does the sign mean?
   ○ **a.** One-way street ahead.
   ○ **b.** Pass other cars on the right.
   ○ **c.** Left turn only.
   ○ **d.** You cannot go straight ahead.

Check your answers below.

1. b 2. d 3. d 4. c 5. b 6. c 7. a 8. a 9. c 10. d

8 correct	**CONGRATULATIONS!** You pass! Get your driver's license.
Below 8 correct	**SORRY.** You're not ready to drive. Study for two more weeks. Then, come back and retake the test.

A. Look at the street map. Then, read the driving directions from the starting point.

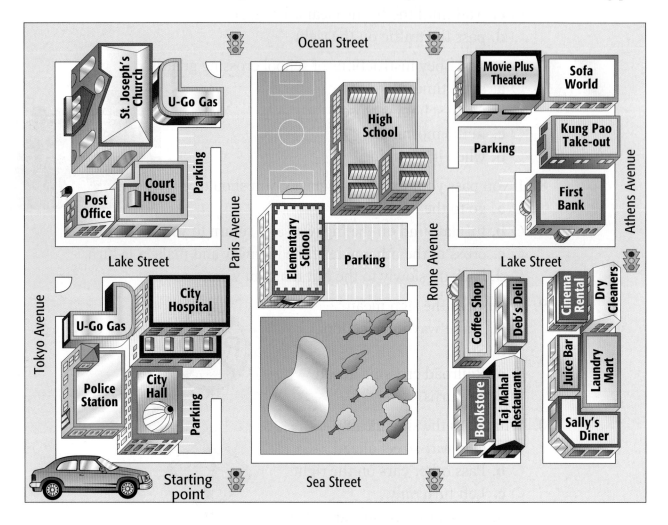

Conversation 1

A: My sofa is getting old. I need to buy a new sofa. How do I get to Sofa World? I heard that there's a great selection of sofas there.

B: That's right. Sofa World has a large selection of sofas. You're on Sea Street. Go to the first traffic light and turn left. That's Paris Avenue. Traffic is usually light. Take Paris straight to Ocean Street. There's a gas station on your left and a soccer field on your right. Turn right. Go through one traffic light. Sofa World is the second building on the right. It's on the corner of Ocean Street and Athens Avenue.

Conversation 2

A: I have to pick up sandwiches for a meeting at my office. How do I get to Deb's Deli? I heard that I can get a great sandwich there.

B: That's right. The sandwiches are delicious. It's easy. This is Sea Street. Go to the second light, turn left. That's Rome Avenue. Go to the next corner. That's Lake Street. It's difficult to park around there, so you should park in the municipal parking lot on the corner. Deb'si Deli is across the street from the parking lot.

B. In your notebook, write directions from school to your home or workplace. Include the names of important streets and landmarks such as gas stations, banks, and stores.

C. Unnecessary sentences. When you write a story or composition, it is important to include details to help the reader understand. It is also important to stay on topic. Do not include unnecessary information that may confuse the reader. Read each paragraph. ~~Cross out~~ the unnecessary sentence(s). Why did you cross out each sentence?

1. I think that all people should wear seat belts. Seat belts save lives. Three years ago, I was in an accident. I was on my way to work on a cold, snowy winter day. I don't like winter because I am from a warm country, and it doesn't snow there. The road was icy, but I was driving a little too fast. When I stepped on the brakes to stop at a stop sign, the car slid. I couldn't stop the car, and I slid through the stop sign into the intersection. I hit a truck. I had on my seat belt, so I wasn't hurt. The other driver didn't have on his seat belt. He had to go to the hospital for his injuries.

2. I think that the new cell-phone laws are ridiculous. My parents gave me a cell phone when I got my driver's license. I have a part-time job, and I have to work in the evenings. It was very difficult for me to find a job, so I want to keep this job until I finish high school. I always call my mother from my car to tell her that I'm on my way home. My cell phone is very cute. It's red, and it plays my favorite song when it rings. A few months ago, I had a flat tire on the way home. I used my cell phone to call my father. He called our auto association to come and help me. Then, my father called me back and kept talking to me as he drove to my location to wait with me. I was very nervous and scared. I was very happy to have my cell phone.

D. Edit. Find and correct the mistakes.

1. She must puts money in the parking meter.
2. Can you driving a stick shift?
3. Drivers has to follow the traffic rules.
4. I didn't have to took the test in English.
5. The baby should to ride in the back seat.
6. He better not take another day off, or he'll lose his job.
7. We had not buy a new car because we found a used one in good condition.

Looking at the Internet

Many states have Web sites for the Department of Motor Vehicles. The Web sites give information to current drivers as well as potential drivers. Search the Internet to find your state's Department of Motor Vehicles. Here's an example: Search "Florida" and "Motor Vehicles." Share the information you find with your classmates.

A. Traffic regulations. Fill in the blank in each sentence with the correct modal. There's more than one correct answer.

must must not	has to doesn't have to	have to don't have to	should shouldn't	had better had better not

1. You _____ take the written test in English.

2. You _____ drive over the speed limit.

3. Learners _____ get permits before they can drive.

4. Children under seven _____ ride in car seats.

5. You _____ drive and talk on a cellular phone.

6. You _____ use a hands-free cellular phone.

7. Drivers _____ drink and drive, or they will lose their licenses.

8. You _____ wash your car.

9. You _____ change your car's oil every 3,000 miles.

10. Bicycle riders _____ ride in the same direction as cars.

B. Compare the driving rules in the state where you live now to the driving rules in your native country. Add an appropriate verb.

can	can't	must	must not	have to	don't have to

1. In this state, I _____ a seat belt.

2. In my country, I _____ a seat belt.

3. In this state, children _____ in car seats.

4. In my country, children _____ in car seats.

5. In this state, drivers _____ auto insurance.

6. In my country, drivers _____ auto insurance.

7. In this state, you _____ obtain a license when you are _____ years old.

8. In my country, you _____ obtain a license when you are 16 years old.

In your notebook, write two more rules about driving in your country.

Grammar Summary

Modals are a special group of verbs. Each modal carries its own meaning. For example, *Emilio goes to school* is a fact. *Emilio has to go to school* shows that it is necessary for Emilio to go to school. The meaning changes when you use a modal verb.

▶ **1.** ***Have to* and *must*** Use *have to* and *must* to express rules, obligation, or necessity.

I **have to wear** a seat belt.

I **must stop** at a red light.

He **had to pay** his traffic fine.

▶ **2.** ***Don't have to/Doesn't have to/Didn't have to*** The negative form of *have to* shows that an action is not necessary.

You **don't have to be** 21 years old to drive.

She **doesn't have to get** 100% correct on the written test.

I **didn't have to get** a visa before I came here.

▶ **3.** ***Must not* and *cannot*** *Must not* and *cannot* show that an action is against the law or rules.

You **cannot go** through a red light.   You **must not go** through a red light.

Students **cannot copy** from other students.   Students **must not copy** from other students.

▶ **4.** ***Can***

   a. *Can* shows ability or possibility.   *Cannot* shows inability or no possibility.

   I **can drive** a truck.   He **cannot drive** a stick shift.

   I **can meet** you after class.   They **cannot take** more than four classes.

   b. *Can* also shows that an action is permitted.

   I **can park** here.   He **can use** his father's car.

▶ **5.** ***Should*** *Should* expresses an opinion or advice. *Shouldn't/Should not* shows that something is <u>not</u> a good idea.

I **should buy** a smaller car.   You **shouldn't buy** a larger car.

He **should study** English.   She **shouldn't study** in the cafeteria.

▶ **6.** ***Had better/Had better not*** *Had better/had better not* expresses a strong warning. *Had better* is stronger than *should*, and it expresses the idea that something bad might happen.

I **had better renew** my license this week.   You **had better not** park here.

(Meaning: My license will expire this week.)   (Meaning: Your car will be towed away.)

Sports

A. Match. Write each word from the box under the correct picture.

football	bowling ball	golf ball
tennis ball	soccer ball	volleyball
basketball	baseball	ping pong ball

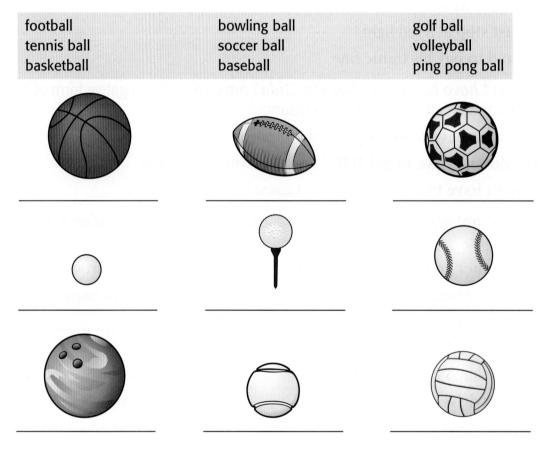

_____   _____   _____

_____   _____   _____

_____   _____   _____

B. Discuss.

1. What sport do you play?

2. Are you on a team?

3. How long have you been playing _____?

4. How often do you play _____?

5. Did you play a sport in high school?

6. Did you ever win a competition?

7. What sport do you enjoy watching?

8. What is your favorite team?

9. Who is your favorite player?

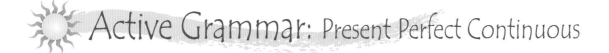
The **present continuous** describes what a person is doing now.
The **present perfect continuous** tells *how long* a person has been performing that action.
   He's **playing** soccer now.
   He's **been playing** soccer for an hour.

I You We They	have	been	**playing** tennis **watching** the game	for an hour. for two hours. since 2:00.
He She	has			

Contractions
I have—I've
you have—you've
he has—he's
she has—she's
we have—we've
they have—they've

A. Read and complete.

It's 5:00.

Carl <u>is playing</u> basketball.

Carl <u>began</u> to play basketball at 4:00.

He <u>has been playing</u> basketball for an hour.

He<u>'s been playing</u> basketball since 4:00.

It's 3:00.

The men <u>are playing</u> soccer.

They <u>began</u> to play soccer at 1:00.

They <u>have been playing</u> soccer for two hours.

They<u>'ve been playing</u> soccer since 1:00.

It's 12:00.

The women _____ tennis.

They _____ to play tennis at 10:00.

They _____ tennis for two hours.

They _____ tennis since 10:00.

It's 5:00.

I _____ golf.

I _____ to play golf at 2:00.

I _____ golf for three hours.

I _____ golf since 2:00.

Active Grammar: For and Since

A. Write each word or phrase under the correct column.

For
For shows an amount of time:
for a few minutes
for three days

Since
Since tells when an action started:
since 2000
since Monday
since she moved to the city

✓ she began to play tennis   he joined the team   several days

✓ three hours   a long time   I was a child

a few minutes   about two weeks   many years

2:00   he broke his arm   Saturday

For	Since
three hours	she began to play tennis
_____	_____
_____	_____
_____	_____
_____	_____
_____	_____

B. Complete the sentences using *for* or *since*.

1. She's been playing professionally ___for___ five years.

2. You've been hitting better _____ you took lessons.

3. He's been working out _____ 8:00 this morning.

4. The team has been practicing _____ about three hours.

5. She's been riding her bicycle _____ two hours.

6. He's been speaking with the coach _____ he got on the field.

7. The players have been listening to the coach _____ 30 minutes.

8. He hasn't been running well _____ he hurt his leg.

9. The fans have been watching the game _____ 4:00.

10. He's been playing golf _____ he was a child.

What have you been up to?

A. Pronunciation. Listen and repeat.

1. **a.** She's taking tennis lessons.   **b.** She's been taking tennis lessons.
2. **a.** She's learning how to drive.   **b.** She's been learning how to drive.
3. **a.** He's playing baseball.   **b.** He's been playing baseball.
4. **a.** I'm looking for a new apartment.   **b.** I've been looking for a new apartment.
5. **a.** She's recovering from her accident.   **b.** She's been recovering from her accident.
6. **a.** He's studying Chinese.   **b.** He's been studying Chinese.
7. **a.** He's working hard.   **b.** He's been working hard.
8. **a.** I'm training for a new job.   **b.** I've been training for a new job.

Listen again. Circle the sentence you hear.

Practice these sentences with a partner.

B. Listen to the conversation. Then, practice the conversation with a partner.

A: Hi, Juan. What've you been up to?

B: I've been painting the house.

A: And how about the family?

B: We're all fine. Maribel is 16 now, so she's been learning how to drive.

A: I've been through that! And your parents? How have they been enjoying their retirement?

B: They've been traveling. They're in China now.

A: Say "Hi!" to them for me!

B: I will.

C. Form sentences with these cues. Use the present perfect continuous tense. Then, develop a conversation similar to the one in Exercise B.

1. put in a lot of overtime
2. look for a job
3. coach my son's baseball team
4. travel
5. put in a new bathroom
6. take dance lessons
7. practice for my driving test
8. go out with someone new
9. study for my final exams
10. play a lot of golf

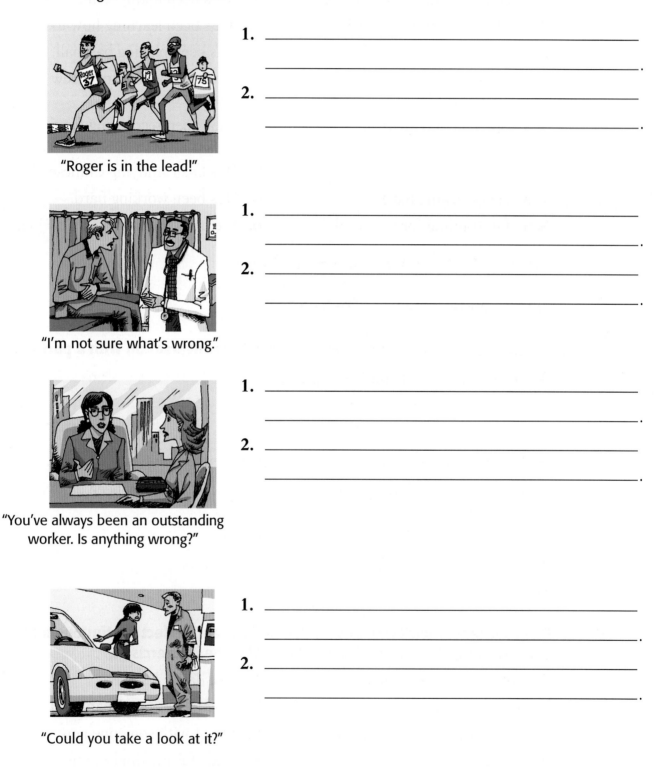

D. Student to student dictation.

Student A: Turn to page 246. Read the sentences to Student B.

Student B: Look at the pictures below. Listen to Student A and write each sentence next to the correct picture. When you finish, change pages. Student B will read eight new sentences.

"Roger is in the lead!"

1. _____ .

2. _____ .

"I'm not sure what's wrong."

1. _____ .

2. _____ .

"You've always been an outstanding worker. Is anything wrong?"

1. _____ .

2. _____ .

"Could you take a look at it?"

1. _____ .

2. _____ .

Active Grammar: Questions and Answers

Have you **been watching** the game?	Yes, I **have**.	No, I **haven't**.
Have they **been watching** the game?	Yes, they **have**.	No, they **haven't**.
Has she **been watching** the game?	Yes, she **has**.	No, she **hasn't**.
Has he **been watching** the game?	Yes, he **has**.	No, he **hasn't**.

How long	have	you they	been watching	the game?
	has	he she		

A. Listen to this interview between Robert and a reporter. Then, answer the questions.

1. How old is Robert?

2. What did he just win?

3. How long has he been playing tennis?

4. Who taught him how to play?

5. Does he take private lessons?

6. How long has he been taking private lessons?

7. How often do his parents want him to practice?

8. What is his dream?

B. Listen to this interview between Anna and a reporter. Then, use the cues to ask and answer questions.

1. About how old / Anna?

2. What / she / just win?

3. she / have / good coach?

4. How long / she / work with her coach?

5. she / work with a new choreographer?

6. she / do the same routine?

7. she / practice / triple jump?

8. When / try the triple jump in competition?

choreographer—
a person who coordinates
music and dance

C. Ask your teacher these questions. If your teacher answers _Yes_, ask a question with _How long_.

> **Student:** Are you reading anything good now?
> **Teacher:** Yes, I'm reading _River Town_ by Peter Hessler.
> **Student:** How long have you been reading that book?
> **Teacher:** Well, I got it out of the library two weeks ago and I've been reading it for about a week.

1. Do you play a musical instrument?
2. Do you wear contacts?
3. Do you play a particular sport?
4. Do you live in this city?
5. Do you drive?

6. Do you take vitamins?
7. Do you have a hobby?
8. Do you work at this school full time?
9. Are you studying a foreign language now?
10. Are you reading anything good now?

D. Sit in a group of four or five students. Write each person's name in the first column of the chart. Answer these five questions. Use the chart to record each person's answers.

1. How long have you been living in the United States?
2. How long have you been driving?
3. How long have you been studying English?
4. How long have you been attending this school?
5. How long have you been working in the United States?

Students' Names	Question 1	Question 2	Question 3	Question 4	Question 5
1.					
2.					
3.					
4.					
5.					

Use the information in your chart to complete these sentences.

1. _____ has been living in the United States the longest.
2. _____ has been driving longer than _____.
3. _____ doesn't drive.
4. _____ has been studying English for _____.
5. _____ has been studying English since _____.
6. _____ has been attending this school the longest.
7. _____ doesn't work.
8. _____ has been working longer than _____.

☀ Well-known Athletes

A. Read the information about these athletes. Ask and answer questions using the information in the boxes.

Possible questions

Who's this?

What sport does he/she play?

How old is he/she?

How long has he/she been playing _____?

What country is he/she from?

Tiger Woods
Born: 12/30/1975—USA
Started to play when he
was one year old

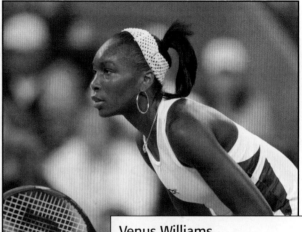

Venus Williams
Born 6/17/1980—USA
Began to play at age three

Ronaldo
Born: 9/22/1976—Brazil
Began to play professionally
in 1990

Pyrros Dimas
Born: 1972 in Albania of
ethnic Greek parents
Three Olympic gold medals
for Greece
Began to lift weights in 1991

The Big Picture: The Soccer Game

players
fans
announcer
coach
referee
concession workers

A. Label these people in the picture.

 B. Listen to a description of this scene. Then, answer the questions.

1. Who's playing?
2. Which team is in the lead? What's the score?
3. How long have they been playing?
4. How many minutes are left in the game?
5. How many fans are watching the game?
6. What have the concession workers been doing?
7. What have people been buying?
8. Has there been any fighting on the field?
9. What have the coaches been doing?
10. Which player has everyone been watching?

C. Complete the sentences using the correct verb in the present perfect continuous tense.

buy	run	wait	shout
watch	describe	call	make
	be	cheer	

1. The fans _____ have been making _____ a lot of noise.

2. The fans _____ a lot of soda and water.

3. People _____ in line to buy food.

4. An announcer _____ the game.

5. The players _____ up and down the field.

6. A few of the players _____ each other names.

7. The coach _____ instructions.

8. Everyone _____ player number 7.

9. The players _____ fast and accurate.

10. The fans _____ for their favorite teams.

D. Match the short answers with the questions.

1. Is the stadium full? _____ a. Yes, there are.

2. Did the game start at 2:00? _____ b. Yes, he has.

3. Are there more than twenty thousand fans? _____ c. Yes, he does.

4. Have the fans been cheering? _____ d. Yes, it is.

5. Are the fans hot? _____ e. Yes, it did.

6. Has the coach been giving instructions? _____ f. Yes, they are.

7. Do the Stars have four goals? _____ g. No, it isn't.

8. Does player number 7 have the ball? _____ h. No, they haven't.

9. Is the score 4-1? _____ i. Yes, they have.

10. Have the refs been calling many illegal plays? _____ j. No, they don't.

Reading: Lance Armstrong

A. Before You Read.

1. Look at the picture of Lance Armstrong. What is his sport? Have you ever heard of this athlete?

2. The Tour de France is one of the most difficult cycling races in the world. What do you know about this event?

Soccer, baseball, basketball . . . millions of people follow these sports and watch their favorite teams on TV. Cycling doesn't have the media coverage of some other sports, but most people can name the number one cyclist in the world—Lance Armstrong. His story is amazing for both his athletic **accomplishments** and his difficult road to **achieving** them.

Lance Armstrong was born on September 18, 1971, in Plano, Texas, and raised by a single mother. He began riding at an early age and was entering triathalons (running, swimming, and cycling competitions) before he was a teenager. By the age of 20, Armstrong was the U.S. National Amateur Cycling Champion.

From 1991 to 1996, Lance Armstrong continued to enter and win races. In 1993, he became the U.S. Pro Champion, and he won one million dollars in the Thrift Drug Triple Crown. In 1995, he won the Classico San Sebastion in Italy—the first American ever to win that race. By 1996, Armstrong was the number one cyclist in the world.

However, in October 1996, Armstrong began to lose energy and feel sick. A visit to the doctor brought terrible news. Armstrong had cancer, and it had spread to his lungs, brain, and abdomen. Armstrong **feared** he might never race again or that he might not even **survive**. He was **facing** the most difficult **challenge** of his life. In the months after his diagnosis, Armstrong had three major operations and then months of strong chemotherapy. In 1997, the doctors declared that Armstrong was cancer free.

Armstrong states that the cancer was a "wake-up call." Cancer gave him the strength to fight, to get back on his bicycle and win. He says, "Anybody who lives with cancer is a hero." Armstrong **founded** the *Lance Armstrong Foundation*, a nonprofit organization that raises money for cancer research, awareness, and early **detection**.

As Armstrong grew stronger, he entered the world of bicycling competition again, winning more titles and races. He returned to the U.S. Postal Service team, this time with a strong belief in himself and a **determination** to win. In 1999, Armstrong won the Tour de France, a three-week event, which takes riders more than two thousand miles through the valleys and high mountains of France. He won the event again in 2000, 2001, and 2002. On the Internet, it is possible to follow Armstrong's career since 2002 and to learn about the work of the *Lance Armstrong Foundation*.

B. Vocabulary. Look at the words in bold print in the reading. Write each word from the reading next to its definition.

1. strong will   _____determination_____

2. looking at   _____

3. live   _____

4. was afraid of   _____

5. the discovery of a problem   _____

6. started an organization   _____

7. difficult problem   _____

8. reaching a goal   _____

9. successes   _____

C. Sentence sense. It is possible to understand the meaning of a sentence even when you do not understand every word. Read the sentences from the story and circle the sentence with a similar meaning.

1. Cycling doesn't have the media coverage of some other sports.
   a. You don't see a lot of bicycle racing events on TV.
   b. Bicycling, like other sports, is popular with TV viewers.

2. His story is amazing for both his athletic accomplishments and his difficult road to achieving them.
   a. In bicycling, the roads are often high and difficult.
   b. Armstrong had some difficult times on his way to becoming a top athlete.

3. In 1995, he won the Classico San Sebastion, the first American ever to win that race.
   a. Americans always come in first in the Classico San Sebastion.
   b. This was the first time that an American won the Classico San Sebastion.

4. Armstrong feared he might never race again or that he might not even survive.
   a. Armstrong was afraid that he was going to die.
   b. Armstrong was afraid to get back on his bicycle and race again.

5. Armstrong was facing the most difficult challenge of his life.
   a. It was very difficult to win bicycling competitions
   b. Facing cancer was more difficult than competing in a bicycle race.

6. Armstrong states that the cancer was a "wake-up call."
   a. Cancer helped Armstrong to become a more serious bicyclist.
   b. Armstrong could finally forget about having cancer.

7. He returned to the U.S. Postal Service team, this time with a strong belief in himself and a determination to win.
   a. Armstrong believed that he could win competitions again.
   b. Armstrong believed he would be strong enough to race again.

Writing Our Stories: A Friendly Letter

A. Read this letter from Maria to her friend in Ecuador.

November 12

Hi Paula,

Sorry I haven't written for so long. I have been very busy and I have lots of news for you.

This year, school is much better. It was very difficult last year because my English wasn't too good. Now, I feel much more comfortable here. I'm studying business and hotel management. My courses are really interesting and I've been doing well. My roommate is American, so I've been speaking English every day, all day. She's really nice.

I met someone really special! My roommate lifts weights and she talked me into going over to the gym with her. You know me, I never exercise! The second day I was there, the guy on the treadmill next to me started to talk to me. I went back at the same time the next day, and we just continued talking, so I began to use the gym every day! I've never been so healthy! Ron and I have been going out for three months. Ron is on the tennis team at college, so I've been going to lots of tennis matches. He's been trying to teach me how to play tennis, but I'm not very good!

Thanksgiving is a big American holiday and I have two invitations for dinner. I might visit my roommate's family in Boston or I might meet my boyfriend's family in New York. I'm not sure yet.

What have you been doing? How is school this year? Please write and tell me about everyone! I miss you!

Love,
Maria

B. Compound sentences. We can combine two short sentences with words like *and*, *but*, *so*, and *or*. Each part of the new sentence has a subject and a verb. Remember to use a comma.

Some friends are coming from Brazil, **and** they are going to visit me next week.
I've been trying to learn Japanese, **but** I don't have anyone to speak to.
I've been taking tennis lessons, **so** my game is improving.
My parents are going to fly to the U.S., **or** I'm going to fly to Brazil.

In your notebook, combine these sentences.

1. My sister and brother are going to arrive tomorrow. They are going to stay with me for a week.

2. I might major in art. I might study graphic design.

3. I've been calling Jack for a week. He hasn't returned my calls.

4. Bill hasn't been attending soccer practice. The coach is going to suspend him from the team.

5. Julie hasn't been feeling well. She made a doctor's appointment.

6. Ben wanted to attend private college. He couldn't afford the tuition.

7. I bought a digital camera. My roommate is going to show me how to use it.

8. My boyfriend is going to make dinner tonight. We're going to order take-out food tonight.

C. Write an informal letter to a friend. Tell him/her what you have been doing.

D. Edit. Find and correct the mistakes in these sentences.

1. I been playing a lot of soccer.

2. He has been show me how to play golf.

3. She been very busy lately.

4. We have been going out for the first day of school.

5. He have been doing well in class.

6. She is going out with him since September.

7. They have been living in Tampa since six months.

8. She has been worked at a restaurant for two months.

9. What you have been doing?

10. Have you see any of our old friends?

www Looking at the Internet

What athlete do you admire? Click on *Search* and enter the name of the athlete. Find a photo of the athlete and print it. Tell your classmates the name of the athlete, the sport he or she plays, the team he or she plays for, and two or three interesting facts about the athlete.

Practicing on Your Own

A. (Circle) the sentence that shows the same meaning.

1. Tara began to play volleyball at 1:00. It's 3:00 and she is still playing volleyball.
   a. Tara has been playing volleyball for two hours.
   b. Tara played volleyball for two hours.

2. Tom played tennis in the park from 4:00 to 5:00. Then, he went home.
   a. Tom has been playing tennis for an hour.
   b. Tom played tennis for an hour.

3. Yesterday Martin rode his bicycle from 8 A.M. to 1 P.M.
   a. Martin has been riding his bicycle for five hours.
   b. Martin rode his bicycle for five hours.

4. The soccer stadium is full. The fans took their seats an hour ago and they are watching the game.
   a. The fans watched the game for an hour.
   b. The fans have been watching the game for an hour.

5. Juan lifts weights at the gym every day from 7:00 to 8:00. It's 7:30 now.
   a. Juan lifted weights for 30 minutes.
   b. Juan has been lifting weights for 30 minutes.

6. That was a very long basketball game. I got to the arena at 4:00 and the game ended at 7:00.
   a. I've been sitting in the arena for three hours.
   b. I sat in the arena for three hours.

B. Complete these questions and answers.

1. **A:** How long _____has he been playing_____ golf? (play)

   B: He _____ golf for seven years.

2. **A:** How long _____ in Chicago? (live)

   B: I _____ here for five years.

3. **A:** How long _____ to the news? (listen)

   B: They _____ to the news for an hour.

4. **A:** How long _____ these pains in your back? (have)

   B: I _____ these pains for two weeks.

5. **A:** How long _____ to hear about the job? (wait)

   B: She _____ for a week.

6. **A:** How long _____ for the test? (study)

   B: I _____ for three hours.

Grammar Summary

▶ **1. Present perfect continuous**

The present perfect continuous talks about an action that started in the past and continues in the present. The action is not yet complete.

He **has been watching** the game since 8:00.

They **have been playing** tennis for an hour.

I You We They	**have**			since 8:00.
		been	**playing**	
He She It	**has**			for two hours.

▶ **2. *For* and *since***

For shows an amount of time.

for an hour

for three days

Since tells when an action started.

since 12:00

since the game started

▶ **3. *Yes/No* questions**

Have you **been practicing** all afternoon?	**Yes**, I **have**.	**No**, I **haven't**.
Has she **been playing** tennis since 2000?	**Yes**, she **has**.	**No**, she **hasn't**.
Have they **been running** for two hours?	**Yes**, they **have**.	**No**, they **haven't**.

▶ **4. *How long* questions**

***How long* has** she **been playing** basketball?

***How long* have** they **been running**?

Changes

A. Family reunions. Discuss these questions.

1. How large is your family?

2. How do you keep up-to-date on what is happening in your extended family?

3. When do you see your whole family?

4. What is a family reunion? Did you ever have a family reunion? If so, give some details.

> **Immediate family:** The family you live with.
>
> **Extended family:** The whole family! Count your parents, grandparents, brothers and sisters, children, aunts and uncles, and cousins.

B. A phone call. Listen to Kathy and Gloria talk about the plans for a family reunion. Then, read each sentence and ⊙ircle T for *true* or F for *false*.

1. Kathy and Gloria haven't spoken for a long time.	T	F
2. Their family has become very large.	T	F
3. The family has just had a reunion.	T	F
4. Angela has sent out the invitations already.	T	F
5. Gloria has just become a grandmother.	T	F
6. Michael has just retired.	T	F
7. Michael has opened a small business.	T	F

Active Grammar: Present Perfect

A. <u>Underline</u> the present perfect tense in the sentences below. (Circle) *for* or *since*.

> The **present perfect** tells about an action that began in the past and continues into the present.
>   They **have lived** in this country for five years.
>   She **has worked** at that company since she graduated from college.
>
> The present perfect can also talk about the recent past. These sentences often use *just, recently,* or *lately.*
>   I **have** just **quit** my job.
>   He **hasn't felt** well *lately.*
>
> Use the past participle form of the verb with *have / has.*

I You We They	have haven't	been friends with him gone out with him	for two years.
He She	has hasn't	worked with him	since January.

1. Kathy and Gloria <u>haven't spoken</u> **(for)** **/** **since** several months.

2. Michael <u>has managed</u> a small business **for** **/** **since** three years.

3. Tuan and Lana have been married **for** **/** **since** 1989.

4. Henry has belonged to the volunteer fire department **for** **/** **since** 2000.

5. Joanna has sold life insurance **for** **/** **since** ten years.

6. Rita has been divorced **for** **/** **since** six months.

7. Richard has owned his own business **for** **/** **since** he moved to Ohio.

8. Tom has been in college **for** **/ since** six years.

9. Anna has walked two miles a day **for** **/** **since** she had her heart attack.

10. Brian hasn't found a job **for** **/** **since** he graduated from college.

B. *Since.* Make sentences with the information on the left and the *since* clauses on the right. Many combinations are possible.

1. I haven't had a good night's sleep   since I fell in love.

2. I have had several complaints from my neighbors   since I had the baby.

3. I have lost 10 pounds   since I joined the health club.

4. I've made several new friends

5. I haven't been able to concentrate on my job   since I bought a dog.

C. Listen and repeat.

Simple form	Simple past	Past participle	Simple form	Simple past	Past participle
be	was/were	been	leave	left	left
bear	bore	born	lose	lost	lost
become	became	become	make	made	made
begin	began	begun	meet	met	met
break	broke	broken	pay	paid	paid
bring	brought	brought	put	put	put
buy	bought	bought	quit	quit	quit
come	came	come	read	read	read
do	did	done	say	said	said
drink	drank	drunk	see	saw	seen
drive	drove	driven	sell	sold	sold
eat	ate	eaten	send	sent	sent
fall	fell	fallen	sit	sat	sat
feel	felt	felt	sleep	slept	slept
find	found	found	speak	spoke	spoken
forget	forgot	forgotten	spend	spent	spent
get	got	got/gotten	take	took	taken
give	gave	given	teach	taught	taught
go	went	gone	tell	told	told
grow	grew	grown	think	thought	thought
have	had	had	understand	understood	understood
hear	heard	heard	win	won	won
know	knew	known	write	wrote	written

D. Complete the sentences with the correct form of the verbs in the present perfect.

1. I (know) _____ *have known* _____ Juan for ten years.

2. She (fall) _____ in love.

3. He (make) _____ the soccer team at high school.

4. Stanley (get) _____ just _____ his driver's license.

5. Silvia (find) _____ a new job recently.

6. Henry (become) _____ a model.

7. My sister (come) _____ just _____ from Japan.

8. They (sell) _____ their house recently.

9. My uncle (buy) _____ an airplane!

10. My mother (be) _____ a teacher since 1990.

E. Pronunciation. Listen to the stress as each speaker <u>clarifies</u> the information. <u>Underline</u> the word that is stressed.

1. **A:** I hear that David has bought a sailboat.

   B: Not exactly. He's bought a <u>motorboat.</u>

2. **A:** I hear that Amy has moved to North Carolina.

   B: Close. She's moved to South Carolina.

3. **A:** I hear that Nora has gotten her driver's license.

   B: No, just the opposite. She's lost her driver's license.

4. **A:** I hear that Joe and Tom have opened an Italian restaurant.

   B: Not Italian. They've opened a Mexican restaurant.

Practice the sentences above with a partner. Then, complete these conversations and practice them with a partner.

5. **A:** I hear that Paul has made the baseball team.

   B: No, he's made the _____ team.

6. **A:** I hear that Alex and Kathy have gotten a cat.

   B: Not exactly. They've gotten a _____.

F. Changes. Describe five changes in these people's lives.

1.

Allen ten years ago

Allen today

2.

Mary and Tom five years ago

Mary and Tom today

G. Find someone who . . . Stand up, walk around the classroom, and ask your classmates about their activities this month. Try to find someone who answers *Yes* to each item. Write that student's name on the line.

> Have you changed jobs?   No, I haven't.   (Continue to ask other students!)
> Have you changed jobs?   Yes, I have.   (Write that student's name.)

1. buy / any new clothes?   _____

2. see / a good movie?   _____

3. go / to a party?   _____

4. move?   _____

5. have / a haircut?   _____

6. take / a test?   _____

7. be / late for class?   _____

H. Conversation. Write a conversation with one student who answered *Yes* to one of the questions above. Then, read your conversation to the class.

> A: Have you bought any new clothes?   B: Yes, I have.
> A: What did you buy?   B: I bought a pair of jeans.
> A: Where did you get them?   B: At Shoppers' World.

A: Have you _____ ?

B: _____ .

A: _____ ?

B: _____ .

A: _____ ?

B: _____ .

I. Contrast—present perfect and simple past.

> The **present perfect tense** tells about actions that began in the past and continue into the present.
>   I ***have lived*** in this country for three years.
>   She ***has lived*** in that apartment since she graduated from college.
>
> The **present perfect tense** describes events in the recent past.
>   He ***has found*** a new job.
>   They ***have*** just ***won*** the lottery.
>
> The **past tense** describes an action completed in the past. The time is stated or known.
>   She ***graduated*** from college in 2001.
>   They ***moved*** to New Mexico two years ago.

Complete the sentences using the correct form of the verbs in the past or the present perfect.

1. Dave moved into his apartment one year ago.

   He (live) _____has lived_____ in his apartment for a year.

   The landlord (just / increase) _____ his rent by $200!

2. My mother and father (be married) _____have been married_____ for a long time.

   They (get) _____ married in 1950.

3. I (join) _____ the Democratic Party ten years ago.

   I _____have belonged_____ to the Democratic Party for ten years.

4. She _____began_____ to work at the nursing home three years ago.

   She (work) _____ at the nursing home for three years.

5. I (take) _____ my examination two weeks ago.

   I (just / receive) _____ my grade.

6. Carol (look) _____ a new job for several months.

   She (quit) _____ her job four months ago.

7. Richard (start) _____ his diet two months ago.

   He (lose) _____ fifteen pounds since he started his diet.

8. George (drive) _____ his convertible for over 25 years!

   He (buy) _____ it in 1975.

9. I (take) _____ my first art class five years ago.

   Since that time, I (paint) _____ over one hundred pictures.

10. Sofia (have) _____ a heart attack last month.

    She (negative - eat) _____ any fried foods since then.

11. They (move) _____ to California in 2001.

    They (live) _____ in Los Angeles since they arrived.

12. Sherry and Kathy (be) _____ best friends for a long time.

    They (meet) _____ for the first time when they were in high school.

Active Grammar: Already and Yet

> **Already** shows that an action is completed. Use **already** in affirmative sentences. You can use the present perfect tense or the past tense.
> She **has already bought** the invitations.   She **already bought** the invitations.
> She **has bought** the invitations **already**.   She **bought** the invitations **already**.
> She **has already bought** the invitations.   She **already bought** the invitations.
>
> **Yet** shows the action has not been completed. Use **yet** in negative sentences and in questions. You can use the present perfect tense or the past tense.
> Has she **sent** the invitations **yet**?   Did she **send** the invitations **yet**?

A. Reunion plans. Listen to the conversation between Angela and Gloria. Check the things that Angela has already completed.

Completed	Not completed	Things to do for the reunion
✓		form a committee to help plan the reunion
		set a date
		make the invitations on the computer
		find the addresses of relatives who have moved
		send the invitations
		plan the activities and games
		order the cake
		plan the menu
		buy the decorations
		hire two people to help cook, serve, and clean up

B. The to-do list. Discuss each item on Angela's list using *already* or *yet*.

> She has **already** formed a committee to plan the reunion.
> They haven't sent the invitations **yet**.

C. My goals. Before you came to the United States, what were three of your goals? Did you want to learn English? Did you want to buy a car? Write three of your goals below.

1. _____
2. _____
3. _____

Read each goal to your group. Explain whether you have accomplished that goal since you came to this country. Use *already* or *yet* in your answer.

D. After the party. George and Monica had a party and almost all of the guests have left. They have just begun to clean their home. Use the cues below to talk about their progress. What have they done? What haven't they done?

put away the food	collect the cans and bottles
clear off the table	blow out the candles
take down the decorations	eat the last piece of cake
sweep the floor	close the windows
wash the dishes	get Monica's brother to leave
empty the garbage can	turn off the stereo

E. What have you done today? Ask one another about your day so far.

Have you gotten your mail yet?
Yes, I have. I got it at 10:00. *or*
No, I haven't. I don't get my mail until 4:00.

go to work   get your mail   eat a piece of fruit

buy anything   do your homework   exercise

make a phone call   take a shower

make your bed   speak in class   watch TV   read the newspaper

The Big Picture: Gossip

A. Discuss this vocabulary.

gossip	clinic	grounded
broken off	face-lift	date / go out with

B. Gossip. Listen to these people talk about their friends, family, and coworkers. Label each person in the pictures.

Rosa	Paul	Grandpa	Diana	Mary	Amy

1. _____

2. _____

3. _____

4. _____

5. _____

6. _____

C. Answer these questions about the gossip you heard.

1. Who has had a face-lift?
2. Who has just been promoted?
3. Who has begun to date a much older man?
4. Who has broken off her engagement?
5. Who has bought a red convertible?

6. Who has just been in an accident?

7. Who has just been at a clinic?

8. Who has been grounded?

9. Who has fallen in love with a neighbor?

10. Who has left to travel across the country?

11. Who has taken away their daughter's cell phone?

D. Read these statements. Circle *T* for *true* and *F* for *false*.

1. Diana still has Chris's ring.	T	F
2. Rosa looks wonderful!	T	F
3. Rosa told all her friends that she had a face-lift.	T	F
4. Amy's parents have taken away her cell phone.	T	F
5. This is the first time that Amy has gotten in trouble.	T	F
6. Paul has been promoted.	T	F
7. Paul has the best sales record in the company.	T	F
8. Mary is dating a man who is much older than she is.	T	F
9. Grandpa has bought a new car.	T	F
10. Grandpa now has gray hair.	T	F

E. Surprise intonation. To show surprise and interest, a listener often repeats a few words of a speaker's conversation with question intonation. Listen and repeat the surprise intonation.

1. **A:** He bought a new convertible. **B:** A new convertible?

2. **A:** He left yesterday. **B:** He left?

3. **A:** He's just been promoted. **B:** Promoted?

4. **A:** She's run off with a man twice her age. **B:** Twice her age?

Listen and show surprise at statements 5–10.

F. Write three statements with surprising news. Tell your partner the news. Your partner will show surprise at the information.

1. _____ .

2. _____ .

3. _____ .

Reading: A Family Newsletter

A. Skimming for the main idea. The first four sections of this family newsletter on page 127 talk about a specific event. Look quickly at the four sections and write the events they describe.

Section 1: <u>Plans for the family reunion</u>   Section 3: _____

Section 2: _____   Section 4: _____

B. Skimming for details. Look quickly through the information in the newsletter. Answer these questions.

1. What are the dates for the family reunion?

2. Where is the barbecue on Saturday?

3. Where is the family going on Sunday?

4. What did Debbie major in? Does she have a job yet?

5. How old is Grandma Nelson?

6. Where did Fred and Ann move? What did Fred buy?

7. Where are they volunteering?

8. What kind of an operation did Laura have?

9. What kind of information is Karen looking for?

C. Vocabulary. Match these words from the newsletter with their meanings. Then, complete the sentences below with the words in their correct form.

<u>d</u> **1.** adjust to	**a.**	contribute money or time
_____ **2.** hassle-free	**b.**	became
_____ **3.** elderly	**c.**	job possibilities
_____ **4.** turned	**d.**	meet or handle changes in your life
_____ **5.** chip in	**e.**	in the future
_____ **6.** ahead	**f.**	easy
_____ **7.** leads	**g.**	people who are very old.

1. Sunday is the only _____ day of the week.

2. All the children _____ to buy their parents a trip to Bermuda.

3. My sister, who just had twins, has many sleepless nights _____.

4. I'm 19. I'll _____ 20 on March 5.

5. Greg has just graduated with a degree in physical therapy. He is looking into several _____.

The Nelsons in the News

Circle August 14th and 15th on your calendars! This year's reunion committee includes Doris, Frank, Lynn, and Roberto. For Saturday, we've already reserved ten tables in Essex Park, close to the children's playground and across from the pond. We'll all **chip in** for the chicken and burgers and each family will bring a salad and dessert. Most people have asked us to plan Sunday as a day at the beach. People have requested a relaxing, **hassle-free** day. We're talking to different delis in the area and are planning to order a large picnic lunch. Look at the next issue for more details! We'd love your suggestions and comments. Call Angela at 555-8739.

Congratulations to Debbie Nelson. After eight years at college, sometimes full-time, sometimes part-time, Debbie has just completed all her course work in social work. She will graduate in May. Debbie has accepted a position at Atlantic Community Services, where she will be working with troubled teens.

Grandma Mayra Nelson **turned** 99 on January 2nd. She lives with her daughter, Eva, and son-in-law, Brad. Mayra enjoys TV, her flower garden, and visits from her four children, 12 grandchildren, and 30 great-grandchildren. She will become a great, great-grandmother in March! Mayra says that she is looking forward to her 100th birthday. She tells her children, "I expect a big party to celebrate my wonderful family."

Hi everyone!
Our new home in Florida is only five blocks from the beach. After working for 40 years, Ann and I were wondering how we would **adjust to** retirement. It wasn't hard! Ann has joined a tennis group and she plays three mornings a week. I've bought a little fishing boat and you'll find me on the water two or three mornings a week. I haven't caught "the big one" yet, but I'm planning to! Ann and I are also volunteering at the local community center. We deliver Meals on Wheels to the **elderly** one day a week. Two days a week, we read with children in an after-school program for kids who need extra help with their schoolwork. Don't worry—we haven't forgotten about all of you. We'll be coming up for the family reunion. If you are planning a trip to Florida, we'd love to see you. Our number is 555-3494.

Fred

Send your get-well cards to Laura. Her knee replacement went well, but she has several months of physical therapy **ahead**. Her address: 346 Windsor Avenue.

Karen is looking for job **leads**. Her company closed its doors last month, leaving 75 accountants looking for work. If you have any suggestions, please call her at 555-9087.

Congratulations to Todd! He has been accepted to Duke University, his first-choice college.

A. Newsletters include information about family events, both large and small. Did anyone in your extended family recently . . .

☐ graduate   ☐ celebrate a birthday   ☐ lose a job

☐ get married   ☐ celebrate an anniversary   ☐ accept a new job

☐ get engaged   ☐ take a vacation   ☐ have an accident

☐ get divorced   ☐ move   ☐ have an operation

☐ have a baby   ☐ retire   ☐ pass away (die)

Other: ☐ _____

Tell the class about one of these events.

B. Read this news article from a family newsletter.

Henry has just accepted a position as distribution manager at Davis and Bates. Davis and Bates is a growing furniture manufacturer in the West. Henry will coordinate all the company's deliveries. Currently, the company employs 25 people in its distribution center. They are planning to expand this to 50 employees. Henry is selling his house, and he will leave for California next month. His wife, Paula, and their two children will move to California after they sell their house.

C. Getting the facts. When reporting facts, it is important to get all the details. Specific facts provide interesting and clear information. Read the examples. Then, use your imagination to write specific facts about each statement.

1. Thomas graduated from college.

   Thomas graduated from the University of Maryland in May with a degree in biology.

   _____

2. Tuan and Lana had a baby.

   Tuan and Lana had an eight-pound baby girl on September 18th. They have named the

   baby Kathy, after Lana's mother.

3. Linda celebrated her birthday.

_____

_____

4. Tom was in a bad car accident.

_____

_____

5. Ken and Susan celebrated their wedding anniversary.

_____

_____

6. Karin and Juan have just returned from a wonderful vacation.

_____

_____

D. A news article. Write a short factual article about an event in your family, your class, or your school.

E. Edit. Find and correct the mistakes in these sentences.

1. She have just found a new job.
2. They haven't gotten married already.
3. They get married on October 10.
4. They has just celebrated their tenth wedding anniversary.
5. Jason has come already home from the hospital.
6. They have lived in the same house for 1990.
7. Olga has graduated from Duke University last month.
8. Ron has take a job in Arizona.
9. Grandma Barnes pass away on June 15.
10. The whole family have just enjoyed a wonderful family reunion.

Looking at the Internet

Click on **Search** and enter the words "family reunion." What kinds of services can you find at a family reunion Web site? What can you buy to make the reunion more fun or more memorable? Tell your classmates what you found.

A. A changed city. Last year, Tamara returned to her native country for the first time in ten years. Complete these sentences about the changes in her hometown. Use the present perfect tense.

1. Ten years ago, there were two doctors. Now there is a small clinic with six doctors. The health care system (improve) _____ has improved _____.

2. The population (increase) _____ from 25,000 to 50,000.

3. Many new restaurants (open) _____.

4. The unemployment rate (decrease) _____ from 15 percent to 9 percent.

5. Tourism (become) _____ a major industry.

6. The city (hire) _____ fifteen new police officers.

7. The crime rate (drop) _____ substantially.

8. Many new businesses (move) _____ into the area because of the strong economy.

9. Her quiet village (change) _____ into a busy, noisy town.

B. A changed student. Tommy had a difficult first semester at college and is now on academic probation. He's changed and become a serious student. Compare his first and second semesters at school using the present perfect tense.

First Semester: The "old" Tommy

1. He missed ten days of school.

2. He was late for his classes.

3. He failed every test.

4. He didn't ask for extra help.

5. He didn't do his homework.

6. He failed two courses.

7. He didn't study for tests.

8. He didn't write any papers.

Second Semester: The "new" Tommy

1. He has missed only one day of school.

2. _____.

3. _____.

4. _____.

5. _____.

6. _____.

7. _____.

8. _____.

Grammar Summary

> **1. Present perfect**

  a. The present perfect tense tells about an action that started in the past and continues into the present. The action is not completed.

    They **have lived** in Miami for six years.

    He **has owned** that company since he moved to Wisconsin.

  b. The present perfect describes actions in the recent past. It is often used with *just, lately,* and *recently.* If the sentence gives a specific time or date, use the past tense.

    She **has just found** a new job.

    She **found** a new job last week. (This sentence gives a specific past time.)

    I've spoken to him recently.

    I **spoke** to him yesterday. (This sentence gives a specific past time.)

  c. The present perfect is used with *already* and *yet.*

    She **has already bought** her plane ticket.

    I **haven't registered** for my classes **yet**.

> **2. Statements**

Use **have** or **has** and the past participle to form the present perfect.

I You We They	**have** **haven't**	**worked** here **known** him	for two years.
He She	**has** **hasn't**	**been** married	since 2001.

> **3. Yes/No questions**

Have	I you we they	**worked** here **known** him	for two years?
Has	he she	**been** married	since 2001?

9 Job Performance

A. Discuss the different jobs in the pictures.

1. What is the job title for each person?

2. Does this person work in production or service?

3. What skills does this person need for the job?

4. Would you like this kind of work? Why or why not?

B. Sit in a group of two or three students. Talk about your jobs.

1. What company do you work for?

2. What product does this company make or what service does it provide?

3. How many employees work for your company?

4. What kinds of positions does your company have?

5. Is there a human resources or personnel office?

6. How long have you worked there?

7. What do you do? What are your job responsibilities?

8. What benefits do you receive?

9. How often do you receive a performance evaluation?

Active Grammar: *How long* and *How many*

> ***How long*** asks about an amount of time.
>   How long **has** she **been repairing** TVs?   She's been repairing TVs for two hours.
>
> ***How many*** asks about a specific number.
>   How many TVs **has** she **repaired**?   She **has repaired** four TVs.
>
> When we use the **present perfect**, it shows that the action is <u>not yet completed.</u>
> The person is still working or performing the action.
>
> **Note:** When we use the **past**, it shows that the action is <u>completed.</u>
>
>   How many TVs **did** she **repair**?   She **repaired** 25 TVs. (Her work is finished.)

A. Read this conversation.

A: What is Harry doing?

B: He's registering students for classes.

A: How long has he been sitting at the registration counter?

B: He's been sitting there for two hours.

A: How many students has he registered so far?

B: He's registered 18 students so far today.

B. Ask and answer questions about each picture. Use Exercise A as an example.

What is he/she doing?

How long has he/she been _____?

How many _____ has he/she _____?

Active Grammar: Repeated Past Actions

Indefinite time expressions and adverbs of frequency

We use the **present perfect** to talk about *repeated past actions*. These actions have occurred several times and may occur again. In these sentences, we are interested in the action, and not in the time of the action. We often use indefinite time expressions and adverbs of frequency in these sentences.

1. Place most indefinite time expressions at the end of a sentence.

from time to time	a few times	once
two times so far this month	so far	twice

   I have missed work **from time to time.**   I have missed work **two times this month.**

2. Place adverbs of frequency before the main verb.

always	often	seldom
frequently	sometimes	never

   I have **never** been late for work.   I have **seldom** missed work.

A. Ask your teacher about his/her job and interests.

1. How long have you been teaching at this school?
2. Have you ever worked at a different school?
3. Have you ever taught any other subjects?
4. Have you ever studied another language?
5. Have you ever had a different kind of a job?
6. Have you ever gotten stuck in traffic on your way to work?
7. Have you ever visited _____?
8. Have you ever eaten _____ food?
9. Have you ever acted in a play?
10. Have you ever played on a sports team?

B. Ask and answer these questions about work.

A: Have you ever taken a personal day?
B: Yes, I've taken one personal day this year.

1. call in sick?
2. have an accident at work?
3. quit a job?
4. receive a raise?
5. get a promotion?
6. receive a performance evaluation?
7. complain to your boss?
8. complain about your boss?
9. work a double shift?
10. attend a training program?
11. have a problem with a coworker?
12. (be) laid off?

Ask your partner two more questions about work.

Time expressions are usually placed at the end of a sentence.

I began to work here **in 2000**.   I have worked here **for two years**.

Pay attention to the placement of adverbs of frequency and indefinite time expressions in the present perfect tense.

1. Place adverbs of frequency before the main verb.

    Laura has **never** received a warning at work.

2. Place **just, already**, and **finally** before the main verb. **Already** can also be placed at the end of the sentence.

    Henry has **just** gotten a raise.   I've **already** had dinner. OR
                                              I've had dinner **already**.

3. Place **yet, recently**, and **at last** at the end of the sentence.

    I've spoken to him **recently**.   Bill hasn't finished the report **yet**.

4. Place indefinite time expressions at the end of a sentence.

    I have changed jobs **twice**.   She's taken four breaks today **so far**!

A. Make four sentences about each picture using the cues. Place the adverbs and time expressions in the correct place in the sentences. Use the simple past or the present perfect.

go on a job interview

1.

| twice | just |
| yesterday | last week |

take a vacation

2.

| never | last summer |
| two years ago | recently |

get a promotion

3.

| last year | yet |
| twice | in 2002 |

complete the order

4.

| yesterday | finally |
| an hour ago | already |

B. Pronunciation: Simple past tense versus present perfect tense. Listen and repeat.

> **Note:** Sometimes it's difficult to hear if a person is using the past or present perfect. It's important to know which one is being used because it can change the meaning.

1. a. I sold five cars.   b. I've sold five cars.
2. a. She worked five hours.   b. She's worked five hours.
3. a. They made 500 donuts.   b. They've made 500 donuts.
4. a. She walked five miles.   b. She's walked five miles.
5. a. I helped 10 customers.   b. I've helped 10 customers.
6. a. He planted five trees.   b. He's planted five trees.
7. a. She read 20 pages.   b. She's read 20 pages.
8. a. I cleaned seven rooms.   b. I've cleaned seven rooms.
9. a. He typed four reports.   b. He's typed four reports.
10. a. I checked in 50 passengers. b. I've checked in 50 passengers.

Listen again and ⟨circle⟩ the sentence you hear.

Practice these sentences with a partner.

C. Listen to each sentence. ⟨Circle⟩ the letter of the sentence that shows the correct meaning.

1. a. The doctor is still seeing patients.
    b. The doctor is finished seeing patients for the day.
2. a. Benji is still ironing shirts.
    b. Benji is finished ironing shirts for the day.
3. a. The men are still planting trees.
    b. The men are finished planting the trees.
4. a. The teacher has more papers to correct.
    b. The teacher finished all the papers.
5. a. Carlos is finished for the day.
    b. Carlos is still in his truck, delivering packages.
6. a. Mary is not going to call any more people today.
    b. Mary will call 100 more people.
7. a. She retired from the hospital.
    b. She's still working at the hospital.
8. a. He will drive farther today.
    b. He's going to stop for the day.
9. a. There are still customers in line.
    b. She is going home because the bank is now closed.

> We use the **past tense** to describe an action that occurred at a <u>specific</u> time or event.
>
> I **ate** lunch at La Salsa last Friday. The food was delicious.
>
> We can use the **present perfect** to describe an action that occurred at an <u>unspecified</u> time in the past. The sentence does not talk about a specific event or time. The action is more important than the exact time.
>
> I've **eaten** at La Salsa. The food is delicious.

A. Complete the sentences with the past or the present perfect of the verbs in parentheses.

1. Bob _____ (receive) a raise last year.

2. Bob _____ (receive) two raises this year and it's only July.

3. Laura _____ (have) six job interviews so far this year.

4. Laura _____ (have) a job interview in Dallas yesterday.

5. I _____ (hear) that song a hundred times.

6. I _____ (hear) that song a few minutes ago.

7. Sarah _____ (take) two sick days when she had the flu.

8. Sarah _____ (take) two sick days this year.

9. We _____ (hire) three new workers, and we need one more.

10. We _____ (hire) the four new workers that we needed.

B. Ask and answer the questions. Be careful of the tense!

1. Have you missed any days of school this year?

2. How many days have you been absent so far?

3. Why did you miss class last week?

4. How many different jobs have you had in your life?

5. Where do you work now? How long have you been working there?

6. Where did you work before this?

7. Why did you leave that job?

8. How many different countries have you lived in?

9. Have you ever traveled to _____?

10. Where did you go on your last vacation?

Job Performance

A. Read George's job description. Then, listen as he describes his job. Answer the questions.

Job Description for Metro Transit Drivers

1. Report to work on time and in full uniform.
2. Drive carefully and obey all traffic and safety laws.
3. Pick up and discharge passengers at designated bus stops.
4. Collect correct fares.
5. Greet and treat passengers with courtesy.

Company policy: Employee pay starts at $9.00 an hour. All employees with good evaluations receive a pay increase of $0.50 a year. If the employee has no accidents in five years, pay will increase to $13.00.

George's Salary (1998–2003)

1998	1999	2000	2001	2002	2003
$9.00	$9.50	$10.00	$10.50	$11.00	$13.00

1. How long has George been working for Metro Transit?
2. What year did he begin to work there?
3. How much was his starting salary?
4. Has his salary increased each year?
5. Has he ever had an accident?
6. What year is it?
7. How many pay increases has George received since 1998?
8. What is his salary now?

B. Complete this information about George and his job. Use the past or present perfect form of the verbs in parentheses.

1. Before he started at Metro Transit, George _____ (work) as a school bus driver.

2. He _____ (negative—like) the noise on the school bus.

3. He _____ (see) an ad in the newspaper for Metro Transit.

4. He _____ (apply) for the job and _____ (receive) a job offer the next week.

5. When George began at Metro Transit, he _____ (earn) $9.00 an hour.

6. He _____ (receive) a pay raise every year since then.

7. His performance evaluations _____ always _____ (be) very good.

8. He _____ (have) two or three passenger complaints, which is less than the company average.

9. George _____ only _____ one serious problem at work. (have)

10. Two years ago, he _____ (get) a ticket for speeding.

11. He _____ (pay) a fine of $200 and the company _____ (charge) him another $250.

12. George _____ always _____ polite and courteous to the passengers. (be)

C. **Employee performance.** These four insurance agents have been working for CarCo for one year or more. Look at the chart and answer the questions about their job performance.

Employee	Years at CarCo	Policies Last Year	Policies This Year to Date	Customer Complaints This Year
Jeff	3	125	43	2
Katie	1	67	40	5
George	4	55	22	0
Ellen	2	88	35	10

1. Who has worked at CarCo the longest?

2. How long has George worked there?

3. Is George the best agent at CarCo? Why or why not?

4. Who wrote the most policies last year? Who wrote the fewest?

5. Who has written the most policies so far this year?

6. Which agent has received the fewest complaints?

7. Ellen has sold many policies so far this year. Why is the boss dissatisfied with her performance?

8. George has never received a customer complaint. Why is the boss dissatisfied with his performance?

9. Katie has worked at CarCo for only one year. How would you evaluate her performance?

10. Who is the best agent at CarCo?

A. Evaluation forms. Mr. Davis owns a large jewelry store. Every six months he evaluates his employees. Today he is talking to two employees, Katie and Amy. Read the job description and look at the evaluation forms. Discuss any new words or phrases.

Davis Jewelry: Sales Assistant

Assist customers in making jewelry selections

Maintain and restock displays

Perform sales transactions accurately

Follow all store procedures and policies

B. Katie's evaluation. Listen as Mr. Davis evaluates Katie and check the appropriate boxes. He will focus on Katie's strengths and areas that need improvement. If Mr. Davis does not mention an area, you can check that she meets expectations. Then, answer the questions about her evaluation.

	Exceeds Expectations	Meets Expectations	Requires Improvement	Unsatisfactory
General				
Reports to work as scheduled				
Appearance is neat and appropriate				
Shows initiative				
Maintains displays on a daily basis				
Customer service				
Assists customers in a professional manner				
Uses effective sales techniques				
Transactions and procedures				
Performs sales transactions accurately				
Reports messages and information effectively				

1. Is Mr. Davis pleased with Katie's work?
2. Has she always arrived on time? Has her on-time arrival improved?
3. Does she show initiative at work? Explain your answer.
4. How are Katie's sales?
5. Has she used effective sales techniques? How do you know?
6. What has happened when she has overcharged the customers? What has happened when she has undercharged the customers?
7. When does Katie make mistakes in her sales transactions?
8. What has Mr. Davis decided to do?
9. Does Katie like her job?

C. Amy's evaluation. Listen as Mr. Davis evaluates Amy and check the appropriate boxes. He will focus on Amy's strengths and areas that need improvement. If Mr. Davis does not mention an area, you can check that she meets expectations. Then, answer the questions about her evaluation.

	Exceeds Expectations	Meets Expectations	Requires Improvement	Unsatisfactory
General				
Reports to work as scheduled				
Appearance is neat and appropriate				
Shows initiative				
Maintains displays on a daily basis				
Customer service				
Assists customers in a professional manner				
Uses effective sales techniques				
Transactions and procedures				
Performs sales transactions accurately				
Reports messages and information effectively				

1. Is Mr. Davis pleased with Amy's appearance?
2. Why doesn't Mr. Davis like Amy's nails?
3. How has Amy shown initiative?
4. Has Amy ever thought of studying art or design?
5. How are Amy's sales?
6. Has she always used effective sales techniques?
7. In what other area does Amy need improvement?
8. What kind of mistakes has Amy made on the phone?
9. Why has this caused a problem?
10. What does Mr. Davis want Amy to do?
11. Does Amy like her job?

Reading: The Changing Workforce

A. Before You Read. Match each vocabulary word with its meaning.

_____ **1.** to outnumber   **a.** to grow larger

_____ **2.** to age   **b.** to have a greater amount or number

_____ **3.** to increase   **c.** equal

_____ **4.** to be in demand   **d.** to get older

_____ **5.** to account for   **e.** to stay

_____ **6.** to remain   **f.** to be needed or required

The workforce of the United States includes everyone who is now working and everyone who is looking for a job. The Bureau of Labor Statistics evaluates the current workforce and employment opportunities, and it makes predictions about the future.

Between 2000 and 2010, approximately 17 million new workers will enter the workforce, bringing the total number of workers in the United States to 168 million. What will this workforce look like? The number of women in the workforce has **increased** steadily from 1945 to the present. Because of this, almost half of all workers will be women (48%). The workforce is **aging**, too. Baby boomers—people born between 1946 and 1964—make up almost half the workforce. As this group ages, more workers will be in their 50s and 60s. The social security retirement age is gradually rising, influencing how long workers **remain** on the job. The workforce will become more ethnically diverse, also. In 2000, 73.1 percent of the workforce was classified as White, non-Hispanic. By 2010, this will fall to 69.2 percent. The Hispanic workforce will soon **outnumber** all other ethnic groups, accounting for 13.3 percent of the total workers. Blacks will make up 12.7 percent and Asians 6.1 percent.

The labor department defines two types of jobs—goods-producing jobs and service-providing jobs. Goods-producing jobs include manufacturing, agriculture, mining, and fishing. There will be almost no growth in goods-producing jobs because of the increasing use of machinery and because most goods are now produced in other countries. Any growth in this area will be for replacement workers, taking the jobs of workers who are retiring or moving to other employment.

Service providers, in industries such as education, health services, finance, transportation, and communications, will **account for** 20.2 million new jobs between 2000 and 2010. Many of these new jobs will require a college degree. Occupations such as computer programmers, educators, professional health-care workers, and librarians are four-year college degree programs. Businesses will be looking for accountants, public-relations managers, and computer information systems managers. There will be at least five million new service jobs such as food preparers, health-care support workers, transportation workers, and security guards. Most of these will require only high school graduation and possibly a short training program. Salespersons and cashiers will also **be in demand**.

Every two years, the United States government publishes the *Occupational Outlook Handbook*, which presents specific information about the job market and the job outlook. Each job is described in detail with job descriptions, training required, salary information, and future prospects. The reference section of every library has this book to help students and workers plan for their future careers.

Source: Bureau of Labor Statistics; *Occupational Outlook Handbook*

B. Understanding numbers. Check the reading again and decide if these statements are true or false.

1. By 2010, there will be about 168 million workers in the U.S.   T   F

2. Soon there will be more women than men in the workforce.   T   F

3. The workforce is growing older.   T   F

4. As the age for social security retirement rises, people will work longer.   T   F

5. The white, non-Hispanic workforce is now 73.1 percent of the labor force.   T   F

6. By 2010, there will be more Hispanic workers than black workers.   T   F

7. There are more Asians than blacks in the workforce.   T   F

8. The number of goods-producing jobs will continue to increase.   T   F

9. There will be 20.2 million new jobs in education and health services.   T   F

10. All new service jobs will require a college degree.   T   F

C. Read the second paragraph again. List three general characteristics of the labor force in 2010.

1. _____

2. _____

3. _____

A. Read.

I am considering a career as a dental hygienist. A dental hygienist usually works in a dentist's office. A dental hygienist removes plaque and deposits from teeth, takes dental X-rays, and explains to patients how to clean and floss their teeth. In some offices, dental hygienists administer anesthetics, fill cavities, and assist the dentist.

All dental hygienists must be licensed by their state. It is necessary to attend an accredited dental hygiene program and to pass a written and a clinical examination. Many community colleges offer dental hygienist programs and most dental hygienists have their associate degree. At school, students study in classrooms, in clinical settings, and in laboratories. They take many science courses, such as anatomy, physiology, chemistry, and radiography. There is a strong job outlook for dental hygienists. In this field, many people work part-time and the hours can be flexible. The average salary is about $25.00 an hour.

I'm interested in this career because I like working with people and helping people. The working conditions are clean and pleasant. My favorite subject in high school was biology and I did very well. I'm a little concerned about chemistry, because I didn't do well in that subject. I don't have the time to attend college for four years. An occupation that only requires a two-year program and has a good salary and job prospects is appealing to me.

B. Thinking about jobs. What are you good at? Check your job skills.

☐ selling	☐ designing	☐ repairing things
☐ planning	☐ calculating	☐ inspecting
☐ managing money	☐ researching	☐ teaching
☐ writing reports	☐ supervising people	☐ public speaking
☐ organizing	☐ managing people	☐ helping people
☐ operating equipment	☐ programming	☐ using software

Check the job values that are the most important to you:

☐ salary   ☐ benefits

☐ job status   ☐ job security

☐ promotion possibilities   ☐ job training

C. Researching a job. Choose a career that sounds interesting to you. Look in the *Occupational Outlook Handbook* in the library or online (www.bls.gov). Or, use America's Career InfoNet online (acincet.org). Find out the following information about a career. Take short notes.

Career title:	
Nature of the work (job description):	
Working conditions:	
Education or training required:	
Earnings:	
Job outlook:	

D. Writing: Looking at careers. Write a paragraph or two describing the job you researched. Then, explain why this career is or is not a good job choice for you.

E. Edit. Find and correct the mistakes in these sentences.

1. I have never take a sick day.

2. She has gotten along with her coworkers always.

3. He has spoken to the boss a few minutes ago.

4. She has receive an award as the top salesperson twice this year.

5. Have you never attended a sales meeting?

6. They have never went on a job interview.

7. She have not always followed company policies.

 Looking at the Internet

Many Web sites contain helpful information about jobs, requirements, training, salaries, and job outlooks. Check one of these sites. What jobs have the best job outlook for the future?

Occupational Outlook Handbook   www.bls.gov

American's Career InfoNet   www.acinet.org

Practicing on Your Own

A. An evaluation. Rewrite the sentences. Put the adverb or time expression in the correct place in the sentence.

1. Susan has worked overtime. (several times this month)

    _____.

2. She has followed company policies. (always)

    _____.

3. She has spoken to the human resources department about a promotion.
    (already)

    _____.

4. We have received a complaint about her work. (rarely)

    _____.

5. She has taken an advanced software course. (recently)

    _____.

6. She has been able to solve problems. (usually)

    _____.

7. She has completed a sales management course. (just)

    _____.

B. Evaluation reports. The owner of Excel Electronics is writing her monthly evaluation reports on two of her employees. Karl is going to receive a promotion. David is going to lose his job. Using the present perfect, compare the two workers.

Karl	David
1. He has always arrived on time.	**1.** _David has been late ten times._
2. He has taken one sick day.	**2.** _____.
3. He has sold 150 televisions.	**3.** _____.
4. _____.	**4.** He has made mistakes on seven bills of sale.
5. He has always written the correct address on delivery notices.	**5.** _____.
6. He has often worked overtime.	**6.** _____.

Grammar Summary

▶ **1. *How many* questions**

We often use the present perfect with *How many* questions. In these sentences, the person is still working or performing the action.

What is Stella doing?   She is repairing TVs.

How many TVs **has** she **repaired**?   She **has repaired** seven TVs.

Note: When we use the past tense, it shows that the action is completed.

How many TVs did she repair yesterday?   She repaired ten TVs.

▶ **2. Repeated past actions**

We use the present perfect to talk about repeated past actions. These actions may have occurred several times in the past and may occur again. We are more interested in the action than the time of the action. We often use indefinite time expressions or adverbs of frequency in these sentences.

Have you ever visited Vietnam? No, I haven't.

Have you ever gotten a promotion? Yes, I've gotten two promotions.

I **have** seldom **taken** a sick day.

I **have taken** three sick days this year.

I **have taken** a sick day from time to time.

▶ **3. Past actions**

We can use the present perfect to talk about actions that happened in the past. In these sentences, we are interested in the action, not the specific time that the action occurred.

She **has spoken** to the boss.

He **has gotten** the job.

Note: Use the past tense to talk about actions that occurred at a specific time in the past. We often use past time expressions in these sentences, or the speakers know the time that the action occurred.

She **spoke** to the boss yesterday.

He **got** a new job last month.

▶ **4. Present perfect with adverbs**

We often use the present perfect with the following adverbs:

already	I **have** *already* **filled** that order.
	I **have filled** that order *already*.
yet	She **hasn't completed** the report *yet*.
finally	The company **has** *finally* **given** the workers a raise.
at last	The new computers **have arrived** *at last*.
just	He **has** *just* **received** a large order.
recently	I **have changed** jobs *recently*.
	I **have** *recently* **changed** jobs.

Regrets and Possibilities

A. Read the thoughts and discuss each picture.

Active Grammar: Past Modals—*Should have*

A. Review the past participle forms. Write the correct past participle form of each verb.

Simple Form	Past participle	Simple form	Past participle
buy	bought	leave	
try		meet	
drive		see	
forget		lose	
fill		pay	
send		sleep	
eat		spend	
break		tell	
feel		write	

B. Listen and complete.

1. I _____ should have bought _____ a new one.
2. I _____ a used one.
3. She _____ harder.
4. I _____ for so many courses.
5. I _____ earlier.
6. I _____ to bring it.
7. They _____ the tank.
8. He _____ without a license.
9. We _____ the check on time.
10. She _____ it.

C. Complete each sentence. Use *should have* and the correct form of the verb.

> **Past Modal: *Should have***
>
> ***Should have*** expresses a regret about a **past action**.
>
> **should + (not) have** + past participle
> I **should have studied** more. (Meaning: I didn't study enough.)
> We **should have brought** warm clothes. (Meaning: We didn't bring warm clothes.)
> They **shouldn't have left** their umbrellas at home. (Meaning: They didn't bring their umbrellas.)

1. I took too many courses and now my grades are falling.

   I _____ (take) so many courses.

2. Akiko forgot to bring her book, and she needs it for the exam.

   She _____ (forget) her book.

3. Sandra's cellular phone rang during the exam.

   She _____ (turn off) her
   phone before the exam.

4. Jim stayed up very late. The next morning, he overslept and was late.

   He _____ (stay up) so late.

5. Marie wanted to take a psychology course, but she registered too late.

   She _____ (register) earlier.

6. Paul didn't type his paper and received a low grade.

   He _____ (type) his paper.

D. What should they have done? Look at each picture. Make a statement about each picture. Use *should have* and your imagination.

bring	put	remember	take	wear	eat

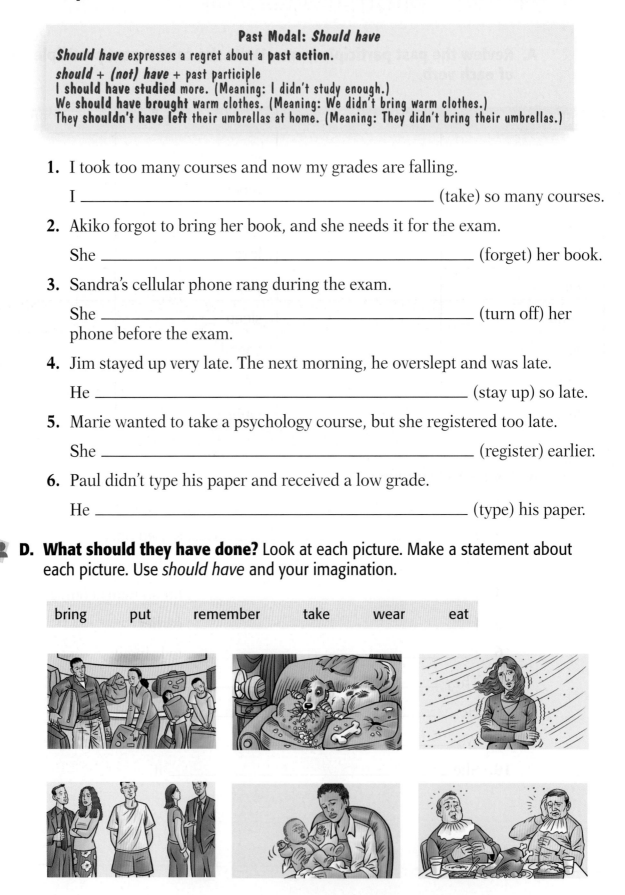

☀ *May have, might have, and could have*

> **Past modals of possibility**
>
> ***May have, might have, could have*** all express possibility about a past event.
> They have similar meanings. ***Could have*** also expresses a choice.
>
> | I
You
He
She
We
They | may have
might have
could have | gone to the movies.
forgotten to bring it.
been busy.
lost her key. |
> |---|---|---|

A. Match each statement with the correct statement of possibility.

__e__ **1.** Frank didn't come to work yesterday.

a. He might have had a job interview.

____ **2.** I wonder where the neighbors went.

b. They may have gone to Florida.

____ **3.** I saw Tariq with a strange woman. Who was she?

c. She might have bought her a teddy bear.

____ **4.** Marco was wearing a suit yesterday. He usually wears jeans.

d. You could have left them in the restaurant.

____ **5.** Madeline was in a toy store yesterday. What did she buy for her niece?

e. He may have been sick.

____ **6.** Anna isn't happy with her new job.

f. She could have taken that other job.

____ **7.** I can't find my keys.

g. That might have been his sister. I hear that she's in town.

B. Read each sentence. With a partner, write two possibilities in your notebook. Use *might have*, *may have*, or *could have* and an appropriate verb.

> The teacher was late to class.
> *The teacher might have gotten stuck in traffic.*

1. A classmate missed an important exam.
2. A classmate looked ill yesterday. Today, she didn't come to class.
3. A friend was at a travel agency last Saturday.
4. A strange woman was talking to your friend's husband.
5. A friend called you to pick her up at a hospital emergency room.
6. A very large package was delivered to your neighbors.

Must have—Deduction

Must have expresses a probability or deduction based on a past event.

I You He She We They	must have must (not) have	been sick. lost (her) keys. broken (his) leg. had an appointment.

A. Listen to a man calling 911 to report a problem in his apartment. Choose from the box below, and write the letter of the correct deduction on the space provided.

1. __g__　　2. ____　　3. ____　　4. ____

5. ____　　6. ____　　7. ____　　8. ____

a. The burglar must have used it to hide the other clothes.

b. The burglar must have taken it.

c. The burglar must have gotten scared and left through the window.

d. The burglar must have scared the cat.

e. The burglar must have dropped the gloves when he left.

f. The burglar must have been hungry.

g. Someone must have broken in.

h. The burglar must have put on one of your suits.

B. Pronunciation: Past modals. Listen and repeat.

1. You must've left your book at home.

2. She might've studied French.

3. I should've made an appointment.

4. We could've gone on a vacation.

5. He must've had to work.

6. She couldn't have walked that far.

7. We shouldn't have spoken to her.

8. They shouldn't have arrived late.

9. He may not have had an opportunity.

10. I must not have heard you.

Practice saying the sentences with a partner.

C. Pronunciation: Word stress. Listen to the conversation and <u>underline</u> the stressed words.

A: <u>Hi</u>, Julia. <u>Why</u> didn't you <u>come</u> to my <u>party</u>? Everyone <u>missed</u> you.

B: <u>What</u> party?

A: I had a party last Saturday.

B: You should've called me.

A: I did. I left a message on your machine.

B: I changed my number. You could've sent an invitation.

A: I did. I mailed it two weeks ago.

B: You must've sent it to the wrong address. I moved three weeks ago.

A: You should've told me.

B: Sorry. Anyway, how was the party?

A: It was fun. You should've been there.

D. Practice saying the conversation with a partner. Use the correct stress. Substitute your partner's name.

A. Read and look at the pictures.

1. The students are interested.

The professor is interesting.

2. The man is bored.

The woman is boring.

Many adjectives end in either **-ing** or **-ed.**

This is a very **exciting** city, and I am **excited** to be here.
The museum was **fascinating.** I've never been so **fascinated** by a museum before.

B. Listen and repeat. Discuss any new vocabulary.

annoyed	annoying	exhausted	exhausting	interested	interesting
confused	confusing	disgusted	disgusting	surprised	surprising
excited	exciting	embarrassed	embarrassing	frustrated	frustrating
depressed	depressing	frightened	frightening	challenged	challenging

C. Make sentences about each picture. Use adjectives from the list.

The student is confused by the math problem.
The math problem is confusing.

1.

the student / the math problem

2.

the music / the neighbors

3.

the children / the costume

4.

the mother / the triplets

5.

the climber / the mountain

6.

his cooking / his wife

D. Student to student dictation: Good News/Bad News

Student A: Turn to page 247.
Student B: Use the cues in numbers 1–5 to tell Student A what happened last weekend. Student A will be a good listener and give an appropriate response.

1. I / have to work overtime / all weekend
2. I / not find / keys / for two hours
3. not get / the new job
4. my son / win / football championship
5. get / promotion

Student B: Turn to page 247.
Student A: Use the cues in numbers 6–10 to tell Student B what happened last weekend. Student B will be a good listener and respond with an appropriate response.

6. my daughter / get engaged
7. I / get lost in a strange neighborhood / for an hour
8. at the bank / I / cannot express myself in English
9. I / receive a bonus
10. my friends / have a birthday party / for me

E. Read each statement. Give a response with *That must have been* or *You must have been* and an appropriate adjective from the box.

| bored | boring | embarrassed | embarrassing | challenged | challenging |
| frightened | frightening | interested | interesting | disgusted | disgusting |

1. We spent ten hours at the museum. (You)
2. My family and I were fishing when our boat sank. (That)
3. I started a new job, and I had to learn many new things. (That)
4. I ordered soup at a restaurant, and there was a cockroach in it. (You)
5. I was talking about my boss when she walked into the room. (You)
6. We were taking a test when my cell phone rang. (That)
7. I was home alone when I heard someone break a window. (You)
8. I am afraid of heights, and my friends took me to the 45th floor. (That)

A. Mr. Dellaventura is the school counselor at Plains High School. Students come to see him when they have academic or personal problems. Sometimes the teachers send students to see him. Other times, the students come to see him on their own. Listen to Mr. Dellaventura counsel two students. Take notes in the spaces provided.

Notes: Amber	Notes: Miguel

B. Match each student with the correct problems and concerns.

Student	Problems
Amber	**a.** relationship
	b. problems with a class
	c. college plans
Miguel	**d.** poor grades
	e. lost a job
	f. needed a job

C. Listen again to Amber's conversation. Then, answer the questions.

1. What job does Amber have at school?
2. What does the counselor think about Amber's work on the school paper?
3. Why is Amber upset?
4. Is she good at her job?
5. Why is the job important to her?
6. What did Amber do? Why?
7. Is she sorry?
8. What is the counselor going to do to help her?

D. Amber's regrets. Complete the sentences. Use *shouldn't have* or *should have* and the verb in parentheses to express the facts and your opinion.

1. Amber _____ (write) incorrect information.
2. Amber _____ (speak) to her boyfriend about her feelings.
3. Amber _____ (think) more carefully before she wrote the article.
4. In my opinion, the vice principal _____ (take) away her job.

E. Listen again to Miguel's conversation. Then, answer the questions.

1. Is Miguel a good student? Has he improved?
2. Did Miguel do the things that the counselor suggested?
3. What could Miguel have done to improve his math grades?
4. Which is harder for Miguel—speaking English or writing English?
5. Why didn't Miguel get help from a tutor?
6. Where is Miguel working now?
7. What's his schedule?

F. Complete the sentences about Miguel. Use *should have, must have, could have,* or *couldn't have* and the verb in parentheses.

1. Miguel _____ (find) a math tutor, but he didn't need to.
2. Miguel's math instructor _____ (be) pleased at his progress.
3. Miguel _____ (make) a good impression at his job interview.
4. Miguel _____ (find) a different writing tutor.
5. Miguel _____ (get) the job without his counselor's help.

Reading: Weekend and After-School Language and Culture Programs

A. Before You Read.

1. Do you have children, grandchildren, or nieces and nephews?

2. Can the children speak, read, and write your native language?

3. Do you want the children to learn your native language and culture?

Family 1

I'm from Argentina. My family and I are living in the United States. We've been living here for almost three years now. My children can speak English fluently now, and they are in regular classes. I'm disappointed that they don't speak Spanish anymore. They've forgotten our language. I should've done something to help them maintain our language and learn about our Argentinean culture, but it's too late now.

Family 2

My daughter is very excited. This summer, we're going to visit my parents in Korea for the first time. I've been sending her to Korean school every weekend for the past year. Some friends told me that I should've concentrated on her English, but my husband and I decided that we wanted her to learn Korean, too. She's been writing letters to their grandparents, and the grandparents are thrilled to receive a letter that they can read. We made the right decision.

What can immigrant parents do to help their children learn or **maintain** their native language and culture? Children who grow up speaking one language outside the home and a different language inside the home learn to speak two languages. However, it is much harder for them to learn to read and write the language at an advanced level. Therefore, many parents send their children to weekend or after-school language and culture programs for an average of three to five hours a week. The **mission** of most programs is to help children of immigrant parents and/or grandparents learn their native language and culture. There are Polish schools, Chinese schools, Japanese schools, Greek schools, and Korean schools to name a few.

One Korean school in New York City offers six hours of instruction every Saturday. The school teaches reading and conversation, Korean history, Korean **fine arts**, including art, music, and calligraphy. Korean children who were adopted by American couples, Korean-Americans, Koreans, and non-Koreans are among the students who attend the classes.

A Greek school in Chicago teaches Greek language to children in their Greek Orthodox Church community. Most Greek schools are run by a Greek Orthodox Church. The school day lasts two and a half hours every Saturday. The students can learn to read, write, and speak Greek. One school has been in existence since 1922. One parent explained why she sent her daughter to Greek school. She said, "I studied Greek in an after-school program when I was a child, and I wanted my daughter to learn Greek, too. **Besides** learning the culture of my parents, she was also learning another language. The more languages she learns, the better off she'll be in the future." She added, "Sometimes it was a **struggle** to get her to classes, in terms of convenience and other school activities, but I kept her in the classes." When the daughter was older, she even took a trip to Greece with her classmates at the school.

B. Vocabulary. Guessing meaning from context.

1. What can immigrant parents do to help their children learn or **maintain** their native language and culture? *Maintain* means . . .

    a. to repair. **b.** to continue. **c.** to take care of. **d.** to speak.

2. The **mission** of most programs is to help children of immigrant parents and/or grandparents to learn the native language and culture. A *mission* is . . .

    a. a goal. **b.** a map. **c.** a lesson. **d.** a fight.

3. The school teaches reading and conversation, Korean history, Korean **fine arts**, including art, music, and calligraphy. Which of the following is not a *fine art*?

    a. drawing **b.** painting **c.** chemistry **d.** photography

4. **Besides** learning the culture of my parents, she was also learning another language. *Besides* means . . .

    a. but. **b.** in addition to. **c.** next to. **d.** if.

5. Sometimes it was a **struggle** to get her to classes. A *struggle* means . . .

    a. it was easy. **b.** it was confusing. **c.** it was challenging. **d.** it was exciting.

C. Read and discuss the questions.

1. Are you similar to Family 1 or Family 2? Explain your answer.

2. Is it important for you if your children or future children learn to speak, read, and write your native language? Why or why not?

3. How many hours a week do most schools offer lessons?

4. Can American students attend Korean school?

5. What do you think about weekend language and culture schools for children?

Writing Our Stories: My Regrets

A. Read.

It's difficult to move to a new city, especially to a new country. Looking back, there are many things that I should have done to prepare.

First of all, there's the language. I studied English in school, but I didn't take it seriously. I should've taken it more seriously. Also, I could've taken a class before I came here. Of course, now I'm taking English classes. Second, good jobs are hard to find. I finished my degree back in my country, but I didn't bring my transcripts. I should've brought my transcripts with me. I've ordered my transcripts from the university, but it's taking a long time for them to arrive. When they arrive, I may be able to find a job in my field. Finally, I didn't know how to drive when I arrived. In my country, pubic transportaition was very convenient and cheap, but in my state, many jobs are located outside the city. One of my friends is teaching me how to drive so that I will have more job opportunities.

B. Use the following questions to organize your composition.

1. What did you forget to bring with you that you needed?
2. What did you bring with you that you didn't need?
3. What should you have done before you came here?
4. Could you have studied English before you came to this country?
5. Did you forget any important documents that you needed?
6. Did you contact relatives in this country when you were planning your trip?
7. In what city did you live when you first came to this country? Were you happy with your neighborhood?
8. Did you have information about job opportunities before you came to this country? Were you happy with your first job?

In your notebook, write your composition.

C. Using quotation marks. Read each sentence. Add a verb from the list below and add correct punctuation and quotation marks.

> **Use quotation marks when you want to repeat or write a conversation or someone's exact words.** Report conversation or exact words with a verb such as *said, shouted, yelled, cried, asked,* or *complained.* Punctuation of the conversation should be <u>inside</u> the quotation marks.
>
> She said, "I studied Greek in an after-school program when I was a child, and I wanted my daughter to learn Greek, too."
>
> The customer complained, "This doesn't work. I want a refund!"

asked	shouted	explained	said	complained

1. Sylvia _____*shouted*_____, "Stop slamming the door!"

2. Ivan _____ When can I take the test

3. Marlene _____ We should've called the police

4. Juliette _____ Do you have any job openings

5. Karen _____ I must have overslept. I'm sorry I'm late

6. Gustavo _____ I've been living here for two years and you've never come to visit me.

7. José _____ You should have invited her to the party

D. Edit. Find and correct the mistakes.

1. I could've study to be a doctor, but I chose computers instead.

2. We should have not eaten so much. I think I've gained five pounds.

3. You must had enjoyed the party.

4. Peter might has called after 10:00.

5. Edward should enjoyed his surprise party, but he didn't.

6. That TV must have be expensive. It's the newest model.

7. The performance was very excited.

8. My job can be very frustrated.

www Looking at the Internet

Search the Internet for weekend language and culture schools. Use quotation marks to limit your search. For example, try "weekend schools" and "Polish." Find out if there is a school near you. Tell your classmates where it is.

A. Modals—Review. Complete each conversation with the verb in parentheses and an appropriate modal chosen from the list. Use the present or past modal form.

have to had to must (not)	doesn't / don't have to didn't have to	should (not) had better (not)	may (not) might (not) could (not)

1. **A:** Are you free this weekend?

    B: No, I'm not. I _____ (work) overtime.

2. **Driver:** What's the problem, Officer?

    Officer: You _____ (not make) a turn at that corner.

    Now, I _____ (give) you a ticket.

3. **A:** How's the weather?

    B: It's very cloudy. It _____ (rain). You _____

    _____ (take) your umbrella.

4. **A:** Why are you so late?

    B: It's a nice day, so I decided to walk. I _____ (take) the bus instead.

5. **A:** Did you hear? Connie's husband was laid off last week.

    B: She _____ (be) very upset.

6. **A:** Why does Steven wear blue shirts every day?

    B: I don't know. He _____ (like) the color.

7. **Teacher:** This is your last chance. You _____ (not / miss) another class.

    Student: I promise I won't be absent again.

8. **A:** Why didn't Peter take his driving test last Friday?

    B: I'm not sure. He _____ (be) ready.

Grammar Summary

Past modals are formed by using a modal + *(not) have* + the past participle of the main verb.

▶ **1. Should have**   Use *should have* to express a regret about a past action.

I **should have worn** a suit.

(Meaning: I didn't wear a suit. It was a bad idea. I wasn't dressed appropriately.)

She **shouldn't have worn** jeans.

(Meaning: She wore jeans. It was a bad idea. She wasn't dressed appropriately.)

▶ **2. Might have/May have/Could have**   *Might have, may have,* and *could have* express past possibilities. *Could have* also expresses a past choice. *Couldn't have* means impossibility.

He **might have gone** to the movies.

(Meaning: I don't know where he went. Maybe he went to the movies.)

They **may not have taken** the exam yesterday.

(Meaning: Maybe they didn't take the exam yesterday. I don't know.)

I **could have studied** English in my country.

(Meaning: I didn't study English in my country. Classes were available, but I didn't enroll.)

▶ **3. Must have**—Probability and deduction   *Must have* expresses a probability or deduction based on a past event.

We **must have been** out when you called.

(Meaning: We probably weren't at home when you called.)

You **must not have heard** the telephone.

(Meaning: You were at home when I called, but you didn't answer the telephone. You probably didn't hear the telephone ring.)

▶ **4. Must have**—Expressing sympathy or empathy   *Must have* is also used to express sympathy or empathy when participating in a conversation.

A: I had a terrible car accident.　　**A:** I went on a tour of the country last summer.

B: You **must have been** frightened.　　**B:** That **must have been** interesting.

▶ **5. -ing versus -ed adjectives**   Many adjectives end in either *-ing* or *-ed*. A general rule: Use *-ing* to talk about things; use *-ed* to talk about your feelings.

The Museum of Natural History is **interesting**. (Meaning: People like to visit there.)

I'm **bored** when I visit art museums. (Meaning: I don't like to visit art museums.)

Let's Get Organized

A. Comment on the desk in the picture. Answer the questions.

1. Does an organized desk indicate an organized person?

2. What can you infer about the person who works at this desk?

3. Is your desk (or room) organized or disorganized?

B. Are you organized? Take this short quiz. Do you know the exact location of each of these items in your house? Circle Yes or No for each item.

1. postage stamps	Yes	No
2. scissors	Yes	No
3. tape	Yes	No
4. aspirin	Yes	No
5. pencil sharpener	Yes	No
6. car title	Yes	No
7. checkbook	Yes	No

8. rental agreement or deed	Yes	No
9. address book	Yes	No
10. calculator	Yes	No
11. birth certificate	Yes	No
12. last test paper	Yes	No

If you circled all twelve items, congratulations! You are a very organized person. If you circled ten or more items, you are doing well. If you circled fewer than ten items, it's not too late!! This unit and the suggestions of your classmates will have you organized in no time!

Active Grammar: Verb + infinitive

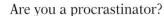

A. Read.

Are you a procrastinator?

Everyone has plans and goals. Some plans are short-term and can be accomplished in a few hours or a weekend: I'm going to wash the car. I plan to organize my closet. I want to gather all my photos from the past five years and put them in a photo album. I need to study for the test next week. I plan to start an exercise program. Some goals are far in the future and will take years to accomplish: I expect to get my nursing degree. I want to start my own business. Do you find yourself making plans but not accomplishing them? Is it difficult to take the first step? Is it impossible to find the time? Could you be a procrastinator? A procrastinator waits for the last minute. A procrastinator believes, "There is always tomorrow."

Verb + infinitives

Use an **infinitive** (*to* + verb) after the following verbs.

agree	forget	manage	remember
ask	hate	need	seem
(be) able to	hope	offer	try
can afford	intend	plan	volunteer
choose	know how	prefer	wait
decide	like	prepare	want
expect	learn (how)	promise	wish
fail	love	refuse	would like

I **plan** *to attend* the school concert.

He **promised** *to baby-sit* for his cousin.

B. Use these cues to describe your weekend plans.

1. would like / visit
2. plan / buy
3. expect / do
4. need / study
5. will try / finish

6. intend / call
7. hope / see
8. promised / help
9. will try / read
10. want / organize

C. Complete these sentences with some of your future goals.

1. I intend _____.

2. I expect _____.

3. I have decided _____.

4. By next year, I will be able _____.

5. I would like _____.

D. My teacher. Ask your teacher these questions.

1. What are your plans for this weekend?
2. Why did you decide to become a teacher?
3. Do you know how to speak another language?
4. Would you like to learn my language?
5. Do you want to live in another country for a few years?
6. Where would you like to travel?
7. Do you plan to teach at this school next year?
8. Do you expect to teach ESL for the next ten years?
9. In addition to teaching, what else do you like to do?
10. Do you plan to stay in this state or to move to another state sometime?
11. Do you know how to cook any ethnic foods?
12. Will you remember to pass me at the end of this class?
13. Would you agree to end class early today?

Distractions and Excuses

A. Read.

It's hard to get started on your plans. It's easy to make excuses! And once you start on a goal, there are always distractions. You sit down to work at the computer, check your e-mail, and then start to chat with friends. A friend calls and wants you to go to the mall. It's time for your favorite TV show.

B. My distractions. Write your top two distractions.

Example: ___the telephone_____

1. _____ 2. _____

C. Student to student dictation.
Student A: Turn to page 248. Read the excuses. Your partners will copy them.
Student B: Listen and copy the excuses you hear. When you finish, change pages.

1. _____.
2. _____.
3. _____.
4. _____.
5. _____.

A To-Do List

A. Read.

You have commitments and appointments. There is homework, a big test, and a composition to write for school. You have many responsibilities at home.

Controlling your time is the key to success. Each day, sit down and write a list of the things you need to do that day. This is your to-do list. Then, number your list in order of importance. What needs to get done first? Do it! Check it off your list, and start number two.

B. Listen to Sergio talk about the things he wants to accomplish today. As you listen, write a to-do list for Sergio.

To Do

C. Talk about the things that Sergio wants to do today. Put his list in order from 1 to 7. Is Sergio realistic? Can he accomplish all of these things today?

D. Write a to-do list for yourself for today or for tomorrow. What is the most important item on your list? Number your items in order of importance.

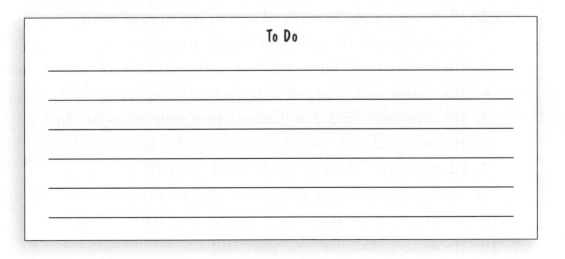

To Do

Active Grammar: Verb + object + infinitive

A. Read.

Mornings are difficult for most people. It's helpful to organize the night before. These suggestions might help:

1. Check your calendar.
2. Lay out your clothes for the next day.
3. Make your lunch.
4. Put all your books and supplies in your bag or backpack.
5. Write your to-do list for tomorrow.

Verb + object + infinitive

Use an **object + an infinitive** after the following verbs:

advise	encourage	hire	remind	urge
allow	expect	invite	require	want
ask	forbid	permit	teach	warn
convince	help	persuade	tell	

My mother **asked** *me to clean* my room.
My teacher **expected** *us to budget* our time.
My brother **persuaded** *me not to quit* school.

B. Advice for Paul. Restate each comment using an infinitive.

1. His teacher said, "Turn in your report on time." (expect)
   His teacher expected him to turn in his report on time.

2. His teacher said, "Don't hand in your report late." (tell)
   His teacher told him not to hand in his report late.

3. His teacher said, "Buy a notebook and organize your papers." (advise)

4. His mother said, "Lay out your clothes the night before." (convince)

5. His sister said, "Buy a wall calendar for your bedroom." (tell)

6. His girlfriend said, "Get everything together before you go to sleep." (urge)

7. His boss said, "Don't be late for work." (warn)

8. His father said, "Turn off your cell phone when you study." (remind)

9. His grandmother said, "Let's clean up your room." (help)

10. His mother said, "Get up earlier." (urge)

C. Problems. Complete these sentences. What advice did each person give?

1. Gloria got a speeding ticket in another state. She doesn't want to pay the fine. She believes that you only need to pay a ticket for the state you live in.

   Her brother convinced _her to sign the ticket and send in the fine._____

2. Your brother lost his credit card.

   You advised _____.

3. Lisa is 24 years old; she's an only child and lives at home. Her company offered her a great job promotion, but she needs to move out of state.

   Her parents expect _____.

   Her boss is encouraging _____.

4. John has begun to hang around with a group of troublemakers. Two of them have dropped out of school and two of them have been in trouble with the law.

   His parents have forbidden _____.

   The baseball coach has invited _____.

   His brother is urging him _____.

5. Your friends are coming to this country for a month. You want to see them, but you don't want them to stay with you because you live in a studio apartment.

   You are going to tell _____.

   You are not going to invite _____.

6. Your sister was accepted to college, but she doesn't have enough money for tuition.

   Your parents have persuaded _____.

   Her teacher advised _____.

D. Answer these questions about growing up.

1. When you were a child, what did your parents forbid you to do?
2. How many hours did they expect you to study?
3. Did your parents help you to do your homework?
4. Did they expect you to come right home after school?
5. When you were a teenager, how did they expect you to help at home?
6. Who taught you how to drive?
7. Did they allow you to go out on Saturday night?
8. Did they encourage you to play a sport?
9. Did you expect your parents to give you an allowance?
10. What did they advise you not to do?

Active Grammar: *Be + adjective + infinitive*

A. Read.

Make a schedule of your day or of your study time. It's easy to say, "I'll get it done sometime today." It's more helpful to make an appointment with yourself. If possible, find a time that is the most productive for you. Maybe that is right after class or as soon as you get home. What is your most productive time?

Be + adjective + infinitive				
Use the infinitive form after these adjectives:				
dangerous	good	important	polite	selfish
difficult	hard	impossible	possible	stressful
easy	healthy	interesting	reasonable	terrible
expensive	helpful	lonely	realistic	thoughtful
foolish	idealistic	necessary	romantic	wonderful

B. Make sentences about the busy pace of daily life in the United States.

It's difficult It's impossible It's hard	to	get started on a project. work and go to school. find time to exercise. stick to a schedule. accomplish everything I need to do. keep my papers in order. get enough sleep. have time for myself.

C. Pronunciation: Stressed syllables. Listen and mark the stressed syllable.

1. dán · ger · ous
2. i · de · a · lís · tic
3. im · pos · si · ble
4. in · ter · est · ing
5. po · lite

6. rea · son · a · ble
7. re · a · lis · tic
8. ro · man · tic
9. stress · ful
10. thought · ful

D. In your notebook, write sentences with the adjectives from Exercise C.

It's dangerous to drive when you are very tired.
It's idealistic to believe the promises of that politician.

E. Use the adjectives to give suggestions for organizing your day.

| helpful | important | smart | necessary |

1. file your important papers   *It's helpful to file your important papers.*
2. check your appointment calendar daily
3. make a to-do list
4. hang a calendar in your kitchen or bedroom
5. plan your day
6. lay out your clothes for the next day
7. schedule your study time
8. organize your desk
9. take a break every two hours
10. post notes on your desk to help you remember things
11. have a pencil sharpener on your desk
12. keep a dictionary on your desk

Give two more suggestions for organizing your day.

F. A study schedule. Ali has a lot of homework this weekend. He likes to study in the morning. Look at his assignments and schedule his study time for Saturday and Sunday. Write the assignments in the chart below. Does he have enough time to complete all his work?

Assignments
Grammar workbook—pages 153 to 156
Read article about Elvis (two pages)
Go to library and research a popular musician
Write a composition about a popular musician
Study infinitives for test on Monday

Saturday	Sunday
9:00	9:00
10:00	10:00
11:00	11:00

🔊 **A. Diana started college last month. Her first math test is tomorrow. Diana is supposed to be studying for her test now. Listen to her telephone conversations.**

B. Listen to the conversation again. As you listen, circle *True* or *False*.

1.	Susan was able to stop and talk with Diana.	True	False
2.	Susan has to study for the math test.	True	False
3.	Diana's father expects her to do well in school.	True	False
4.	Diana called Jacob at his job.	True	False
5.	Jacob needs to write his lab report.	True	False
6.	He plans to see Diana later tonight.	True	False
7.	Alex is at school now.	True	False
8.	Alex asked her to join a study group.	True	False
9.	Katie invited Diana to go to the mall.	True	False
10.	Diana decided to stay home and study.	True	False

C. Listen again as Diana speaks to each person. Then, complete these sentences using the infinitive form.

Susan

1. Susan isn't able _to talk on the phone now._

2. She needs _____.

3. She promised _____.

Dad

4. He expects _____.

5. He reminded _____.

Jacob

6. He plans _____.

7. He encouraged _____.

Alex

8. He asked _____.

9. He volunteered _____.

10. They agreed _____.

Katie

11. She invited _____.

12. Diana decided _____.

D. Diana failed the math test. Her mother asked her the following questions. Ask the questions with these cues and give Diana's answer.

1. Why / agree / go to the mall?

2. When / plan / talk to your teacher?

3. How many hours / plan / study every night?

4. When / expect / organize your room?

5. need / quit your job?

6. expect / pass this course?

E. Working with a partner, write a conversation between Diana and her mother. Diana is upset about the test and her mother is giving her advice.

Reading: Active Learning

A. Active learners. Circle the study techniques you use when studying English. Add two more.

1. I make lists and charts.
2. I write examples of the work we are doing in class.
3. I sit and look at the book.
4. I use an English study site on the Internet.
5. I study with a partner.

6. I try to read the newspaper.
7. I listen to a tape or CD. Sometimes I try to copy the sentences.
8. I repeat the sentences in the book aloud.
9. _____
10. _____

Once you have scheduled your study time, shut out distractions, sit down, and begin your assignments. How can you make the most of your study time? It is helpful to become an active student, both at home and outside of class. These students are all "active learners." How do they approach learning?

Because I'm really **pressed for time**, I have to plan carefully to find study time. One of the only places I have **downtime** is in my car. I made a tape with the verb forms and I play this over and over again. After we study a unit, I record ten or fifteen sentences as examples of the grammar. I **pop** the tape in the car stereo, listen to the sentences, and memorize them as I sit in traffic. I'm sure that drivers in other cars think I'm a crazy guy talking to myself.

For me, it's important to have a study partner. When I'm taking a new class, I look for a person who is serious about studying. After class, we meet in the library and review the material we studied in class. For example, I ask my partner the same questions we practiced in class, and she gives me the answers. Then, we switch roles. Our favorite activity is dictations of the sentences or paragraphs we studied. When we learned the past participles, we gave each other quizzes. I think this is the best way to study because we are using our grammar.

I enjoy **breaking** news stories so I'll choose one or two major stories. First, I'll watch the news on TV and look at the action to get the idea of the story. Then, I will read newspaper articles about the story. Finally, I'll look on the Internet. There are several great sites on news where I can look at the story and see photographs or video clips. Some of the sites even have audio. I've been able to **improve** my vocabulary and to learn some interesting information.

Country music is my ticket to English. Country music is easy to understand because the songs tell a story. I have CDs by Faith Hill, Reba McEntire, Garth Brooks, Tim McGraw, and lots of other popular country singers. I listen to their music, copy the words, and sing along with the **lyrics.** Many of the CDs have **inserts** with the words so that I can follow along. At other times, I'll ask an American student if she can help me figure out the words.

B. Vocabulary. Match each boldface word or phrase with the word or phrase that has the same meaning.

_____ 1. I'm **pressed for time**.   **a.** current

_____ 2. I have **downtime** in my car.   **b.** papers with the words

_____ 3. I **pop** the tape into the car stereo.   **c.** words

_____ 4. I sing along with the **lyrics**.   **d.** make better

_____ 5. Many of the CDs have **inserts**.   **e.** I'm very busy.

_____ 6. I enjoy **breaking** news stories.   **f.** free time

_____ 7. I've been able to **improve** my vocabulary.   **g.** put

C. Discuss the meaning of each verbal phrase in the box . Then, write only the correct preposition in each sentence.

| look at   look in   look on   look for |

1. He's looking _____ the map of Africa to find the capital of Kenya.

2. He looked _____ the dictionary to find the meaning of the word.

3. She is looking _____ a study partner to practice her English with.

4. After I look _____ the computer screen for a long time, my eyes get tired.

5. They look _____ Web to find movie times.

6. I need to look _____ information about the election.

7. You can look _____ the newspaper to find the movie times.

8. You can look _____ the Internet to find the best prices for airline tickets.

D. Discuss your learning strategies. How would you approach each assignment?

1. You are going to have a test on infinitives.

2. You need to write a composition about the pros and cons of living in a large city.

3. You failed your last test on the present perfect.

4. You would like to improve your vocabulary.

Writing Our Stories: Study Time

A. Read.

My study area is a large table <u>in the corner of my bedroom</u>. There's a large desk lamp in the corner. <u>On the left side of my desk</u> is my high school graduation present—a laptop computer. My printer is in back of the computer. Above the desk, attached to the wall, is a long, narrow shelf, about 6 inches wide. It holds envelopes, a pencil sharpener, a small clock, a jar with pens and pencils—everything I need—all in easy reach. To the right of my desk is a small bookcase for my books and notebooks and papers. I keep a large calendar over my desk for my work schedule and appointments.

I like to study in the evening from 7:00 to 9:30. I check my assignments, open my books, and begin. I always do my writing first because it's my least favorite assignment. When that is finished, I relax a little and start my reading assignments. I leave my grammar and vocabulary for last because that is the easiest homework for me.

It's difficult to study after 9:30 because I share my bedroom with my older sister. When she gets home from work at 9:30, she likes to watch TV in the bedroom or talk on the phone with her boyfriend. That's the time that I get on the Internet, e-mail my friends, and try to ignore her!

B. Writing. Describe your study area and your study time.

1. Draw a picture of your study area. It could be your kitchen table, a desk in your bedroom, or the school library.

2. Look at the picture. Does it include everything you use? Where are your books, your pencils, your dictionary, your backpack? What other unusual items are in the picture?

3. Carefully describe your study area. Details add interest. Give locations.

4. Describe how you organize your study time. If you are completely disorganized, it is still important to describe your study area and time. Understanding what you do is the first step to making changes.

C. Preposition review. First, underline the prepositional phrases in the description on page 176. Then, describe the locations in this picture. In some of the sentences, the location is at the beginning of the sentence. In other sentences, the location is at the end.

1. My stereo is _____ .

2. My telephone is _____ .

3. There's a small clock _____ .

4. _____ is a photo of my girlfriend.

5. My laptop computer sits _____ .

6. I'm always hungry when I study, so there's always a bag of potato chips _____ .

7. The wastebasket that is _____ often overflows with paper.

D. Edit. Find and correct the mistakes in these sentences.

1. I like study on the kitchen table.

2. It's difficult find time to study.

3. My mother told to be home by 12:00.

4. Is impossible to complete all this homework.

5. She promised to helped me.

6. My father encouraged my sister to do his best.

7. The teacher urged to us to use the computer lab.

8. My grandfather offered pay my tuition.

www Looking at the Internet

Many Web sites help students organize their busy lives. Other sites help students with time management and study skills. Find an idea to help you better organize your time by entering one of these phrases in the *Search* box:

  time management and study skills
  time management and college

A. Use the cues. Write the question and give an answer about your weekend plans.

1. How many hours / need to study?

   A: <u>How many hours do you need to study this weekend?</u>

   B: <u>I need to study for three hours this weekend.</u>

2. Where / plan / go?

   A: _____?

   B: _____.

3. Who / expect / visit?

   A: _____?

   B: _____.

4. What movie / would like / see?

   A: _____?

   B: _____.

5. What / hope / do?

   A: _____?

   B: _____.

B. Rewrite each sentence, using the verb in parentheses. You will need to change the wording in some of the sentences.

1. Luis's parents said, "We know you will do well in college." (expect)

   <u>Luis's parents expect him to do well in college.</u>

2. Laura's father said, "Take art lessons." (encourage)

   _____.

3. My brother said, "You should become an engineer." (tell)

   _____.

4. My high school counselor said, "Apply for a scholarship." (advise)

   _____.

5. My friend said, "Don't turn in your paper late." (warn)

   _____.

Grammar Summary

► **1. Verb + infinitive**

Use an infinitive (*to* + verb) after the following verbs:

agree	forget	manage	remember
ask	hate	need	seem
(be) able to	hope	offer	try
can afford	intend	plan	volunteer
choose	know how	prefer	wait
decide	like	prepare	want
expect	learn (how)	promise	wish
fail	love	refuse	would like

I **hope to finish** this report by 5:00.

He **forgot to do** his homework.

I **know how to organize** my time.

► **2. Verb + object + infinitive**

Use an object + infinitive after the following verbs:

advise	encourage	hire	remind	urge
allow	expect	invite	require	want
ask	forbid	permit	teach	warn
convince	help	persuade	tell	

My parents **didn't permit me to go** out during the week.

The school **required all students to wear** uniforms.

My classmate **helped me to understand** the math problems.

► **3. *Be* + adjective + infinitive**

Use the infinitive form after these adjectives:

dangerous	good	important	polite	selfish
difficult	hard	impossible	possible	stressful
easy	healthy	interesting	reasonable	terrible
expensive	helpful	lonely	realistic	thoughtful
foolish	idealistic	necessary	romantic	wonderful

It**'s important to have** clear plans and goals.

It **was difficult to accomplish** my goals.

12 Becoming a Citizen

A. New citizens. Listen to Marco and Luciana's story about becoming citizens of the United States.

1.

2.

3.

4. INS Office

5.

6.

Citizenship Process

1. Fill out the application for citizenship.
2. Send application, three photographs, copies of requested documents, and check(s) to your regional Immigration and Naturalization Service (INS) office. Send your letter via certified mail.
3. Have your fingerprints taken.
4. Go for your citizenship interview and English test.
5. Take the Oath of Allegiance to the United States at your swearing in ceremony.

B. Discuss these questions about citizenship.

1. Are you a citizen? Is anyone in your family a citizen?

2. What are the benefits of becoming a citizen?

3. What are the responsibilities of being a citizen?

Active Grammar: Verb + Gerund

> **Verb + gerund**
>
> Use a **gerund** (simple verb form + *ing*) after the following verbs:
>
> | | | | |
> |---|---|---|---|
> | admit | consider | imagine | recommend |
> | anticipate | delay | like | regret |
> | appreciate | discuss | love | resent |
> | avoid | dislike | miss | start |
> | begin | doesn't / don't mind | postpone | stop |
> | can't help | enjoy | practice | suggest |
> | can't stand | finish | quit | understand |
> | continue | hate | recall | |
>
> They **missed** *seeing* their family for holidays and celebrations.

A. Listen to these sentences about Marco and Luciana. Fill in the gerund you hear.

1. Marco and Luciana discussed _____ citizens.

2. They delayed _____ the process because Luciana's English was not strong.

3. Luciana regretted _____ English classes earlier.

4. She began _____ English at a local adult school.

5. A friend recommended _____ in a citizenship class.

6. They didn't mind _____ class one night a week.

7. Marco and Luciana enjoyed _____ about U.S. history.

8. They practiced _____ one another questions.

9. Luciana couldn't help _____ nervous before the test.

B. Restate these sentences. Use gerunds.

1. People discuss (leave) their countries for many years before making a final decision.

2. They anticipate (have) a better life for their children.

3. New immigrants can't help (worry) about money and work.

4. Some immigrants begin (study) English soon after they arrive.

5. Other students postpone (enroll) in English classes.

6. Many new immigrants start (work) in low-paying jobs.

7. They imagine (find) better jobs.

8. In the first year, many new immigrants consider (return) to their countries.

9. They miss (see) their families.

10. They can't stand (hear) English all day!

11. Older immigrants recommend (find) friends and activities in the United States.

12. They suggest (start) English classes.

C. Before coming to the United States. Sit in a small group. Use the verbs in the box to talk about your preparations to come to America. All these verbs are followed by gerunds. You might want to use some of the cues below to help recall your plans.

anticipate	discuss	recall	start
begin	finish	regret	stop
continue	quit	remember	

apply	work	learn (English)
save (money)	contact (relatives)	say good-bye
live	fill out	shop
take	buy	call
find out	write	pack

A: I began learning English. How about you?

B: No, I didn't study English. I regret not taking classes.

A: I continued working until the week before I left.

B: Me, too. I couldn't stop working.

D. After coming to the United States. What do you like about the United States? What don't you like? Write two or three items in each column.

like/enjoy	don't mind	dislike/don't like	can't stand

Sit in a small group of three or four students. Compare your information and discuss the similarities and differences.

A: I can't stand wearing a heavy winter coat and hat and gloves.

B: Why?

A: I come from a tropical country. I don't like heavy clothing.

Active Grammar: Preposition + Gerund

> **Preposition + gerund**
> Use a gerund (simple verb form + *ing*) after the following prepositions:
> after   besides   in addition to   while
> before   by   instead of   without
>
> After *studying* the citizenship book, she easily passed the test.

A. Citizenship. Restate these sentences about citizenship. Use a gerund.

1. Before I applied for citizenship, I lived here for ten years.

   Before applying for citizenship, I lived here for ten years.

2. After I obtained the application for naturalization, I had my fingerprints taken.

3. After I filled out the application, I wrote the check.

4. Before I sent in the paperwork, I had the required photographs taken.

5. After I sent in the papers, I waited a long time.

6. While I waited, I studied for the citizenship test.

7. Before I took the Oath of Allegiance, I took and passed the citizenship test.

8. After I took the Oath of Allegiance, I was a citizen.

B. Time line. The time line shows Jarek's activities from 1990 to 2002. Use the information to complete the sentences.

> 1990—applied for a visa
> 1993—received his visa
> 1994—arrived in the United States
> 1995—began to study English; worked as a taxi driver
> 1997—began to work at an auto body repair shop
> 1999—applied for citizenship
> 2000—became a citizen
> 2001—met Dorota
> 2002—married Dorota; opened his own auto body repair shop

1. After _____ waiting _____ for three years, Jarek received a visa.
2. After _____ in the United States, Jarek found a job as a taxi driver.
3. Instead of _____ English in Poland, Jarek waited until he came to the United States.
4. While _____ as a taxi driver, Jarked studied English.
5. After _____ a taxi for two years, Jarek got a job in an auto body repair shop.
6. Before _____ Dorota, Jarek became a citizen.
7. After _____ Dorota, Jarek opened his own auto body shop.

Active Grammar: Verb + Preposition + Gerund; Be + Adjective Phrase + Gerund

Verb + preposition + gerund

Use a **gerund** (simple verb form + *ing*) after the following verbs and prepositions:

adjust to	complain about	give up	succeed in
approve of	concentrate on	insist on	suspect of
argue about	count on	keep on	talk about
believe in	depend on	look forward to	think about
blame for	dream about	plan on	warn about
care about	forget about	prevent from	worry about

New immigrants **plan on** *working* hard.

Be + adjective phrase + gerund

Use a **gerund** (simple verb form + *ing*) after the following: *be* + adjective phrase:

afraid of	good at	interested in	tired of
capable of	guilty of	opposed to	upset about
famous for	in favor of	proud of	

Antonio **was in favor of** *coming* to America, but his wife wasn't.

A. Complete these sentences about your experiences and feelings before and after coming to the United States. Use a gerund in each sentence. Then, read your sentences to a partner.

Before coming to the United States . . .

1. I dreamed about _____.

2. I planned on _____.

3. I looked forward to _____.

4. I worried about _____.

5. I was interested in _____.

After coming to the United States . . .

6. I am proud of _____.

7. I have adjusted to _____.

8. I often complain about _____.

9. I think about _____.

10. I'm tired of _____.

B. Pronunciation: Linking. When a word begins with a vowel, link it with the word before. Listen to this conversation. Then, practice the conversation with a partner.

A: I thought life here was going to be easy. I just can't adjust to living here. I'm upset_about leaving my family.

B: You'll_always miss them. I plan_on visiting my family once_a year.

A: And I'm afraid_of losing my job.

B: Yesterday you were complaining_about working so much_overtime!

A: I gave_up working_at my family's business to come here.

B: You weren't interested_in working there. And you plan_on_opening your_own business someday.

A: I'm tired_of listening to English_all day! I'm thinking_of going back to Korea.

B: You've_only been here for nine months. Forget_about going back. Concentrate_on learning English_and making_a few friends.

C. I agree/I disagree. Eight commonly discussed issues are listed below. Use the phrases in the box, all requiring gerunds, and state your opinion. Give your reasons.

I agree with	I disagree with
I am in favor of	I don't agree with
I approve of	I'm opposed to
	I'm against
	I object to

1. Limit new immigration
2. Mandate English only in government offices
3. Issue national identity cards
4. Prohibit the sale of automatic weapons
5. Increase the tax on cigarettes
6. Allow prayer in public school
7. Institute national health insurance
8. Raise the retirement age

Name two more controversial issues in your city, state, or in the nation. Give your opinion of the issue.

Active Grammar: Contrast—Infinitives and Gerunds

A. Contrast—Gerund or infinitive? Do you use a gerund or an infinitive after these verbs? Read each sentence and use the correct form of the word in parentheses.

1. It was impossible (find) a job in my country.
2. I miss (see) my family and friends.
3. I intend (visit) my native country next year.
4. I expect my cousin (arrive) soon.
5. Have you ever considered (become) a citizen?
6. How long do you plan (stay) in this country?
7. How long do you plan on (work) at your current job?
8. My parents appreciate (receive) a check from me each month.
9. She's proud of (start) her own import business.
10. I promised (write) my grandparents often.
11. Besides (have) difficulty finding a job when I first arrived, I didn't like (live) with my uncle.
12. Carlos enjoys (read) books about American history.
13. My uncle refused (change) his long name when he came here.
14. Sometimes I regret (come) to this country.
15. I sometimes complain about (come) here, but then I remember the reasons that I came.
16. In addition to (sponsor) his sister, Andres is supporting his parents.
17. I have invited my cousins (live) with me their first month in the United States.

B. Ask and answer the questions with a partner or a small group.

1. When do you anticipate finishing your English studies?
2. When do you intend to visit your country?
3. Have you ever considered becoming a citizen?
4. What do you sometimes worry about?
5. What do you miss doing since you came here?
6. What do you enjoy doing in this country?
7. What do you dream about doing?
8. What do you advise new immigrants to bring with them?
9. Why did you decide to come to the United States?
10. Would you encourage your brother or sister to come to live here?

C. Listen: Citizenship decisions. Listen to each of these immigrants speak about citizenship. Then, answer the questions. Many include a gerund or an infinitive.

1. Why did they decide to come to the United States?
2. What was he concerned about?
3. Where was he able to find a good job?
4. What does he appreciate having?
5. What can he afford to do?
6. Why is he thinking about becoming a citizen?
7. Who does he want to sponsor?

8. How long has she been living in the United States?
9. What country is she from?
10. What does she enjoy doing?
11. Where has she been dreaming about retiring?
12. Where do her children want to live?
13. What is her situation?
14. What do you think she should do?

D. Listen to Martin talk about becoming a citizen. Then, complete the questions.

1. How old _____ he when _____?
2. _____ it easy for him _____ English?
3. What _____ he able_____?
4. Where _____ work?
5. What _____ the people in his office enjoy_____?
6. Who _____ him _____ a citizen?
7. _____ difficult _____ for citizenship?
8. What _____ able _____ in November?

Now answer the questions.

A. Look at the pictures. Who is running for office? What are the people doing?

B. Listen and retell the story about the local political campaign.

C. Listen again and (circle) *True* or *False*.

1. Manuel is a citizen.	True	False
2. Manuel has always been involved in politics.	True	False
3. Manuel votes in every election.	True	False
4. Manuel and John are good friends.	True	False
5. Manuel's and John's families enjoy spending time together.	True	False
6. John owns a computer company with Manuel.	True	False
7. John hires senior citizens for his bookstore.	True	False
8. John is running for mayor.	True	False

D. Complete the sentences.

donate	give	have
organize	set	shake
spend	work	

1. John complained about _____ hands.
2. John is looking forward to _____ interviews.
3. Andrea is good at _____ people.
4. Their friends have been talking about _____ a voter registration drive.
5. They're thinking about _____ up tables at the supermarkets.
6. They are not worried about _____ too much money.
7. John's friends have insisted on _____ services.
8. Kathy quit _____ to help with her husband's campaign.

E. Ask and answer questions about the story. Use the cues provided and the names in the box. You will need to use different verb tenses.

Who enjoys spending time together?

The families do.

1. who / enjoy / spend time together
2. who / interested in / work on the campaign
3. who / quit / work
4. who / interested in / make signs
5. who / insist on / donate services
6. who / like / help John practice for the debate
7. who / enjoy / stuff envelopes

Manuel
Andrea
Kathy
friends
volunteers
the children
the families

Reading: The Citizenship Test

A. Before You Read.

1. What is the U.S. Citizenship Test?

2. Do you know anyone who has taken the test?

3. What is the best way to prepare for the test?

B. The U.S. Citizenship Test. This test is required for anyone who wants to become a U.S. citizen. An INS examiner asks a citizenship applicant a group of questions from a list of 100 questions. The questions are about U.S. history and government.

Read each sample question of the Citizenship Test. Fill in the circle next to the correct answer.

1. What are the colors of the United States flag?
   - ○ **a.** red and white
   - ○ **b.** red, white, and blue
   - ○ **c.** red and blue.
   - ○ **d.** red, white, blue, and black

2. What do the stars on the flag mean?
   - ○ **a.** There is one star for each one hundred citizens.
   - ○ **b.** There is one star for each citizen.
   - ○ **c.** There is one star for each state of the union.
   - ○ **d.** There is one star for each president.

3. How many states are there in the United States?
   - ○ **a.** 48
   - ○ **b.** 49
   - ○ **c.** 50
   - ○ **d.** 51

4. What is the 4th of July?
   - ○ **a.** Memorial Day
   - ○ **b.** President's Day
   - ○ **c.** Flag Day
   - ○ **d.** Independence Day

5. From whom did the United States win independence?
   - ○ **a.** Ireland
   - ○ **b.** Great Britain
   - ○ **c.** France
   - ○ **d.** Germany

6. Who was the first president of the United States?
   - ○ **a.** Abraham Lincoln
   - ○ **b.** John Adams
   - ○ **c.** George Washington
   - ○ **d.** Benjamin Franklin

7. Who becomes the president of the United States if the president should die?
   - ○ **a.** the secretary of state
   - ○ **b.** the defense secretary
   - ○ **c.** the first lady
   - ○ **d.** the vice president

8. Who makes the laws in the United States?
   ○ **a.** judges   ○ **c.** the president
   ○ **b.** congress   ○ **d.** the governors

9. Who was president during the Civil War?
   ○ **a.** Abraham Lincoln   ○ **c.** Richard Nixon
   ○ **b.** George Washington   ○ **d.** Franklin D. Roosevelt

10. What is the 50th state of the union?
    ○ **a.** Alaska   ○ **c.** Puerto Rico
    ○ **b.** Hawaii   ○ **d.** Florida

11. Who is the commander-in-chief of the U.S. military?
    ○ **a.** congress   ○ **c.** the president
    ○ **b.** the secretary of defense   ○ **d.** the U.S. citizens

12. In what month do we vote for the president?
    ○ **a.** January   ○ **c.** July
    ○ **b.** April   ○ **d.** November

Check your answers below.

1. b   2. c   3. c   4. d   5. b   6. c   7. d   8. b   9. a   10. b   11. c   12. d

C. Written English testing. In order to become a citizen, you must be able to speak, read, and write basic English. These are a few examples of the types of sentences that an INS officer may ask you to read or write. The sentences may be about history and government or about everyday life. Practice reading and dictating the sentences to a partner.

1. All United States citizens have the right to vote.

2. Martha Washington was the first first lady.

3. Our government is divided into three branches.

4. People vote for the president in November.

5. The president lives in the White House.

6. I am too busy to talk today.

7. My car does not work.

8. She can speak English very well.

9. The man wanted to get a job.

10. You drink too much coffee.

Writing Our Stories: A Political Platform

A. Read the two different political platforms. Which person would you vote for?

I believe in improving our community by attracting development to our town. I'm in favor of lowering taxes in order to attract much needed new businesses, including the new paint factory, to our town. Our town must begin building the factory right away. We need new jobs for our citizens. I'm opposed to building a new library. We already have a library. The new library can wait, but jobs can't. In addition to creating jobs, I'm in favor of increasing parking meters to fifty cents per half hour. I manage a successful business, and the downtown areas need income to improve parking and the sidewalks. I have fifteen years of experience on the town council. You can count on me to serve you.

Douglas McMurphy

It's time for a change. The citizens of this town are used to hearing the same promises. They're tired of seeing heavy traffic and breathing factory pollution. They miss having peace and quiet in their community. We don't need more development. Instead of building a paint factory, we should start building a new library. As a former high school teacher and member of the Board of Education, I'm proud of the improvements we've made in educating our children. More students are applying to college than ever before. Imagine having a place where adults and children can enjoy reading, using free computer facilities, and listening to authors read from their books. A vote for me is a vote for education in a livable community.

Angela Luisa Velez

B. Pretend that you are a political candidate and you are running for a town council seat. In your notebook, write a paragraph describing your political platform. What is your opinion on (1) the new paint factory, (2) building a new library, and (3) raising parking meter prices to fifty cents per half hour? Choose one other issue that you want to discuss. Use the vocabulary below in your platform.

be opposed to	be in favor of	believe in

C. Sentence fragments. Read each sentence. Circle *Fragment* or *Correct*.

A *sentence fragment* is an incomplete sentence. Here are two examples:

Because traffic will increase.   **incorrect; incomplete idea**
I'm opposed to building the mall
  because traffic will increase.   **correct**

Will be good for the town.   **incorrect; missing subject**
A new library will be good for the town.   **correct**

1. After the airplane landed.   Fragment   Correct
2. He regrets not studying English before.   Fragment   Correct
3. When I considered leaving my country.   Fragment   Correct
4. Because I needed to learn English.   Fragment   Correct
5. I dislike taking the bus instead of driving myself. Fragment   Correct
6. I recall filling out an application when I arrived.   Fragment   Correct
7. Is easy to learn English.   Fragment   Correct

D. Edit. Find and correct the mistakes.

1. The mayor isn't interested in run for another term.
2. The students have finished to read two novels.
3. Because I haven't registered to vote yet.
4. I'm tired of walk in the snow.
5. I've missed see my family.
6. The council is opposed building a new parking garage.
7. When I arrived in this country.
8. My daughter can't stand wears heavy winter clothes.

www Looking at the Internet

Search the Internet for information on the citizenship process. Try to find a practice test that you can do online. Enter "citizenship test," or "how to become a citizen." Take the test and see how you do.

Practicing on Your Own

A. Complete each sentence with the gerund form of the verb in parentheses.

1. Before _____ (register) for classes, she had to complete an application.

2. She couldn't stand _____ (wait) in the long lines to register.

3. She postponed _____ (look) for a job until she knew her schedule.

4. She bought her textbooks after _____ (attend) her first class.

5. After she began _____ (study), she had more confidence.

6. She liked _____ (go) to class and _____ (meet) new people.

7. She missed _____ (see) her family, so she started _____ (send) them e-mails every other day.

8. In class, she practiced _____ (speak), _____ (read), and _____ (write).

9. She believed in _____ (work) as hard as possible to achieve her goals.

10. After _____ (study) for a year, she was ready to enroll in an accounting degree program.

B. Contrast. Complete each sentence with the correct form of the verbs in parentheses. Use the gerund or the infinitive form.

1. After _____ (arrive) in this country, he lived with his brother's family.

2. He didn't mind _____ (take) care of his nieces and nephews.

3. He didn't know how _____ (speak) much English, but he could read.

4. His brother persuaded him _____ (enroll) in English classes.

5. Instead of _____ (work) full-time, he decided _____ (take) a part-time job at his brother's company.

6. He has enjoyed _____ (study) and is a good student.

7. He has been trying _____ (speak) as much English as possible.

8. He anticipates _____ (finish) his English classes in a year.

Grammar Summary

▶ 1. Verb + gerund

Use a gerund (simple verb form + *ing*) after certain verbs. A list of some of the verbs is on page 181.

They **discussed coming** to the United States.

I **miss seeing** my family.

My friends **suggested starting** English classes.

▶ 2. Preposition + gerund

Use a gerund (simple verb form + *ing*) after most prepositions. A list of common prepositions that are followed by gerunds is on page 183.

Before coming to this country, I was a full-time student.

After arriving at the airport, my relatives took care of everything for me.

▶ 3. Verb + preposition + gerund

Use a gerund (simple verb form + *ing*) after most verb phrases with a verb and a preposition. A list of verbs + prepositions is on page 184.

I **look forward to visiting** my family.

I **dream about opening** my own business.

I **plan on voting** in the next election.

▶ 4. *Be* + adjective phrase + gerund

Use a gerund (simple verb form + *ing*) after the verb *be* + adjective phrase. A list of the adjective phrases is on page 184.

I **am good at following** directions.

The politician **is in favor of lowering** taxes.

We **are opposed to building** the new factory.

13 Business and Industry

A Product Map

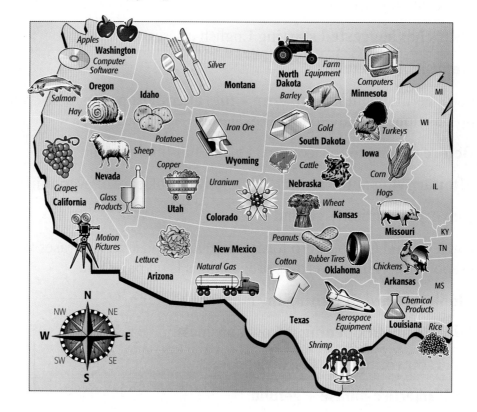

A. Map study. Look at the map of the western half of the United States and answer the questions.

1. Find California. Which state is located north of California?

2. Find Kansas. Which state is located west of Kansas?

3. Find South Dakota. Which state is located north of South Dakota?

4. Find Wyoming. Which state is located west of Wyoming?

5. Find Montana. Which state is located south of Montana?

6. Find Minnesota. Which state is located south of Minnesota?

7. Find Oklahoma. Which state is located south of Oklahoma?

8. Find Arkansas. Which state is located south of Arkansas?

Talk about the map and the products of each state.

Active Grammar: Passive Voice

A. Product map vocabulary. Review the vocabulary with your teacher.

mine	catch	grow	manufacture	produce	raise

B. Write each product from the box next to the correct verb.

✓uranium	apples	shrimp
computers	farm equipment	rubber tires
lettuce	turkeys	natural gas
movies	✓copper	sheep
salmon	potatoes	cattle

mine   _uranium, copper_ _____

catch   _____

grow   _____

manufacture   _____

produce   _____

raise   _____

C. Look at the product map. Read and (circle) *True* or *False*.

> **Passive Voice: *Be* + Past Participle**
> The **active voice** emphasizes the **subject** that **performs** the action.
> The **passive voice** emphasizes the **subject** that **receives** the action.
>
> | **Active** | **Passive** |
> |------------|-------------|
> | Fishermen **catch** salmon in Oregon. | Salmon **are caught** in Oregon. (*Fishermen* is understood.) |
> | Miners **mine** copper in Utah. | Copper **is mined** in Utah. (*Miners* is understood.) |

1. Grapes are grown in California.   (True)   False

2. Silver is mined in Montana.   True   False

3. Potatoes are grown in New Mexico.   True   False

4. Peanuts are grown in Oklahoma.   True   False

5. Turkeys are raised in Utah.   True   False

6. Gold is mined in Iowa.   True   False

7. Cattle are raised in Nebraska.   True   False

8. Rice is grown in Louisiana.   True   False

9. Grapes are grown in Minnesota.   True   False

10. Movies are produced in California.   True   False

D. Active or passive. Circle the correct form of the verb.

> Farmers grow corn in Iowa.   **Active**—the subject performs the action.
> Corn is grown in Iowa.   **Passive**—the subject receives the action.

1. Farmers **(grow)** / **are grown** corn in Texas.
2. Gold **mines** / **is mined** in South Dakota.
3. Ranchers **raise** / **are raised** cattle in Nebraska.
4. Workers **mine** / **are mined** uranium in Nebraska.
5. Turkeys **raise** / **are raised** in Minnesota.
6. Farmers **grow** / **are grown** lettuce in Arizona.
7. Iron ore **mines** / **is mined** in Wyoming.
8. Ranchers **raise** / **are raised** hogs in Missouri.
9. Farmers **grow** / **are grown** apples in Washington.
10. Computers **manufacture** / **are manufactured** in Minnesota.

E. Ask and answer questions about each of the products.

> **Is** milk **produced** in Wisconsin?
> Yes, it is.
>
> **Are** tires **manufactured** in Wisconsin?
> No, they aren't.

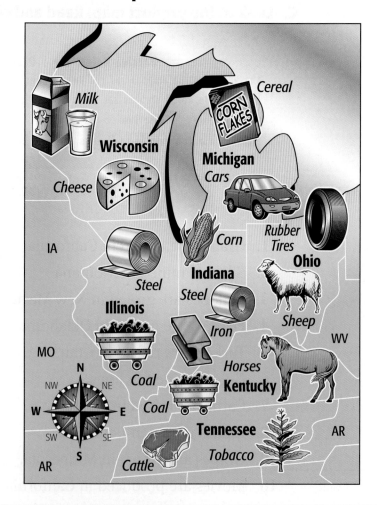

Choose a State: A Research Assignment

A. Work together in a group of three or four students. Choose a state to research. Go to your school library or use the Internet to find out the answers to the questions. Draw an outline of the state in the space below. Then, mark the places and location of products on your map.

1. What is the state capital? Where is it located? Put a star next to the location of the state capital.

2. Mark the bordering states. Then, mark three major cities in your state on your map. Where are they located?

3. What is the largest airport in the state? Mark its location on the map.

4. Draw in one or two major rivers or bodies of water. Label them.

5. What farm products are grown in the state? What major industries are located there?

B. Tell your classmates about your state. Use verbs from the box.

border	locate	grow	manufacture	produce

_____ *is located* in the east / west / north / south.
_____ *is bordered by* (name of bordering states).

C. Well-known companies. Read the list of products. Can you name a major company that each item is produced by? Use the verbs in the box to talk about the products with your partner.

design	refine
deliver	manufacture
make	produce

Copy machines *are manufactured by* _____.
(name of company)

1. copy machines
2. razors
3. stereos
4. cell phones

5. jeans
6. baby food
7. disposable diapers
8. cosmetics

9. gasoline
10. soda
11. packages
12. cameras

D. Write the names of four products that you or you and your family use in your home. Then, complete the sentences. Use one of the verbs from Exercise C and the name of the company. Read the sentences to a partner.

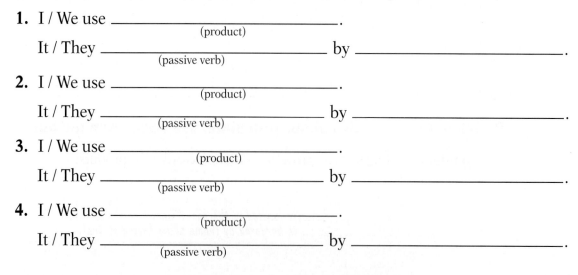

1. I / We use _____.
   (product)
   It / They _____ by _____.
   (passive verb)

2. I / We use _____.
   (product)
   It / They _____ by _____.
   (passive verb)

3. I / We use _____.
   (product)
   It / They _____ by _____.
   (passive verb)

4. I / We use _____.
   (product)
   It / They _____ by _____.
   (passive verb)

A. Listen and write the questions. Then, look at the product map of a few Asian countries and write the answers to the questions.

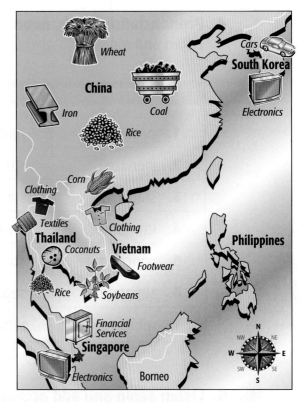

1. Where are electronics manufactured?

   They are manufactured in South Korea.

2. _____ ?

   _____ .

3. _____ ?

   _____ .

4. _____ ?

   _____ .

5. _____ ?

   _____ .

6. _____ ?

   _____ .

7. _____ ?

   _____ .

8. _____ ?

   _____ .

Describing Processes

A. Pronunciation: Verb, noun, and adjective forms and syllable stress.
Listen and repeat.

	Verb	Noun	Adjective
1.	pasteurize	pasteurization	pasteurized
2.	sterilize	sterilization	sterilized
3.	stabilize	stabilization	stabilized
4.	immunize	immunization	immunized
5.	concentrate	concentration	concentrated
6.	separate	separation	separated
7.	refrigerate	refrigeration	refrigerated

B. Listen again and add accent marks to show which syllables are stressed.

pasteurize—to partially sterilize a liquid, such as milk, to kill bacteria; milk is pasteurized

C. Gathering chocolate beans. Look at the pictures on the next page. Use the cues from the box and write each sentence under the correct picture.

1. ripe pods / gather / every few weeks during the season

2. pods / cut down / from the cacao trees

3. pods / split open / and / seeds / remove

4. seeds / put in large wooden boxes for fermentation

5. the seed pulp / drain / for six to eight days

6. seeds / dry / by machine or the sun

7. seeds / put / into large sacks

8. beans / export / to chocolate makers all over the world

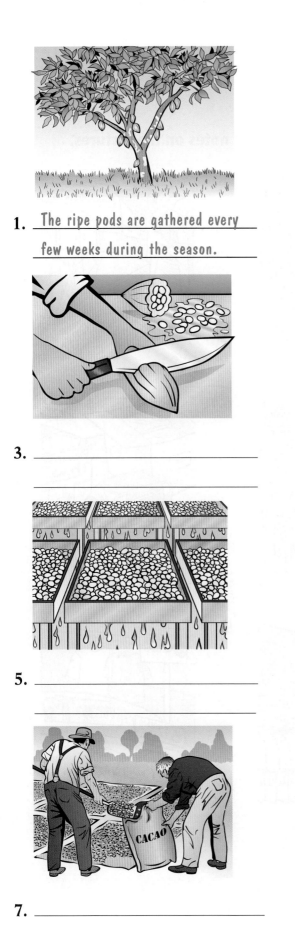

1. The ripe pods are gathered every few weeks during the season.

2. _____

3. _____

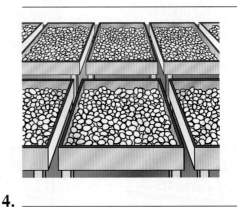

4. _____

5. _____

6. _____

7. _____

8. _____

The Big Picture: T-shirts—From the Field to Your Closet

A. Talk about the pictures. Then, listen and take notes on the pictures.

1.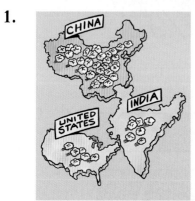

2.

3.

4.

5.

6.

7.

8.

9.

B. Listen again and answer the questions about how a T-shirt is made.

1. What are the three top cotton-producing nations in the world?
2. How is the cotton picked in China—by hand or by machine?
3. What happens at the ginner?
4. Where are the bales of cotton sent?
5. What percent of the cotton fabric is dyed different colors?
6. Does one person complete an entire T-shirt? Explain your answer.
7. What is the original cost for a T-shirt?
8. Why is the T-shirt price increased at the warehouse?
9. How much is the price increased at the department store?
10. How long does it take before a T-shirt is sent to a discount store?

C. Fill in the verbs. Some of the verbs are passive; others are active. Then, put the sentences in chronological order from 1–9.

_____ **a.** The fabric _____ (send) to a sewing plant.

_____ **b.** The T-shirts _____ (ship) to a warehouse.

_____ **c.** The spinners _____ (knit) the yarn into fabric.

__1__ **d.** The cotton ____is picked____ (pick) by the workers.

_____ **e.** The dye houses _____ (dye) the shirts different colors.

_____ **f.** The ginners _____ (clean) the cotton.

_____ **g.** The T-shirts _____ (sew) together on a line.

_____ **h.** The printers _____ (embroider) designs on the shirts.

_____ **i.** The bales of cotton _____ (sell) to spinners.

D. Sentence completion. Complete the sentences according to the story.

1. Before the cotton is put into bales, it _____.
2. When the fabric is sent to a dye house, it _____.
3. After the T-shirts are sewn, they _____.
4. After the patterns are cut, the workers _____.
5. When the T-shirts are sent to the warehouse, the price
   _____ over 200 percent.
6. Before a T-shirt is discounted, the store _____
   it for the full price.
7. The T-shirts are discounted after they _____.
8. The unsold T-shirts are discounted for $14 or less when _____
   _____.

Reading: An Alternative Energy Source

A. Before You Read.

1. What do you do to save energy in your home?
2. Can you list two sources of energy?
3. How can today's cars save energy?

Automobile companies have already begun to manufacture "hybrid" cars—cars that use two sources of power. These cars use typical fuel, such as gasoline, but the cars also have batteries to supply power to an electric motor. Hybrid cars send fewer pollutants into the air. A few automobile manufacturers are trying to provide automobiles for environmentally-minded consumers, but what about the power companies that supply electricity? Consumers need energy to run their microwaves, DVD players, computers, and other possessions. What is a green, or environmentally safe, source of energy?

A significant source of green energy is wind. Windmills have been around for hundreds of years. Traditionally, windmills have been used to pump water for farmers. Today, millions of windmills and wind turbines are found throughout the United States and the world. In California, there are more than fifteen thousand wind turbines to generate power for its increasing population. One percent of California's power is generated by wind turbines. In West Texas, wind energy turbines have become a source of income for people who own groups of wind turbines, or wind farms.

Wind is different from other energy sources, such as coal and gas, which cause pollution and use up the world's natural resources. Wind has an advantage—it does not generate harmful emissions like coal and gas do. The average household consumes approximately 10,000 kwh (kilowatt-hours) of electricity. A 10-kw wind turbine generates enough power to serve a typical household for a year. Wind energy is also included as one of the options in "green power" plans in some of today's electric companies. Customers can choose to use a certain amount of wind energy every month instead of conventional energy. California, Colorado, and Texas are some of the states that offer "green power" options to their customers. The top three users of wind energy in 2002 were Europe, the United States, and India. In fact, ten percent of Denmark's energy is powered by the wind.

Although wind energy is a clean source of energy, not everyone is in favor of wind turbine generators. First of all, opponents of wind energy say that large birds may fly into the moving blades and be killed. Advocates of wind energy say that more birds are killed by automobiles than by wind turbines. Second, opponents say that wind turbine generators are noisy and disturb residents. Advocates say that there are no studies that prove that residents suffer any problems because of wind turbine farms. A wind turbine is no louder than a refrigerator. Third, residents complain that the wind turbine farms are ugly and reduce housing prices. In fact, one wind advocacy group says that the oldest wind farm in Cornwall, England, has attracted over 350,000 visitors. In addition, there has been no evidence that housing prices have been affected by wind turbine farms.

B. Sentence sense. (Circle) the sentence with the closest meaning to the original.

1. A significant source of green energy is wind.

   a. Wind energy is a clean source of energy.

   b. Wind energy is not popular.

   c. Wind energy is not an environmental source of energy.

   d. Wind energy is not good for the environment.

2. Wind energy is included as one of the options in "green power" plans.

   a. Energy consumers can choose wind energy to power their homes.

   b. Consumers must use wind energy.

   c. Consumers must paint their houses green.

   d. Wind energy is more expensive than other plans.

3. Wind energy has an advantage—it does not generate harmful emissions like coal and gas do.

   a. Wind energy sends pollution into the air.

   b. Wind energy is like coal and gas; all three pollute the air.

   c. Wind energy pollutes as much as coal and gas do.

   d. Unlike coal and gas, wind energy does not pollute the environment.

C. Pro or con. Read each statement. Write *pro* if the statement is positive about wind energy, and write *con* if the statement is negative about wind energy.

1. These windmills send no pollutants into the air. _____

2. Coal and gas cause pollution and use up the world's natural resources. _____

3. Wind energy does not generate harmful emissions. _____

4. Wind energy is a clean source of energy. _____

5. Wind turbine generators are noisy and disturb neighborhoods. _____

6. A wind turbine is no louder than a refrigerator. _____

7. Wind turbine farms are ugly and reduce housing prices. _____

Writing Our Stories: Business and Industry in My Country

A. Read.

I am from Tokyo, Japan. Tokyo is located in the eastern part of Japan on Honshu, the largest of the four islands in Japan. Tokyo is also the capital city. Japan is an island. It is bordered by the Pacific Ocean to the east, the Sea of Japan to the west, and the China Sea to the southwest. Because much of Japan is mountainous, the Japanese people live in a small area of the country. Japan has a very large population of 126,974,628 (2000), and we need to import many products, such as wood and natural gas, for our people.

Rice is an important product for the Japanese people. Rice is grown in many parts of Japan. Many vegetables, including sugar beets and radishes, and fruit, such as apples, are grown on Japanese farms. Fishing is also a large industry. In fact, Japan is known to supply about 15 percent of the world's fish. Many resources are imported because our country has very few natural resources. Oil, wood, and iron ore are some of the products that are imported.

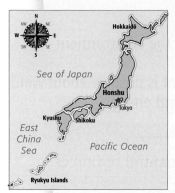

Japan is best known for its automobiles and electronics. In fact, three of the largest automobile companies in the world are Japanese. Japan is also known for its consumer electronics. For example, DVD players, portable stereos, and televisions are manufactured by Japanese companies. Look in your home. How many Japanese-made electronics can you find?

B. Draw a map of your country. Show the bordering countries. Then, add products and natural resources. Use the following questions to guide you in writing a paragraph about your country's industry and products.

1. What city are you from, and where is it located?

2. What are three major products that are produced in your country?

3. What are the major industries in your country?

4. What natural resources are found in your country?

C. For example, such as, and including.

> For example, such as, and including introduce examples.
>
> Many minerals, **such as** copper and iron ore, can be found in my country.
> Many industries are in trouble right now. **For example**, two steel plants
> have laid off workers.
> Tourists can visit a number of famous places in Japan, **including** Kyoto
> and Mt. Fuji.
>
> **Note:** *Including* and *such as* are not used at the beginning of a sentence.

Complete the sentences with examples.

1. Dye houses dye the T-shirts a variety of colors, such as _____
    and _____.

2. T-shirts are sold at discounted prices at many stores, including
    _____, _____, and _____.

3. There are many countries represented in my class. For example, there are
    students from _____, _____, and _____.

4. The United States has many natural resources, such as _____,
    _____, and _____.

5. Agricultural products, including _____ and _____,
    are grown in my state.

D. Edit. Find and correct the mistakes.

1. Coffee is grow in South and Central America.

2. Italy is bordering by Switzerland, Germany, Austria, and Slovenia.

3. The cacao pods carefully picked, and then they are opened.

4. After the cotton picked, it is sent to the ginner.

5. Computer software develops in Washington.

6. Dairy cows raised by farmers.

7. France and Italy is known for their fashions.

8. Wind energy turbines are locate in many parts of Europe.

www Looking at the Internet

Search for a process on the Internet. Type a phrase in quotation marks such
as "How candy is made," or "How orange juice is made." How many steps
are involved in the process? Share the information with your classmates.

A. Complete the sentences about the product map of European countries.

design
raise
produce
grow
assemble
manufacture
build

1. Watches _____ in Switzerland.

2. Automobiles _____ in _____
   _____ .

3. Glass and crystal _____ .

4. Ships _____ .

5. Footwear _____ .

6. Iron and steel _____ .

7. Sheep _____ .

8. Citrus fruit _____ .

9. Chemicals, such as pharmaceuticals, _____ .

10. Clothing _____ .

B. Complete the questions and answers about the product map of Europe.

1. (watches) Where are watches designed and manufactured?
   Watches are designed and manufactured in Switzerland.

2. (software) _____ ?
   _____

3. (citrus fruit) _____ ?
   _____

4. (aircraft) _____ ?
   _____

5. (automobiles) _____?
_____

6. (footwear) _____?
_____

7. (textiles) _____?
_____

8. (glass and crystal) _____?
_____

Grammar Summary

> **1. Active and passive voice**

Active: **Farmers grow** grapes in California.

The active voice emphasizes the **subject** that **performs** the action.

Passive voice: **be** + past participle

Grapes are grown (by farmers) in California.

The passive voice emphasizes the **subject** that **receives** the action.

> **2. Uses of the passive voice**

a. Use the passive voice to emphasize the product, the action, or the process.

Oranges **are transported** to processing plants.

b. Use the passive voice when the person who performed the action is unknown or understood.

Coffee beans **are roasted** before they are processed into powder or bars. (understood)

The milk **was spilled** all over the floor. (unknown)

c. Use the passive voice for general statements of fact.

Windmills **are found** throughout the United States and the world.

> **3. Passive and by**

Use **by** to introduce a known person, company, or performer of the action.

Movies **are produced by** both small and large movie studios.

> **4. Questions**

Cattle **are raised** in Texas.	**Are** cattle **raised** in Texas?	Yes, they are.
Grapes **are grown** in California.	Where **are** grapes **grown**?	In California.
Lettuce **is grown** in Arizona.	What **is grown** in Arizona?	Lettuce.

14 Technology Today

 Listen to the information about inventions in the late twentieth century. After you listen, write the name of the inventor or company under each invention.

anti-shoplifting device	747 Jumbo Jet	video games	artificial heart
1965	1970	1972	1978

hepatitis B vaccine	roller blades	space shuttle	personal computer
1980	1980	1981	1981
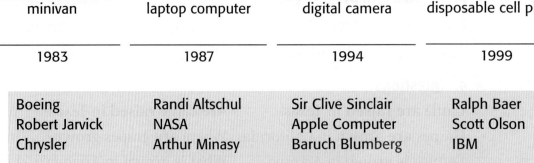			
minivan	laptop computer	digital camera	disposable cell phone
1983	1987	1994	1999

Boeing	Randi Altschul	Sir Clive Sinclair	Ralph Baer
Robert Jarvick	NASA	Apple Computer	Scott Olson
Chrysler	Arthur Minasy	Baruch Blumberg	IBM

Active Grammar: Passive Voice—Past Tense

Subject	be	Past participle	
The space shuttle	was	built invented	in 1976. by NASA.
747 jumbo jets	were	developed designed	in 1970. by Boeing.

A. Complete this information about the inventions on page 212. Use the passive voice.

1. The first anti-shoplifting device (invent)_____was invented_____ by a consultant for the New York City Police Department, Arthur Minasy. These tags (attach) _____ to store merchandise. When a customer bought the item, the tag (remove) _____. The tag set off an alarm if a customer walked through the door without paying.

2. The Boeing 747 (design) _____ as a wide-body airliner for intercontinental flights. Eight hundred and thirty-seven of these (build) _____ by Boeing. The runways of several major airports (extend) _____ in order to accommodate these larger planes.

3. The first family of personal computers (make) _____ by IBM. The personal computer (develop) _____ by a team of engineers.

4. Before 1994, film _____ (use) for photographs. The technology for digital imagery _____ (develop) by both NASA and by private industry. In 1994, the first digital cameras for the consumer market _____ (introduce).

B. Answer these questions about the inventions on page 212. Use the passive voice.

1. When was the first artificial heart invented?
2. Why was it invented?
3. By whom was the artificial heart invented?
4. When was the minivan introduced?
5. What consumer group was it designed for?
6. By whom was the laptop computer invented?
7. When was the disposable cell phone invented?
8. When was the digital camera invented?
9. When were roller blades invented?
10. Why are they also called in-line skates?

A. Read this paragraph about the Model T. The verbs in the passive voice are <u>underlined</u>.

The automobile <u>**was developed**</u> before 1900 and cars <u>**were already used**</u> in Europe on a limited basis. In America, Henry Ford **developed** a more affordable car in 1908 called the Model T. The first moving assembly line <u>**was installed**</u> in his factory in 1913. This **reduced** the cost and time of producing a car. A Model T car <u>**was assembled**</u> in 93 minutes and **cost** $850. By 1927, more than fifteen million cars **were** on the roads in America.

(Circle) *A* for active voice or *P* for passive voice.

1. The first cars did not have windshield wipers.	Ⓐ	P
2. People got out of their cars to clean their windshields.	A	P
3. The first windshield wipers were invented by Mary Anderson.	A	P
4. They were operated from the inside of the car.	A	P
5. The electronic ignition system was invented by Kettering and Coleman.	A	P
6. Before this, people turned a crank to start their engines.	A	P
7. Before 1929, people could not listen to the radio in their cars.	A	P
8. The first car radio was designed by Paul Galvin.	A	P
9. The radio was not installed at the automobile factory.	A	P
10. Car owners took their cars to a separate company for radio installation.	A	P
11. Turn signals were invented by Buick in 1938.	A	P
12. They were developed by a team of engineers.	A	P
13. Before this, people used their hands to signal a turn.	A	P

B. Talk about each advance in car and traffic technology using the chart below. What did people do before each item was invented?

> The electronic ignition system was invented by Charles Kettering and Clyde Coleman in 1911. Before that, people turned a crank by hand in order to start their cars.

Invention	Inventor	Year
windshield wipers	Mary Anderson	1903
electronic ignition system	Charles Kettering and Clyde Coleman	1911
automatic traffic signal	Garrett Morgan	1923
car radio	Paul Galvin	1929
parking meter	Carlton Cole Magee	1932
turn signals	Buick	1938
car air-conditioning	Packard	1940
air bags	General Motors	1973

C. Complete the sentences about the inventions in the chart using the passive voice.

1. One of the first automatic traffic signals ___was developed___ (develop) by Garrett Morgan.

2. He _____ (issue) a patent in 1923.

3. Before this, many people _____ (kill) in traffic accidents.

4. Three positions _____ (feature) on this device: Go, Stop, and All-Direction Stop. The All-Direction Stop allowed pedestrians to cross safely.

5. Morgan's device _____ (use) until today's system of red, yellow, and green lights.

6. The first parking meters _____ (install) in Oklahoma City.

7. They _____ (meet) with angry resistance by drivers.

8. Several of the first parking meters _____ (destroy) by angry groups.

9. Air bags _____ (invent) by General Motors.

10. Air bags _____ (offer) as an option in 1973 Chevys.

11. For more than ten years, air bags _____ (negative—consider) important by drivers. Now they are standard equipment in most cars.

D. Write these sentences about medical history and advances in medicine using the passive voice. The sentences are in the simple present tense or the past tense.

1. In early times, the medicine man cured people.

   In early times, people were cured by the medicine man.

2. The Romans began the first hospitals.

   _____.

3. Germs cause many diseases.

   _____.

4. Many years ago, hospitals did not sterilize equipment.

   _____.

5. Today, doctors and hospitals sterilize all equipment.

   _____.

6. Sir Alexander Fleming discovered penicillin in 1928.

   _____.

7. Bernard Fantus established the first blood bank in the United States in 1937.

   _____.

8. Ian McDonald invented ultrasound in 1958.

   _____.

9. Sound waves create pictures of internal organs.

   _____.

10. Baruch Blumberg developed the hepatitis B vaccine in 1963.

    _____.

11. Most colleges require students to have the hepatitis B vaccine.

    _____.

12. Doctors implanted the first artificial heart in Barney Clark in 1982.

    _____.

13. Doctors performed the first laser surgery to correct vision in 1987.

    _____.

14. Doctors perform many operations on an outpatient basis.

    _____.

Passive and *Wh-* questions

A. Pronunciation: Compound nouns. Listen and repeat the names of these inventions.

> **Note:** The first word receives more stress than the second word.

1. SAFety razor
2. AIR-conditioner
3. LIE detector
4. MIcrowave oven
5. BALLpoint pen

6. PARKing meter
7. CONtact lenses
8. SEAT belt
9. LAser printer
10. CELL phone

Sit with a partner. Pronounce these inventions that are related to the computer.

1. FLOPpy disk
2. KEYboard
3. INKjet printer
4. LAPtop computer
5. E-mail

6. HARD drive
7. WEB page
8. JOYstick
9. TOOLbar
10. SOFTware

B. Questions in the passive. Read the examples in the box. Then, ask and answer questions about these inventions.

What's this?	It's a pop-up toaster.
By whom was it **invented**?	It was invented by Charles Strite.
When was it **invented**?	It was invented in 1919.
What is it **used** for?	It is used to toast bread.

Charles Strite–1919

King Gillette–1904

Ladislo Biro–1938

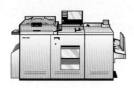

Chester Carlson–
1949

Marion Donovan–
1950

Zenith Electronics–
1950

C. More inventions. List ten inventions in your classroom or that you have in your handbag or your backpack. Then, answer the questions about each invention.

1. _____   6. _____

2. _____   7. _____

3. _____   8. _____

4. _____   9. _____

5. _____   10. _____

1. What is the name of this invention?
2. How many years ago do you think it was invented?
3. What is it made of?
4. What is it used for?
5. What did people use before we had this invention?

Can you think of a problem or job you would like to solve? Can you think of a way to make your life or your work easier? Can you think of an invention that would save time in your life? Brainstorm some ideas for useful inventions.

at home	at work	at school	in your car
at the airport	at the store	at the bank	at the supermarket

D. Student to student dictation.

Student A: Turn to page 249. Read the questions.

Student B: Read each of these responses. Then, listen and write the number of each question next to the correct response. When you finish, change pages. Then, compare answers.

_____ **a.** Because she had a heart attack.

_____ **b.** Because there are heavy thunderstorms in the middle part of the country.

_____ **c.** Because he had three car accidents and four speeding tickets.

_____ **d.** Because she robbed a convenience store.

_____ **e.** Because he didn't pay his rent for five months.

_____ **f.** Because the boss has received several complaints about her work.

_____ **g.** Because she has four credit cards already and she's maxed out on all of them.

_____ **h.** Because we have a foot of snow on the ground.

_____ **i.** Because you forgot her birthday.

_____ **j.** Because they're repairing the bridge.

E. Listen to Hui-Fen describe school in Taiwan. Then, answer these questions.

1. Where was Hui-Fen educated?
2. What were some of the rules in her school?
3. How were students punished if they did not do their homework?
4. When were students allowed to date?
5. What language is spoken at home in Taiwan? In what language are students educated?
6. When is school closed?
7. What other information do you remember about Hui-Fen's education?

F. Interview another student in your class. If possible, interview a student from another country.

1. When were you born? Where were you born?
2. Where were you raised?
3. Were you educated in private school or in public school?
4. Were you involved in any after-school sports or activities?
5. Were you required to wear a uniform?
6. Were you allowed to date?
7. Was school ever cancelled? If so, why?
8. Was school closed in July and August?
9. What language was spoken in class?
10. What languages were taught?
11. Were students expected to stand when they answered a question?
12. How many hours of homework were you assigned?
13. Was homework given every night?
14. Were you kept after school if you didn't do your homework?
15. How often were exams given?

Write two things about your education and your partner's education that were the same.

1. _____

2. _____

Write two things about your education and your partner's education that were different.

1. _____

2. _____

A. Look at the pictures and listen to a short history of some of the inventions and ideas that have made shopping easier.

B. Listen again. Complete the chart.

Invention	Date	How did this invention help people?
Catalogs		
Cash register		
Shopping cart		
Credit card		
Bar code (U.P.C.)		
Online shopping		

C. Which invention does each statement describe?

1. Before this invention, all receipts were handwritten.
2. This invention was first used in 1974.
3. With this advance in technology, it's easy to compare prices.
4. This idea was developed by a traveling salesman.
5. This invention was designed by a grocery store owner.
6. This advance was first used by business travelers.

D. Read the questions first. Then, listen again and answer the questions.

1. Why was a traveling salesman necessary?
2. How did Ward travel?
3. How did his idea help his customers?
4. Where did store owners keep their money before 1884?
5. Was a receipt written or printed?
6. How did the cash register make shopping simpler?
7. Why did customers need shopping carts?
8. Who were credit cards first used by?
9. What inventions are used by supermarket checkers?
10. How does the bar code make their job easier?
11. Why do small companies like online shopping?
12. How does online shopping save customers money?

E. Complete the sentences. Verbs may be in the active or passive voice.

1. The first mail-order catalog (print) _____ in 1872.
   Customers (look) _____ through the catalog
   and (order) _____ the items they wanted.

2. Before 1950, customers (pay) _____ for their
   purchases with cash or by check. The first credit cards (issue)
   _____ to business travelers. With a credit card,
   people (negative—need) _____ to carry a lot of
   cash with them.

3. The first U.P.C. scanner (install) _____ in a
   supermarket in Ohio. Today, supermarket clerks simply (scan)
   _____ each item. The price (appear)
   _____ on their cash register's screen.

Reading: Cell-Phone Controversy

A. Before You Read.

1. Do you own a cell phone? Is it a hand-held set or a hands-free set?

2. Do you talk on the phone when you are driving?

3. Does your state have any laws about the use of cell phones when driving?

B. Vocabulary. Match each word with its meaning.

_____ **1.** controversy   **a.** not permitted by law, not allowed

_____ **2.** relationship   **b.** the time it takes to react

_____ **3.** banned   **c.** disagreement or argument

_____ **4.** evidence   **d.** to put a limit on, to control

_____ **5.** distraction   **e.** connection or association

_____ **6.** to contribute   **f.** facts that prove something is true

_____ **7.** to perform   **g.** something that causes a person to lose concentration

_____ **8.** response time   **h.** to be part of the cause or the reason

_____ **9.** to restrict   **i.** to do, to act, to carry out instructions

Cell-phone technology was developed during the 1970s and 1980s. It was not until the 1990s that cell phones came into everyday use. In 1995, 24 percent of adults in the United States reported that they owned a cell phone. By 2002, that number grew to 64 percent. This little invention has produced a major **controversy**. What is the **relationship** between hand-held phones and accidents? Should there be a law against the use of hand-held phones by drivers?

In June, 2001, the governor of the state of New York signed the first law in the United States that **banned** hand-held phones by drivers. Violators are fined $100. At the ceremony, he was joined by individuals and families who had lost a loved one in an accident involving cell-phone use. New York is following the example set by other countries. The use of cell phones by drivers is banned in Portugal. In several other countries, including Italy, Poland, Spain, Slovakia, and Hungary, drivers are required to use hands-free sets.

The phone industry is fighting these laws. They say that there is not enough **evidence** to prove that cell-phone usage causes accidents. A study by the American Automobile Association (AAA), said that other **distractions** are more serious, such as eating, applying make up, or putting a CD into a CD player. In addition, less than 2 percent of all drivers involved in five thousand accidents reported between 1995 and 1999 said that they were distracted by their cell phone.

Other studies show that cell-phone use **contributes** to accidents. The National Police Agency of Japan reported that in 1997, 2,297 accidents were caused by drivers talking on cell phones. Another study in South Africa showed that one out of every four accidents was related to cell-phone usage.

A study at the University of Utah showed that all cell-phone use in cars is a distraction. Sixty-four drivers were asked to **perform** simple tasks, such as changing a radio station, listening to music, talking on a hands-free cell phone, and talking on a hand-held cell phone. Then, researchers measured their **response time** when they were braking or stopping a car. When people were using a cell phone, their responses were much slower. This was true of both hands-free phones and hand-held phones.

What can drivers expect in the years to come? More laws will be passed **restricting** the use of hand-held cell phones. Cell-phone manufacturers will continue to encourage cell-phone safety in their instructions. And cell-phone companies will advertise headsets, car speakerphones, and voice-activated dialing services. You can be sure that companies are busy today, inventing safer ways to use this new technology.

C. Looking at studies. Read each statement about a study in the reading. Then, circle *T* for True or *F* for False.

1. The American Automobile Association said that using a hand-held phone is more distracting than eating in a car.   T   F

2. AAA also reported that almost five thousand accidents were caused by cell-phone use.   T   F

3. Japan stated that 2,297 cell-phone users had accidents in 1997.   T   F

4. Only four accidents in South Africa were caused by cell-phone use.   T   F

5. A study at the University of Utah showed that hands-free cell phones are safer than hand-held cell phones.   T   F

D. Vocabulary. Use a vocabulary word from Exercise B to complete these sentences.

1. TV is a _____ for children when they are doing their homework.

2. The museum _____ the use of cell phones. They are limited to the lobby.

3. What is the _____ between drinking and driving?

4. Poor weather conditions _____ to many accidents.

5. The _____ shows that the car's brakes failed.

6. There is an ongoing _____ about how to spend taxes.

Writing Our Stories: An Opinion Letter

A. Read this letter from an annoyed customer to the owner of a popular restaurant.

25 Glen Street

Tampa, Florida 33615

March 3, 2003

Dear Mr. Lombardi,

opinion ——————— Please consider a ban on cell phones at your restaurant. This past Friday evening, my husband and I were enjoying dinner at your restaurant when a woman at the next table received a cell-phone call. People at the nearby tables soon learned that she was annoyed at her sister for using her credit card. Her loud conversation continued for ten minutes. My husband and I were looking forward to a relaxing evening, a good dinner, and quiet conversation. We didn't pay $47.00 to listen to another customer's personal problems.

reasons

restatement of opinion ——————— Please follow the example of several other restaurants in the city that have posted signs, "Cell-phone usage limited to emergencies only."

Sincerely,

Teresa Santiago

B. Stating an opinion. Should drivers be able to use hand held-cell phones while driving? Write the following reasons under the correct heading on page 225. Add one more reason under each heading.

> a. Drivers need two hands on the wheel.
> b. Drivers spend hours in traffic. Talking to friends gives them a way to pass the time.
> c. There are not enough studies to prove that drivers using hand-held cell phones cause more accidents.
> d. A person talking on the phone is concentrating on the conversation, not the road.

Drivers should be allowed to use hand-held cell phones:

1. _____

2. _____

3. _____

Drivers should not be allowed to use hand-held cell phones:

1. _____

2. _____

3. _____

C. An opinion letter. The legislature in your state is considering a law to ban the use of hand-held cell phones by drivers. Some legislators are in favor of the ban and others are opposed to it. Write a letter to your congressman or congresswoman stating *your* opinion. Follow this form:

1. State your opinion in the first sentence.

2. Give two or three reasons for your opinion.

3. Restate your opinion in the last sentence.

D. Edit. Find and correct the mistakes in these sentences.

1. The accident was causing by a driver talking on a cell phone.

2. The driver distracted when her cell phone rang.

3. Yesterday I was seen an accident.

4. She was bought a headset for her phone.

5. Hand-held cell phones are ban in New York State.

6. The man at the next table was talk on the phone.

7. The people in the theater was annoyed when a cell phone rang.

8. She was gave a ticket for driving while using a cell phone.

www Looking at the Internet

Look at a few stores on the Internet. What do they sell? Are the prices cheaper or more expensive than stores in your area? How much is shipping? Bring in the home page of a store you like. Tell the other students about this site.

A. Read and complete this article about advances in cardiology. Some of the verbs are active; others are passive. Choose the correct verb tense.

Heart disease is the number-one cause of death in the United States. For years, doctors have been developing tests, medications, and procedures to help patients with heart disease. In the most serious cases, a heart transplant (require) _____.

On December 3, 1967, Dr. Christian Barnard (perform) _____ the first heart transplant in Capetown, South Africa. The heart of an auto accident victim (transplant) _____ into the body of Louis Washansky, a 55-year-old man. He (live) _____ for 18 days following the operation.

Since that day, over fifteen thousand heart transplants have been performed. The major difficulty in these procedures (be) _____ the rejection of the new heart by the recipient's body's immune system. In 1969, an anti-rejection drug, cyclosponine, (discover) _____ by Jean-Francois Borel. Today, heart transplants (perform) _____ throughout the world.

The first artificial heart (implant) _____ in Dr. Barney Clark in 1982. This mechanical heart (attach) _____ by tubes and wires to a large machine. The heart (name) _____ the Jarvick-7 after its inventor, Dr. Robert Jarvick. Dr. Clark (live) _____ for 112 days. The next patient survived for 620 days. But research with the new heart (discontinue) _____.

In July, 2001, a new artificial heart, the AbioCor®, (implant) _____ in Robert Tools, a 59-year-old grandfather with severe heart disease. Unlike the Jarvick-7, the AbioCor® is self-contained. A small battery pack (wore)_____ around the waist. Mr. Tools (live) _____ for 151 days. The second recipient is still alive after 16 months. Studies are continuing with this new heart.

B. In your notebooks, write seven questions about this article.

Grammar Summary

► **1. Active and passive voice**

Active: The doctor **performed** the operation.

Passive: The operation **was performed** *by* the doctor.

In an active sentence, the subject (the doctor) performs the action.

In a passive sentence, the process (the operation), the product, or the action is emphasized. Use *by* to show the performer of the action. If the performer of the action is clearly understood, *by* is not necessary.

► **2. Uses of the passive voice**

a. We can use the passive when the subject receives the action.

The nurse **gave** him an injection. (active)

He **was given** an injection. (passive)

b. We can use the passive when the performer of the action is unknown or understood.

The patient **was admitted** to the hospital.

The operation **was performed** yesterday.

c. We can use the passive for general statements of fact.

Blood **is composed** of millions of cells.

► **3. Passive voice—Past tense statements**

Use *was* or *were* and the past participle to form the passive.

| The patient | **was** | treated | at the hospital. |
| The patients | **were** | | at the clinic. |

► **4. *Wh-* questions**

| When
Where | **was** | the patient | treated? |
| By whom | **were** | the patients | |

Country Music

A. Read the names of different types of music. Can you name a performer who plays each type of music? What's your favorite type of music?

rock and roll	classical	jazz	hip-hop
rhythm and blues (R&B)	country	salsa	rap
pop	heavy metal	opera	gospel

B. Look at the pictures. Which type of music is each performer known for?

Bob Marley

Enrique Iglesias

Faith Hill

Shakira

U-2

Celia Cruz

P. Diddy

Mariah Carey

Placido Domingo

Active Grammar: Adjective Clauses with *who*

A. Look at the people in the picture. Describe the country music fans. Complete the adjective clauses.

The man **who is pointing to the boots** is asking, "Are you going to buy those boots?"
The man **who is standing in line** is asking, "How long have you been waiting?"

1. The girl who _____ is saying, "How many shows have you seen?"

2. The couple who _____ is saying, "This is our tenth show."

3. The woman who _____ is saying, "I'm your biggest fan."

4. The woman who _____ is signing autographs.

5. The woman who _____ is taking a picture of her friend.

6. The woman who _____ is saying, "I only bought a few souvenirs."

B. In your notebook, write five sentences describing your classmates.

The student <u>who is sitting next to the window</u> is from _____ .
(name of country)

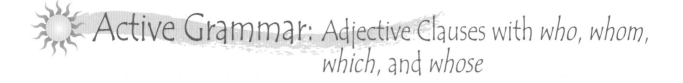

Active Grammar: Adjective Clauses with *who, whom, which,* and *whose*

A. Underline the adjective clauses in the sentences below. **Circle** the relative pronoun and draw an arrow to the noun it modifies.

> **Adjective clauses** begin with relative pronouns such as *who, whom, which,* and *whose.*
>
> **who**—replaces a person   **which**—replaces a thing
> **whom**—replaces an indirect object   **whose**—replaces a possessive
>
> **Note:** For more explanation and examples, refer to the Grammar Summary on page 243.

1. Reba McEntire, who was country music's 1995 entertainer of the year, made more money on her concerts than any other country star.

2. Reba McEntire, whose songs are often about strong independent women, has been in charge of her own career for some time.

3. McEntire, who was forced to sound less country and more mainstream, was not popular for the first thirteen years of her career.

4. McEntire's first husband, whom she divorced in 1987, did not promote her career well.

5. In 1982, McEntire had her first hit song, which was titled "Can't Even Get the Blues."

6. McEntire's fans, to whom she often speaks after shows, are at least 50 percent male.

7. In 2001, McEntire performed in a Broadway show, which brought her new fans.

8. In 2002, McEntire, whose Broadway performance showed her comedic ability, starred in her own TV show.

B. Listen: Country music. Listen to the history of country music. Then, circle *True* or *False* on the next page.

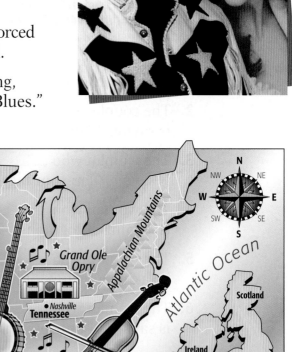

1. Today's country music was originated by immigrants from the British Isles. (True) False
2. The people from Appalachia sang all the time. True False
3. People sang to make their work go more slowly. True False
4. Country music, which the Appalachians sang, was very complicated. True False
5. The banjo, which became popular among country musicians, came from South America. True False
6. The fiddle was the main instrument of country music. True False
7. The first superstars of country music recorded in 1947. True False
8. The Carter Family and Jimmy Rodgers, who all sang country music, became the first superstars of country music. True False

C. Relative pronouns. Fill in the correct relative pronoun from the box.

| who | whose | whom | which |

1. The music, __which__ is called country music, came from the British Isles.
2. The people, _____ immigrated to this country, moved to a land that was similar to their native land.
3. Today's country music began in the Appalachian Mountains, _____ extend from the northeast to the south.
4. The music, _____ was very simple, was sung all the time.
5. The people, _____ immigrated from the British Isles, brought their music with them.
6. The fiddler, _____ instrument was the main country music instrument until the 1930s, made people dance.
7. The fiddler, _____ the community considered a very important part of the music, was necessary in every band.
8. The five-string banjo, _____ came from Africa, was used to play a different kind of music.
9. Jimmy Rodgers and the Carter family, _____ a Virginia record company first recorded, were the earliest superstars of country music.

D. Answer the following questions about you and your classmates. Write your answers on the blanks.

1. What musical instrument do you play? _____

2. Whom do you sit next to in class? _____

3. How long have you been in this country? _____

4. Who has a difficult work schedule? _____

5. Who has long hair? _____

E. With a group of three or four students, complete the sentences. Use the information in questions 1 to 5 from Exercise D.

> **Who plays a musical instrument?**
> Sung Kul, **who is in a band,** is from Korea.
> Beata, **whom I sit next to,** is from Poland.

1. _____, who _____,
   (name of student)

   is from _____.
   (native country)

2. _____, whom _____,
   (name of student)

   is from _____.
   (native country)

3. _____, who _____,
   (name of student)

   is from _____.
   (native country)

4. _____, whose _____,
   (name of student)

   is from _____.
   (native country)

5. _____, whose _____,
   (name of student)

   is from _____.
   (native country)

In your notebook, write five more sentences about your classmates. Use adjective clauses that begin with *who, whom, which,* or *whose*.

A. Complete the sentences about country performer Tim McGraw. Use the information below.

a. Tim McGraw was born in Delhi, Louisiana.

b. He went to Nashville, Tennessee, in the early '90s to start a recording career because the country music industry is primarily located in Nashville.

c. In 1995, McGraw had a hit album.

d. He went on tour in 1996 and performed with Faith Hill.

e. McGraw and Hill married in October, 1996.

f. McGraw and Hill's first child was born in 1997.

g. The couple recorded a duet in 1998. McGraw and Hill's second child was born in the same year.

1. <u>Delhi, Louisiana</u> was the place where _____.

2. He went to _____ where he _____ _____.

3. _____ is the city where the country music industry _____.

4. _____ was the year when McGraw_____.

5. In _____, when _____, he met his future wife, country performer Faith Hill.

6. _____ is the month when McGraw and Hill _____.

7. _____ is the year when their _____.

8. 1998 is the year when _____.

B. Complete the sentences about your life.

1. _____ is the place where I grew up.

2. _____ is the school where I _____.

3. I attend _____, where I study _____.

4. _____ is the year when I _____.

5. _____ is the year when my family and I _____.

6. I began to study English in _____ when I _____.

C. Musical preferences. Complete the following sentences about your musical preferences.

1. _____ is my favorite musician.

2. _____ is my favorite type of music.

3. _____ is my favorite musical group.

4. _____ is my favorite American performer.

5. _____ is my favorite radio station.

6. _____ is my favorite place to go dancing.

D. Rewrite your preferences from Exercise C. Then, discuss your preferences with a partner.

1. _____, who is my favorite musician, is from

   _____.
   (name of country)

2. _____, which is popular in _____,
   (name of country)

   is my favorite type of music.

3. _____, which is my favorite musical group, plays

   _____.
   (type of music)

4. _____, whose music is _____, is
   (adjective)

   my favorite American performer.

5. _____, which is at _____ FM/AM,
   (letters of radio station)   (numbers)

   is my favorite radio station.

6. _____, which is located in _____,
   (name of club)   (name of city)

   is my favorite place to go dancing.

E. Complete the questions on page 235. Then, ask your partner your questions.

Do you know a *music store* where I can buy some country music?

Yes, I do. You should try the CD Den. It's on Broad Street.

1. Do you know a music store where _____?

2. Do you know a movie theater where _____?

3. Do you know a dance club where _____?

4. Do you know a restaurant where _____?

5. Do you know a supermarket where _____?

6. Do you know an auto repair shop where _____?

F. Student to student dictation: Famous musicians.
Student A: Turn to page 250. You will only work on that page.
Student B: Read each sentence below to your partner. Then, listen to your partner's sentence. Use the information in both sentences and write a new, longer sentence with an adjective clause.

1. Elvis Presley was born in Mississippi.

2. Beethoven was first taught music by his father.

3. The Beatles first appeared in America in 1964.

4. Duke Ellington was a famous jazz composer.

5. Selena spoke English as her first language.

6. Mariah Carey is one of the best-selling artists of all time.

Write your new sentences.

1. _____
_____.

2. _____
_____.

3. _____
_____.

4. _____
_____.

5. _____
_____.

6. _____
_____.

A. Talk about the photographs of Fan Fair. What's happening?

B. Listen to the history of the world's biggest country music festival. Take notes of dates, numbers, and places.

Notes

C. Use your notes in Exercise B on page 236 to complete the sentences.

1. _____ fans attend Fan Fair, which is held in Nashville _____.

2. The disc-jockey convention was over _____ years ago.

3. Fan Fair began in _____.

4. Fan Fair is held in _____, when the _____ is better.

5. _____ fans attended the first year.

6. _____ fans attended the following year.

7. Paul McCartney, who is a former_____, attended Fan Fair in _____.

8. Billy Ray Cyrus brought more than _____ reporters in 1992, when he introduced a new _____.

9. Fan Fair, which is now attended by over _____ fans, has more than _____ performers.

10. Tickets can be bought _____ months ahead of time.

D. Listening for details. Read the following questions. Then, listen again to find the answers.

1. Why did the Country Music Association (CMA) and the Grand Ole Opry start Fan Fair?

2. What did fans do at the first Fan Fair?

3. Why was the date changed to June?

4. Where was Fan Fair moved to?

5. Why was it moved?

6. What are some of the surprises that happen at Fan Fair?

7. How many fans attended Fan Fair in 2002?

8. Where is Fan Fair held today?

9. How can fans purchase tickets?

10. Why do fans return to Fan Fair every year?

E. A summary. Use your answers to Exercises B, C, and D to complete the summary of the story in your notebook. The first sentence has been started for you.

The Country Music Association began Fan Fair in...

Reading: Shania Twain

A. Before You Read. Skim the reading to find the answers to the questions. <u>Underline</u> and number the answers.

1. What is Shania Twain's original name?

2. Where was she born?

3. When did her parents divorce?

4. What is the name of Shania's stepfather's Native American tribe?

5. Is she married or single?

Shania Twain was born ①<u>Eilleen Regina Edwards</u> in 1965 in Ontario, Canada, to Sharon and Clarence Edwards. Shania was one of five children—three younger siblings and an older sister. When Shania was only two years old, her parents divorced, and she moved with her mother and two sisters to Timmins, a gold-mining town north of Toronto. Her mother later remarried, and Shania was adopted by her stepfather, who was a member of the Ojibwa Native American tribe. According to some reports, Shania may have lived in and out of poverty.

Shania began performing at a young age. Her mother, whose desire for her daughter to succeed was very strong, took the young singer to many different bars, clubs, and other venues to perform. In high school, Shania joined a local band, with which she performed regularly.

After high school, Shania moved to Toronto, where she continued singing. At age 21, however, her parents were killed in a car crash, and Shania had to take over the role of parent to her younger siblings. Taking care of two teenage brothers and a sister was overwhelming at times. Suddenly, she had to pay bills, keep food on the table, and earn a living. Singing helped Shania to pay the bills.

In 1991, Shania went to Nashville, the home of the country music industry. In 1993, she recorded *Shania Twain*, her first CD. In 1995, her next CD, *The Woman in Me*, which had eight hit songs, sold more than ten million copies. Her third CD, *Come on Over*, was also successful and had another hit song.

Shania and her producer husband, Robert Lange, married in 1993 after a nine-month relationship. Before Lange met Shania, he had already successfully produced albums for rock-and-roll performers. Lange was also the person who produced *The Woman in Me*.

After finishing her 2000 world tour to promote her CD, which was the best-selling album by a female singer, she decided to take a break from performing. She went back to Switzerland, where she and her husband currently reside. In August 2001, they had a son, whom they named Eja. After September 11th, Shania decided to put more emphasis on her family and extended her break until the fall of 2002. Her reappearance in the music world put her face on magazine covers and country music publications. She also began to promote her new album, *Up*, on TV shows.

Some critics say that Shania was not disadvantaged growing up, and she is using her adopted father's Native American heritage to promote her career. Her talent, however, is not in dispute.

B. Scan the reading. (Circle) *True* or *False*.

1.	Shania is the oldest child in her family.	True	False
2.	Shania became responsible for her siblings when she was a teenager.	True	False
3.	Shania has been singing in public since she was very young.	True	False
4.	Sharon Edwards encouraged her daughter to sing.	True	False
5.	Shania's parents were killed in an airplane crash.	True	False
6.	Shania stopped singing after her parents were killed.	True	False
7.	Her first CD was titled *The Woman in Me*.	True	False
8.	Her second CD sold more than ten million copies.	True	False

C. Chronological order. Put the following events in order from 1–9.

_____ **a.** Shania became the "mother" to her siblings.

_____ **b.** She recorded *The Woman in Me*, which was produced by Robert Lange.

_____ **c.** Shania's mother remarried.

_____ **d.** She recorded her first CD.

_____ **e.** She began to perform in public.

__1__ **f.** Shania's parents divorced.

_____ **g.** She moved to Nashville.

_____ **h.** She married Robert Lange.

_____ **i.** Her parents were killed.

D. Complete the adjective clauses based on the reading.

1. In 1991, when Shania _____, she began looking for a record contract.

2. *The Woman in Me*, which _____, had eight hit songs.

3. In 1993, Shania married Robert Lange, who _____.

4. Shania, whose awards include _____, won the 2000 Entertainer of the Year Award from the Country Music Association.

5. After finishing her 2000 world tour, her first child, whom she _____

_____, was born.

A. Read Armin's time line of his life in the United States.

Time Line

July 1993		came to the United States
Aug. 1993		began to promote soccer games in local parks
Jan. 1995		enrolled in English class
Sept. 1995		started selling phone cards
Oct. 1995		quit promotion business
Aug. 1995		bought 10,000 phone cards to sell
Nov. 1995		became successful phone card salesman
July 4, 1996		opened business as distributor
July 1998		entered a partnership with phone card makers
Now		has two offices and a very successful business

B. Read Armin's autobiography, which is based on the time line.

In July, 1993, I emigrated to the United States with my wife and children. We didn't know anyone, but in my country, I used to be a promoter. I tried to continue the same business in this country.

Soccer was popular among the immigrants here, so I began to promote soccer games in the local parks. I arranged for close-circuit TV broadcasts of the games because people were very interested in soccer games, especially professional games between South American teams.

In 1995, a friend of mine told me about phone cards. I offered to sell them for him even though I didn't know anything about phone cards. I was a good salesman and sold more and more cards because I had confidence in myself and my abilities. In October, the promotion business, which wasn't stable, was finished. Sometimes I had no work for two months, so I decided in August to quit the promotion business and to concentrate on selling phone cards. I bought 10,000 cards, which I was able to sell in a short time. In November, 1995, my sales were excellent, and business was strong, so I decided to become a distributor of phone cards.

In July, 1996, I opened an office as a phone card distributor. Many people wanted to sell phone cards, so my business grew quickly. Two years later, I was able to enter a partnership with phone card makers. Today, I have two offices with nine employees and a very successful distribution business, which sells cards in over 5,000 stores.

C. Make a time line. Choose six to ten significant events in your life. Write the year and a phrase about the event on a time line. Use Exercise A as an example.

D. In your notebook, write your autobiography. Use the information in your time line.

E. Run-on sentences. Read the paragraph and correct the run-on sentences. Rewrite the paragraph in your notebook.

> **A *run-on sentence* looks like this:**
>
> **Incorrect:** The Dixie Chicks won the Entertainer of the Year award and Music Video and Vocal Group of the Year and then they won Album of the Year.
> **Correct:** The Dixie Chicks won the Entertainer of the Year award, Music Video of the Year, Vocal Group of the Year, and Album of the Year. Then, they won Album of the Year.
>
> **Incorrect:** The 35th Annual Country Music Association Awards had 1.2 million more viewers than in 2000 because it changed to a different time the host was Vince Gill.
> **Correct:** The 35th Annual Country Music Association Awards had 1.2 million more viewers than in 2000 because it changed to a different time. The host was Vince Gill.

> Vincent Grant Gill was born in 1957, in Oklahoma his father was a judge and his mother was a homemaker when he went to high school he was already busy performing in a band he played the banjo and guitar. After he graduated from high school he started his professional career. He got a recording contract with a record company, where he scored one of his first solo country hits and he moved to a different company in 1989 and won "Single of the Year" award with "When I Call Your Name."

F. Edit. Find and correct the mistakes.

1. The singer who his music I like has written many hit songs.

2. Lyle Lovett, to whom was married Julia Roberts, has acted in movies.

3. Placido Domingo is a famous tenor, whose known worldwide.

4. Faith Hill, whom is married to another country singer, is one of the most popular female country singers.

5. Shania Twain is married to her producer, with him she lives in Switzerland.

6. The Beatles toured all over America, where many fans they had.

 Looking at the Internet

It is easy to find information about your favorite performers on the Internet. Search the Internet to find facts about your favorite musician or singer. Put the name in quotation marks to make sure that you find the person you're looking for. One thing to remember is that fans have Web sites, too. Some of those Web sites may not have the most accurate information. Search for the official Web site. Tell your classmates a few interesting facts you found.

Practicing on Your Own

A. Relative pronouns. Circle the correct relative pronoun.

1. Nashville, **who / which / whom** is located in Tennessee, is known as Music City.

2. For many years, the headquarters of country music has been Nashville, **when / where / which** many of the singers live.

3. Two music producers, Owen Bradley and Chet Atkins, created the Nashville Sound, **whom / which / where** was a more popular and sophisticated sound.

4. Chet Atkins, **whom / who / which** some people say is the most recorded solo artist, built a billion-dollar business and recording center.

5. The idea of the Nashville sound was born **which / when / where** Bradley and Atkins wanted to compete with more popular music.

6. Sixteenth Avenue, **which / where / when** a popular country radio station was started, is called Music Row.

7. After World War II, **which / where / when** people needed some entertainment, the Grand Ole Opry recruited talent to perform country music.

8. Patsy Cline, **which / whose / who** music was produced by Owen Bradley, became one of the most talented Nashville stars.

B. Combining sentences. Read each pair of sentences. Then, combine them into one longer sentence with an adjective clause. Use *who, whose, which, whom, where,* or *when*. Write the sentences in your notebook.

1. Patsy Cline died young. Patsy Cline sang the song "Crazy."
   Patsy Cline, who sang the song "Crazy," died young.

2. Johnny Cash is one of the most famous country singers. Johnny Cash likes to wear black.

3. Reba McEntire has performed in a Broadway musical. Reba McEntire is a popular country music singer.

4. John Lennon was successful after leaving the Beatles. His wife, Yoko Ono, sang with him, too.

5. The five-string banjo was first used in Africa. The five-string banjo became a popular country music instrument.

6. Disco music was popularized in the late 1970s. In the late 1970s, the movie *Saturday Night Fever* was a big hit.

7. Placido Domingo is a famous tenor. Many other artists have performed with him.

8. Trisha Yearwood has earned many awards. Her career started over ten years ago.

Grammar Summary

1. Adjective clauses   An adjective clause describes a noun. It can describe a subject or an object.

The man **who is sitting next to the door** is from Spain.

2. *Who* and *which* clauses   *Who* and *which* can replace a subject.

The man is singing a song. [The man] *who* is wearing a cowboy hat.

The man **who is wearing a cowboy hat** is singing a song.

Country music is very popular. [Country music] *which* started in the Appalachians.

Country music, **which started in the Appalachians**, is very popular.

3. *Whom* and *which* clauses   *Whom* and *which* can replace an object. *Whom* is often used with a preposition. *Whom* is more formal than *Who*.

Many country music performers have attended Fan Fair. The fans admire the [performers.] *whom*

Many country music performers, **whom the fans admire**, have attended Fan Fair.

4. *Whose* clauses   *Whose* shows possession. It replaces possessive nouns and pronouns.

Shania Twain sings to sold-out audiences. [Her] *whose* latest CD was a hit.

Shania Twain, **whose latest CD was a hit**, plays to sold-out audiences.

5. Restrictive versus non-restrictive adjective clauses   There are two types of adjective clauses—restrictive clauses and non-restrictive clauses.

a. A **restrictive clause** is necessary to understand the sentence; therefore, no commas are necessary.

1. The man is from Spain. *Which man do you mean?*

The man **who is sitting next to the door** is from Spain.

2. Providence is the city. *What do you mean?*

Providence is the city **where I went to college**.

b. A **non-restrictive clause** requires commas because the clause contains extra information. The sentence is understandable without the clause. A non-restrictive clause often describes a specific person, place, or thing.

1. Tim McGraw began his career in the 1990s.

Tim McGraw, **who is married to Faith Hill**, began his career in the 1990s.

2. Nashville is the home of country music.

Nashville, **which is located in Tennessee**, is the home of country music.

Appendix A

Unit 4: Comparisons—Global and Local

Page 59

D. Student to student dictation.

Student A: Read sentences 1–6 to Student B. Student B will circle the number of the family that matches the description.

1. The son is as tall as his father.

2. The daughters are older than the son.

3. The sister isn't as old as her brother.

4. This family is as big as family number 1.

5. The mother is older than the father.

6. The son is much taller than the daughter.

Change pages. Student A will turn to page 59.

Student B: Read sentences 1–6 to Student A. Student A will circle the number of the family that matches the description.

1. The son's hair is as red as his mother's.

2. The father is as tall as the mother.

3. The son is the same age as the daughter.

4. This family is the largest.

5. The daughter is one year younger than her brother.

6. The father isn't as old as the mother.

Unit 5: Leisure Activities Page 73

D. Student to student dictation.

Student A: Read questions 1–5 to Student B. Student B will write the questions in the correct space.

1. Who cooked when you were growing up?

2. Who taught you how to cook?

3. Do you watch cooking programs on TV?

4. Is your kitchen big enough for you?

5. What kind of cooking classes did you take before now?

Change pages. Student A will turn to page 73.

Student B: Read questions 6–10 to Student A. Student A will write the questions in the correct space.

6. Does your husband like to cook?

7. What classes did you take together?

8. What was the first dish that you cooked?

9. How does your husband like your food?

10. Why did you decide to go to cooking school?

D. Student to student dictation.

Student A: Read the sentences to Student B.

1. You haven't been coming to work on time.

2. I haven't been feeling well.

3. It's been making a strange noise.

4. They've been running for two hours.

5. I've been having pains in my stomach.

6. It's been leaking oil.

7. They've been drinking a lot of water.

8. We've been receiving complaints about your work.

Change pages. Student A will turn to page 104.

Student B: Read the sentences to Student A.

1. It's been overheating in traffic.

2. I've been having trouble sleeping.

3. The fans have been cheering.

4. You've been making a lot of mistakes in your paperwork.

5. I haven't been eating right.

6. You haven't been getting along well with your coworkers.

7. It hasn't been running smoothly.

8. Roger has been in the lead for 30 minutes.

D. Student to student dictation: Good News / Bad News

Student A: Listen to Student B talk about the weekend. Be a good listener. Give an appropriate response. Use *must have* and an adjective from the box.

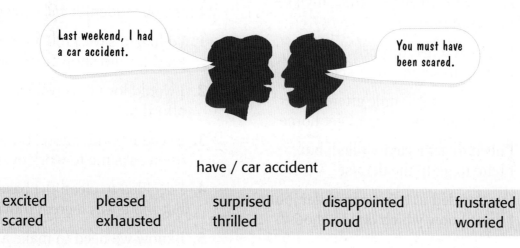

have / car accident

excited	pleased	surprised	disappointed	frustrated
scared	exhausted	thrilled	proud	worried

Student A: Turn to page 155.

Student B: Listen to Student A talk about the weekend. Be a good listener. Give an appropriate response. Use *must have* and an adjective from the box.

C. Student to student dictation.

Student A: Read these excuses to Student B. Student B will copy them.

1. Every time I start to study, my kids interrupt me.

2. I wanted to get up early, but I forgot to set my alarm clock.

3. I want to walk a mile after work, but I'm too tired when I get home.

4. I need to get a cavity filled, but I hate to go to the dentist.

5. I've decided to buy a computer, but I don't know which one to choose.

Student A will now turn to page 166.

Student B: Read these excuses to Student A. Student A will copy them.

1. I'd like to save $100 a month, but I love to shop at the mall.

2. I would love to travel, but I can't afford to.

3. I need to study more, but the boss often asks me to work overtime.

4. I decided to clean the basement, but there was a great movie on TV.

5. I know we need to make a will, but I don't understand legal matters.

D. Student to student dictation.

Student A: Read the questions.

1. Why was his car insurance canceled?

2. Why was she arrested?

3. Why is school closed today?

4. Why was he evicted from his apartment?

5. Why was she taken to the hospital?

6. Why was she fired?

7. Why was she hurt?

8. Why wasn't her credit application approved?

9. Why was the plane delayed?

10. Why is the road closed?

Change pages. Student A will turn to page 218. When you finish, compare your answers.

Unit 15: Country Music Page 235

D. Student to student dictation: Famous musicians

Student A: Work on this page only! Read each sentence below to your partner. Then, listen to your partner's sentence. Use the information in both sentences and write a new, longer sentence with an adjective clause.

1. Elvis Presley sang and acted in movies.
2. Beethoven was a famous classical composer.
3. The Beatles had two lead singers and songwriters.
4. Duke Ellington is still admired today.
5. Selena became famous for her songs in Spanish.
6. Mariah Carey had a number-one hit for ten years in a row.

Write your new sentences.

1. _____
   _____

2. _____
   _____

3. _____
   _____

4. _____
   _____

5. _____
   _____

6. _____
   _____

Unit 1: Education

Page 8

A. Roommates. Sophie and Lizzy are college roommates, but they have very different schedules, habits, and interests. Listen to the two roommates, complete the questions with Do or Does, and then, answer the questions.

Sophie: Hi, I'm Sophie, and I'm a morning person. When the sun comes up, I feel great. I get a lot of things done in the morning, so I take courses early in the morning. I'm finished with my classes by noon. I like to keep everything neat and in order. If things are out of place, I go crazy! My favorite subjects are science and math, so I think I'm going to major in chemistry or computer science. I really like computers and I do all of my work on my computer. I almost never write by hand. Oh, and I always hand in my class work on time. But, my roommate, Lizzie is completely different from me. We get along well, though.

Lizzie: Hi, I'm Lizzie. Sophie and I are complete opposites. She's a morning person, but I'm a night owl. I rarely go to bed before 2 a.m., so I don't get up until noon. I take all afternoon classes. I don't care about keeping my things in order. I can always find my things, even if I have to look on the floor or under the bed. Sophie hates that. She's really neat. My favorite subjects are literature, writing, and art. I love to write and I love to draw. I think I'll major in art history or English literature. I have a computer, but I almost never use it. I prefer to write everything by hand. I only use the computer to type my papers, which are sometimes late. I often have to talk to my professors about my late papers. Sophie is completely different from me, but she's a great roommate.

Page 12

The Big Picture: The University of Texas at San Antonio

A. Listen to the description of this university. As you listen, complete and circle the correct information.

The University of Texas is a large university with many campuses all over Texas. This is a description of the University of Texas at San Antonio, which is located in southeastern Texas.

The University of Texas at San Antonio, or U.T.S.A., is a four-year public university with three campuses. U.T.S.A.'s main campus is located on a suburban campus, 15 miles from downtown San Antonio. The university has a large undergraduate population. It enrolls 12,034 full-time students and 5,391 part-time students. In addition, three thousand students attend the graduate school that offers masters and doctoral degrees. The university employs 963 faculty.

Students who want to attend U.T.S.A. have to follow the same procedures that most college applicants do. First of all, there's an application fee of $25. All students must mail a high school transcript that has all of their grades. All students must complete an application, which they can do online if they want to. The university recommends that students complete four years of English, two years of a foreign language, three years of math, two years of a social science, and two years of a lab science, such as biology or chemistry. The university also recommends prospective students to have one year of fine arts, such as music or art. Most students take the SAT, or Scholastic Aptitude Test, and have total scores of 1000 or above.

Like most other universities, U.T.S.A. offers many academic areas. Students can major in the liberal arts, sciences, or technical fields. Here are just a few of the possible majors: accounting, art history, biology, criminal justice, engineering, and international business.

U.T.S.A. offers many facilities and student services to help the students be successful in their college studies. There are 800 computers available on campus. For students who need extra help or preparation for their college courses, there is a learning center. At the learning center, students can work with tutors to get free help with their homework and talk to counselors about their problems at school. When the students aren't studying, they can take advantage of the many extracurricular activities. There are athletic teams for both men and women. And, there are many student organizations that cover many different interests from drama and theater to science.

To help prepare freshmen or new students for college life, many universities, including U.T.S.A., offer orientation programs. The orientation programs introduce students to life on a college campus, tell students where to go for academic help, and inform students of the many fun activities that are available.

Page 13

C. Listen and write short answers to the questions about the university.

1. Is the university a two-year university?
2. Does the university have only one campus?
3. Is there a graduate school at the university?
4. Does the university require students to pay an application fee?
5. Do future students need three years of a foreign language?
6. Is it a private university?
7. Are there computers on campus for the students?
8. Do students who need academic help pay for the tutoring at the learning center?
9. Are there opportunities for women to participate in sports?
10. Is there an orientation for new students?

Unit 2: Colonial Times (1607–1776)

Page 22

A. Look at the pairs of pictures and listen to the comparison between life in colonial times and life today.

The colonial period in the United States lasted from 1607 to 1776. Most early colonists were men and women from England who decided to start a new life in North America. They settled along the eastern coast of what is now the United States, from Georgia to New Hampshire. Life at that time was very different from today. Most people lived on small farms and were self-sufficient for most of their needs. People grew all of their own food and cooked it over open fires. They didn't go to supermarkets or cook on stoves. When they needed milk, they milked their own cows. They didn't go to the supermarket and buy a carton of milk. Houses functioned without modern conveniences or electricity. Instead of electric lights, people read and worked by candlelight. They didn't sleep on mattresses with box springs. They used to sleep on feather beds. In the evening, instead of watching TV, they read to each other and played games. When people wanted to communicate with friends or relatives far away, they used to write letters. They didn't have telephones or e-mail. For transportation, the people used horses and wagons; they didn't drive cars. Life was slower and simpler, but people worked hard from sunup to sundown.

Page 27

A. Interview. Listen to Eric speak about his childhood in Peru. Complete the questions. Then, ask and answer the questions with a partner.

Oscar: Eric, where were you born?
Eric: I was born in a small town in Peru. On the coast.
Oscar: How many brothers and sisters did you have?
Eric: There were four boys—I was the youngest.
Oscar: Did your grandparents live in the same town?
Eric: My grandparents, my two aunts, my five uncles. We all lived in the same town. And I had lots of cousins.
Oscar: Did you live in the city or the country?
Eric: In the country. My family owned a small farm. In the winter, I had to get up early and milk our cow.
Oscar: How about school? Did you walk to school or take the bus?
Eric: In our town, there were no school buses. I used to ride my bike to school.
Oscar: What did you do after school?
Eric: After school, I played soccer with my brothers and my cousins.
Oscar: How about the summer? What did you do in the summer?
Eric: In the summer, we used to work in the fields with my father.

Oscar: Did you go on vacation?

Eric: We never went on vacation. My mother said that we didn't need a vacation because we lived in the country. A few times each summer, my Mom packed a big lunch and we drove to the ocean.

Oscar: Did you see your relatives a lot?

Eric: All the time. There was always something to celebrate: a birthday, a wedding, or a holiday. We all used to go to my grandparents' house. My mother and aunts used to cook inside and the men barbecued a pig outside. My grandmother always made the desserts. They were wonderful— cakes and rice pudding and *mazamorra morada*.

Page 28

The Big Picture: Benjamin Franklin

A. Listen. Which invention is each sentence describing? Write the number of the correct sentence under each invention.

1. The top half of this invention helps a person to see distance; the bottom half helps a person to see things close up.
2. With this device, you can measure distance.
3. Before this invention, lightning sometimes struck houses and caused fires.
4. Before this invention, people used to have open fires inside their homes.
5. Franklin used this device to map mail routes for towns.
6. This appliance helped people heat their homes safely and with less wood.
7. Franklin cut two pairs of glasses in half and joined them together.
8. This device protects buildings from lightning. It directs lightning into the ground.

B. Note taking. Listen and complete this outline about the life of Benjamin Franklin.

Benjamin Franklin was born in Boston, Massachusetts, on January 17, 1706. At that time, school was not required and Franklin only attended school for two years. For the rest of his life, he continued to read and study on his own, and he even learned five foreign languages. At the age of 12, he began to work at his brother's printing office and learned quickly. By the age of 17, he was an excellent printer. Franklin then moved to Philadelphia in 1728, and at the young age of 22, he opened his own printing shop in that city. He published a newspaper, the *Pennsylvania Gazette*. He knew that many people could not read well, so his publications had many cartoons and pictures.

Benjamin Franklin was respected in Philadelphia and he helped to improve everyday life for the people in the city. In 1732, he started the first public library in America so that people could borrow and read books. In 1736, he helped to organize the first fire department in Philadelphia because most of the houses were wood and there were many fires. Benjamin Franklin was also postmaster in Philadelphia and he helped to set up the routes for the delivery of mail. He also spoke to the officials of the city and encouraged them to pave the streets of the city.

Franklin was also an inventor. He was always asking questions and trying to improve everyday life. At the time, colonial fireplaces sent black smoke throughout the house. Franklin invented a stove that used less wood and gave off more heat. When he was postmaster, he invented the odometer to set up mail routes throughout the city. Franklin wore glasses and became tired of taking his glasses off to see far away, so he invented bifocals. Franklin also experimented with electricity and realized that lightning is a form of electricity. He invented the lightning rod to help protect homes during lightning storms.

As the years passed, Franklin became a leader in the city and in the country. He signed the Declaration of Independence, which stated that the thirteen colonies were a free and independent nation. He served as minister to France during the war with England. When he returned, Franklin signed the Constitution, which established the new government.

Benjamin Franklin died on April 17, 1790, and was buried in Philadelphia.

E. Proverbs. Listen and complete these famous sayings of Ben Franklin. Then, discuss their meanings.

1. A penny saved is a penny earned.
2. Time is money.
3. Early to bed, early to rise, makes a man healthy, wealthy, and wise.
4. Fish and visitors smell in three days.
5. An apple a day keeps the doctor away.
6. Well done is better than well said.
7. There was never a good war or a bad peace.

Unit 3: Family Matters

The Big Picture: The Divorce Agreement

B. Listen for numbers. Listen as the mediator meets with Tom and Amy and reviews their assets. Complete the information below.

Mediator: I have met with you both about your assets. I'd like to review this information with the two of you today. I have a statement for each of you. Tom, your base salary is $42,000 a year.

Tom: Right.

Mediator: You work a lot of overtime, and so you earn between $500 and $1000 extra a month with overtime.

Tom: Yes, usually. But some months, when work is slow, I don't work any overtime.

Mediator: Amy, you have no income. You are a full-time homemaker.

Amy: Yes.

Mediator: You are savers. You have $10,000 in the bank, in a savings account.

Tom: Yes.

Mediator: And you have a house. You bought it for $50,000 ten years ago and today it's worth $120,000. Your monthly mortgage and taxes are $800.

Tom: Yes.

Mediator: OK, now, you have two cars. The minivan is paid off. You have a new car and the payments on that are $300 a month for two more years.

Tom: No, the payments are for just one more year.

Mediator: OK. Let me change that information. Tom, your retirement account is up to $40,000.

Tom: Right.

Mediator: You still have all of the furniture in the house to decide about and you have a lot of electronic equipment, including a big screen TV, a stereo, and a new computer. Did I forget to list any assets?

Tom: We have a dog, a Labrador retriever. He's five years old.

Mediator: We definitely have to decide who will keep the dog.

Mediator: Anything else?

Tom: No.

Amy: No.

D. Listen as the mediator reviews the agreement between Tom and Amy. Complete the information about the agreement.

Mediator: After meeting with you separately and together, it looks like we have a divorce agreement. Now, let's go through the agreement item by item. First, the house. Amy, you'll continue to live in the house. Tom will pay part of the mortgage and taxes—$500 a month. And Amy, you'll pay the other part of the mortgage, $300 a month, and you will take care of all housing costs, including insurance, heat, electricity, and cable. Amy, you can live in the house until the children graduate from high school. That's ten years from now. At the time you sell the house, half the sale will go to Tom and the other half of the sale will go to you, Amy.

Tom: What happens if Amy meets someone and remarries?

Mediator: At that time, she must sell the house and you will divide the sale price. Next, your savings. You'll divide your savings in half. Each of you will have $5,000. Now, let's look at the retirement money. Tom, you have $40,000 in your retirement plan at your company. At this point, we are going to divide this in half and you'll each have $20,000 for your retirement. Any new money in the account is just for Tom. Amy, when you find a job, you need to start your own account and begin to save for retirement. Any questions?

Tom and Amy: No.

Mediator: You have two cars. Tom is in sales and depends on his car. Tom, the new car is yours, and you'll make the rest of the payments on it. Amy, you'll keep the minivan.

Amy: What about the insurance on the cars?

Mediator: You'll each pay your own insurance. You've agreed on the furniture and electronic equipment.

Amy: Yes, I'll keep all the furniture in the house.

Tom: I'll take the electronic equipment.

Mediator: You have agreed on joint custody of the children.

Amy: They'll live with me during the week and continue in their same schools.

Tom: Yes, and they'll live with me on the weekends.

Mediator: Amy, the children will live with you in July and, Tom, they'll live with you in August. Joint custody also means that you have to make all major decisions about the children together. Tom, you will pay child support of $300 a month for each child. That's $600 a month for the children. In addition, for three years you'll pay Amy $400 a month for alimony. This will help with expenses until she can get some more education and some experience at work. Also, Tom, you put in a lot of overtime. All the money that you make in overtime is yours.

Tom: You forgot Rocky.

Mediator: Oh, yes. Tom, we all agreed that you will keep the dog.

Unit 4: Comparisons—Global and Local

Page 56

Listen and complete the comparisons. Use *as many . . . as* and *as much . . . as*.

1. Brazil doesn't have **as many telephones as** Russia does.
2. France has **as many telephones as** it has televisions.
3. India doesn't have **as many cell phones as** it has telephones.
4. Japan doesn't have **as many televisions as** the United States does.
5. Russia doesn't have **as many cell phones as** the other countries do.
6. Brazil has **almost as many Internet users as** France does.
7. Russia has **twice as many Internet users as** India does.

Page 57

B. Pronunciation: *as . . . as* versus *not as . . . as*. Listen to each statement. Circle *same* if you hear *as . . . as*. Circle *different* if you hear *not as . . . as*.

1. My city is as populated as this city.
2. The beaches in my city are as beautiful as this city's.
3. The traffic in this city is as heavy as the traffic in my city.
4. My country isn't as large as the United States.
5. Prices here aren't as cheap as those in my country.
6. The weather in this city is as humid as the weather in my city.

Page 60

The Big Picture: What Happened to My Town?

B. Listen and take notes about the changes in the town. What is different about the town today?

My name's Kenny. I live in a big city now, but let me tell you about where I grew up. I grew up in a small farming community, with a population of only 703 people. There was one high school, and one combination elementary and middle school. There were only 175 students in my whole high school, so we all knew each other. I was in classes with almost the same kids from kindergarten all the way through high school.

I lived in a big house with my parents and five siblings—three younger sisters and two older brothers. I was in the middle. My family had a fruit-tree orchard. We grew apples and pears. My closest neighbors were a mile or two away, so I spent most of my time playing with my siblings or with my best friend. We used to go downtown to hang out. Downtown wasn't a big place. There was one traffic light in front of City Hall. Of course, the mayor was there, but the sheriff's office and the post office were also in the same building. There were only two places to eat downtown. My favorite was Millie's Luncheonette. My mom worked there as a waitress part-time. There was a department store downtown, too. It was the tallest building in town, about three floors. It had everything, and I knew everyone who worked there.

Every Saturday afternoon, my siblings and I could go to the movie theater. There was one movie theater, and it showed only one movie all day. It closed late, at about 10:00. At night, we could ride our bikes home alone. I thought I lived in the best town in the world. Unfortunately, in my second year of high school, my dad sold our orchard and we moved away.

Last year, after 25 years, I went back for my elementary school reunion. What a difference! My parents' old house was surrounded by an entire development of houses. Because of all the new housing, there were many new people in the community. There were two new elementary schools, a new middle school, and the high school was renovated to accommodate 1,000 high school students. Because of the economy, almost all of the farms disappeared, and instead, there were many businesses: factories, a computer manufacturer, and a large pharmaceutical company. And, there's a large shopping mall with fifty stores on the highway. People shop there from all over the area, so traffic is much heavier than it used to be.

Downtown was so different! I didn't recognize it! There was a parking garage where the department store used to be, and there were five traffic lights to control the traffic. The mayor and the sheriff still share the same building, but there's a brand-new post office next to City Hall. It has 10 employees! There are many tall buildings. Some of them have 20 floors! The only thing that was the same was Millie's Luncheonette. The waitresses were older, but they were still as friendly as I remember them.

Unit 5: Leisure Activities

Page 70

A. Who/ Whom/Whose. Listen to these people talk about how they spend their free time. Take notes.

Gina: How do I spend my free time? I like to go dancing. My boyfriend and I go dancing almost every weekend. Every Friday and Saturday night we go dancing at clubs in our area. We meet our friends and we make new friends when we go dancing. We like all kinds of music, but we usually go to clubs that play Latin music or hip-hop. Those are our favorite kinds of music. Oh, and once a month, my boyfriend and I take a dance class together. Dancing is a really good way to keep in shape. I don't need to work out at a gym. Dancing keeps me fit.

Roberto: I spend my time taking care of my tropical fish. I have a large aquarium in my living room, and I have many books about tropical fish and how to take care of them. I also have a few friends who like keeping fish, too. We get together once a week at a coffee shop nearby and talk about what's new with our fish and what new fish we've bought. You'd be surprised to know that keeping an aquarium is a lot of work. I have to change the water regularly and check the water chemistry. I also have to make sure that none of my new fish decide to eat my other fish. But watching my fish is very relaxing after a hard day at work.

Yelena: After I retired, I was bored, and I needed something to do. I live in a senior citizen's apartment building, and one day I saw two men playing chess. It brought back memories for me. My father taught me to play chess when I was a child, and I even joined the chess team in high school, but when I was in university, I didn't have any time for chess. Now that I'm retired, I'm playing again. Chess is a game for people who like to think. I'm getting older, and I need to keep my mind sharp. I play every evening, and tomorrow I'm going to start teaching my grandson how to play.

Page 74

I. An interview: A collector. Laurence collects items of a popular cartoon character. Listen to the interview. As you listen, take notes.

W: So, Laurence, tell me about your collection. How did your collection get started?

M: Well, my sister bought me an old alarm clock for my birthday in 1985.

W: Really? Where did she find it?

M: She found it at a yard sale. I really liked it, and the next thing you know, I was looking for more objects.

W: What was the first thing that you bought for yourself?

M: I bought a 1943 comic book.

W: So, how many objects do you have in your collection now?

M: How many? It's hard to say, . . . I think I have more than two thousand objects.

W: More than two thousand? Where do you keep them all?

M: That's a problem. When we were living in our New York apartment, it was getting crowded, but we moved to a house a few years ago. Now I keep most of my collection in the basement. I keep most things in glass cases so that my family, friends, and I can look at everything. Many things are hanging on the walls.

W: Does your family complain about all of the things that you collect?

M: Not often. Sometimes a closet opens and a lot of stuff falls out. Then, it's a problem.

W: So, where do you find these objects?

M: I get them from many different places. My wife and I go to yard sales, garage sales, and toy shows. Sometimes my friends find something and give it to me. My father and my brother have gotten things for me, too. Once I even got a poster from the parking lot attendant where I park my car every day.

W: That's quite a collection you have. Do you have a favorite object?

M: It's hard to pick a favorite, but I really like a talking toy from 1949.

W: Is there anything in particular that you're looking for now?

M: Well, there's a 1950s cookie jar that I've been looking for.

W: If I find it, I'll let you know.

M: Thanks.

Page 75

A. Pronunciation: Tag questions. Listen and draw an arrow showing the correct intonation. Underline the main verbs.

Example 1: They <u>are having</u> a nice time, aren't they? ↘

Example 2: You <u>don't like</u> to fish, do you? ↗

1. They like to fish, don't they? ↘
2. Fishing isn't expensive, is it? ↗
3. There aren't a lot of boats in the lake, are there? ↘
4. They don't fish every day, do they? ↗
5. They're fishing in a lake, aren't they? ↗
6. It's not a hot day, is it? ↘
7. Fishing isn't tiring, is it? ↗
8. They hope to catch a lot of fish, don't they? ↘

Page 76

The Big Picture: My Hobby

B. Listen and retell the story.

Robert: Hobby? Sure. I have a hobby. My hobby is photography. Six days a week, I work at my father's hardware store. It's the family business. It's a good business, and it's a good job. I like talking with customers, especially our regular customers, and I like to help people with their home improvement projects, but working in a hardware store isn't my dream. My dream is to work as a full-time photographer.

First, I started taking pictures of my friends at parties. I used those one-time use cameras because they were easy to use and pretty cheap. I took pictures on family vacations, too. Then, I decided to buy a real camera with a zoom lens. My pictures started looking more interesting, but I didn't know how to use all of the features of the camera. So, I took a course at the adult community center. The course really helped, and my photos improved. Then, I took another course on black-and-white photography and started taking black-and-white photos, too. I used my family members to experiment with the different film and camera features. I continued to take photography courses and joined a photography club.

Now, I'm learning how to develop my own film. I really like it. I'm thinking about putting a darkroom in one of my closets. A few of my friends have asked me to take their wedding photos, and this weekend I'm going to take photos at my cousin's wedding. I hope I do a good job. If my cousin is happy with the pictures, that will give me the courage to start working professionally. I'm taking a computer course now so that I can learn how to scan photos and put them on a Web site. I want to advertise on the Internet. I'll put some of my best photos on the Internet and maybe someone will hire me.

Page 77

C. Listen and write the questions. Then, circle the answers.

1. Where does Robert work?
2. How many days a week does he work?
3. What is his dream?
4. What kind of camera did he first use?
5. Where did he learn to take better photos?
6. Where is he going to take photos this weekend?
7. What course is he taking now?

Unit 6: Driving

Page 87

C. Listen to Rebecca talk about her schedule. Check the tasks that she has completed.

Uh, let's see, what do I have to do today? Do I need stamps? Hmm. I don't think so. I bought some yesterday. Here they are. OK, so I have to mail my gas bill and my phone bill. I can stop by the post office on the way to the laundromat. I have to do some laundry or I won't have anything to wear. While my clothes are in the wash, I have to go to the supermarket to get some eggs, milk, and something to eat for dinner. Oh, did I deposit my check in my checking account? Yes, I did, and here's the deposit slip from last Saturday. I don't have to visit my parents today. I saw them yesterday morning. Oh, my tooth hurts. I have to make a dentist appointment right away. OK, I think I'm ready to go, but I have to remember to put some gas in the car. I think it's almost on empty.

Page 88

A. Pronunciation: *Can* versus *can't*. Listen to Marcus talk about his driving experience. Complete the sentences with *can* or *can't*.

I'm a terrible driver. I finally got my driving permit three months ago, and it took me three tries to pass the written test. Now, I can only drive with a licensed driver in my car, so my mom or my dad has to drive in the car with me. I can back up, but I can't parallel park. I'm a terrible parker, so I sometimes drive around the corner a few times to find an easy space to park in. I can drive on a busy highway, but I feel nervous. I can't drive at night alone because I'm only 17. I can't drive with the radio on because I can't concentrate. Maybe I need to take the bus.

Page 89

D. Interview: An accident. Listen to Emily talk about her car accident.

A: Hi, Emily. Wow! What happened to your car?
B: You won't believe it. I was in a car accident yesterday.
A: Are you OK?
B: Yeah, I'm fine, but look at my car! It's a mess!
A: It does look pretty bad. What happened?
B: Well, I was waiting for a light on a hill. There was one car in front of me. The driver was an elderly woman and her dog

was sitting on her lap. The dog started barking at a kid on a bicycle and started jumping all over the car. The woman wasn't paying attention and her car started to roll back towards me.

A: Didn't you honk your horn?

B: Of course I did. I couldn't back up, I kept honking my horn. Her car started moving faster and then, it smashed into my car! It crushed the hood.

A: Unbelievable. What happened next?

B: Well, I had to get out of the car and exchange insurance information with the woman.

A: Did you call the police?

B: No, we didn't. No one was hurt and I was late for an appointment, but I had to call my insurance company right away. I just talked to the company and they told me that I had to file a police report. I'm on my way to the police station now.

A: Good luck with your car.

B: Thanks.

Page 91

A. Pronunciation: 'd better/'d better not. Listen and complete the sentences.

1. **I'd better stay** home. I don't feel well.
2. **You'd better put** the baby in the car seat.
3. **She'd better call** the police and report the accident.
4. **We'd better bring** the party inside. It's beginning to rain.
5. **He'd better not eat** another piece of cake. He'll get sick.
6. **You'd better not get** a dog. Your landlord won't allow it.
7. **She'd better slow** down. The roads are icy.
8. **I'd better not buy** that. I can't afford it.

Page 92

The Big Picture: Getting a Driver's License

A. Jennifer is 17 years old and very excited. Listen to Jennifer talk about getting her driver's license. Complete the chart. What does she have to do to get her license?

I am so excited. Tomorrow, my mother's taking me to the Division of Motor Vehicles to get my learner's permit. I have to have my parent's signature on my application because I'm only 16. I have to show proof of my age, too. I grew up in Peru, but I was born here in the U.S., so I can show my U.S. passport. People can also use original birth certificates, a permanent resident cards, or citizenship papers. I'm going to take the written test today. There are 30 questions and signs on the test. I have to get 80 percent correct to pass the test. I speak English well, but my reading is still a little weak. I don't have to take the test in English because the DMV gives the test in 30 languages, including mine—Spanish. I also have to take a vision test to check my eyesight. Then, they are going to take my picture.

After I pay five dollars, I can get my learner's permit. After I get the permit, I can use it for three to six months to practice. I'll need a lot of practice, about 25 hours or more. I was hoping that my older sister could teach me to drive, but in my state, I must have an adult 21 years or older in the car with me. That's the law for people under 18. My sister's only 19, so my mother's going to teach me.

I'm going to practice as much as I can before the road test. My mother will drive me to the road test because I must have a licensed driver 21 years of age or older in the car. My parents will get the auto insurance card, and we need to show the car's registration. Of course, I also have to show my permit. Then, I can take the road test. Wish me luck!

Unit 7: Sports

Page 103

A. Pronunciation. Listen again. Circle the sentence you hear.

1. She's been taking tennis lessons.
2. She's learning how to drive.
3. He's been playing baseball.
4. I've been looking for a new apartment.
5. She's recovering from her accident.
6. He's studying Chinese.
7. He's been working hard.
8. I've been training for a new job.

Page 105

A. Listen to this interview between Robert and a reporter. Then, answer the questions.

Reporter: Congratulations! You just won the state championship.
Robert: Thank you.
Reporter: Robert, how old are you?
Robert: Seven.
Reporter: Seven! And how long have you been playing tennis?
Robert: Since I was three.
Reporter: Who taught you how to play?
Robert: My father. And I take private lessons, too.
Reporter: Here at the tennis club?
Robert: Yes, I've been taking lessons for two years.
Reporter: How many days a week do you play?
Robert: About three or four. I want to practice every day, but my parents say three or four days is enough. I like to play video games with my friends, too.
Reporter: Are you going to continue with your tennis?
Robert: Uh-huh. I'm going to be a professional tennis player when I'm older.

B. Listen to this interview between Anna and a reporter. Then, use the cues to ask and answer questions.

Reporter: Congratulations! You took first place in the competition.
Anna: I'm so excited!
Reporter: No one was surprised when you won today. Your movements are beautiful to watch.
Anna: Thank you. I have a great coach. She's the best!
Reporter: How long have you been working with Ms. Koshevaya?
Anna: For five years now.
Reporter: You've been working with a new choreographer this year, too.
Anna: I really like her. We've been doing a new routine. Last year, I was working with another choreographer, but her style didn't work for me.

Reporter: We hear that you have been practicing the triple jump.
Anna: I've been practicing, but I'm not ready to try it in competition yet. Maybe next season.
Reporter: Thank you, Anna. We wish you the best.

Page 108

The Big Picture: The Soccer Game

B. Listen to a description of this scene. Then, answer the questions.

Today is the championship soccer game between two teams, the Kings and the Stars. The game started at 2:00. It's the second half of the game, with only 10 minutes left to play, and the Stars are in the lead. They're winning 2-1. TV and radio are covering the game and the announcers have been calling the game and describing every play.

The stadium is full, with more than twenty thousand excited fans watching their team in the championship. The fans have been cheering and shouting for their favorite teams. Some of the fans are waving banners and holding up signs.

It's a hot summer day, so the fans have been buying lots of drinks. The concession workers have been walking up and down the stands for an hour, selling soda and water. People have been waiting in line for 10 minutes or more to buy food.

The players are hot because they've been running since the game started. They've been drinking a lot of water and energy drinks. The referees have been watching the players carefully to prevent any illegal play. A few of the players have been calling one another names and pushing hard during the game. But so far, all of the players are still in the game. The coach has been shouting instructions and putting in new players. Both of the goalies are strong and have been stopping goal shots all game, but the players are fast and accurate today. Everyone has been watching the forward for the Stars, Number 7. He's their top player and he now has the ball.

Unit 8: Changes

Page 116

B. A phone call. Listen to Kathy and Gloria talk about the plans for a family reunion. Then, read each sentence and circle *T* for True and *F* for False.

Gloria: Hi, Kathy. This is Gloria.

Kathy: Gloria! How are you? We haven't spoken for ages!

Gloria: I know. We all get so busy. Have you heard? Angela's planning a family reunion.

Kathy: A family reunion? That's great! We haven't gotten together, all of us, for about five years. What's the date?

Gloria: August. I think she said August 15.

Kathy: August 15. That's two months from now. And where's it going to be?

Gloria: At Angela's. She's going to send out the invitations soon. And we'll all help and bring food.

Kathy: Of course. How many of us are there?

Gloria: About 75. Plus two more. My sister, Jenny, just had twins. Two little girls. Identical twins.

Kathy: Beautiful. You're an aunt now. How's Jenny doing?

Gloria: She's tired, but doing well. I help her out a few days a week.

Kathy: Did you hear that Michael has changed jobs?

Gloria: No? What's he doing?

Kathy: He's opened a small business. He's installing big screen TVs and sound systems in people's homes.

Gloria: Wish him my best.

Kathy: I will. It'll be great to see everyone and hear what's happening.

Gloria: See you in August.

Page 122

A. Reunion plans. Listen to the conversation between Angela and Gloria. Check the things that Angela has already completed.

Gloria: How are the reunion plans coming?

Angela: Very well. Everyone wants to help. I asked a few people to help out with the plans, just a small committee, but it's made things much easier.

Gloria: And the date is the fifteenth, right? August 15?

Angela: Yes. We've already made the invitations. Tony's son made the invitations on the computer. We're going to send them out next week.

Gloria: Were you able to find everyone's address?

Angela: I think we have them all.

Gloria: Have you done anything else yet?

Angela: Well, we haven't planned the games or the activities, but we've already planned the menu. We're having chicken on the grill and everyone is going to bring a salad or a side dish. And we're going to order a big cake for dessert.

Gloria: How about decorations?

Angela: We're not going to get too crazy with the decorations. But we have bought some colorful tablecloths and paper products and plastic utensils. There was a big sale after July 4 and we got everything at a good price.

Gloria: Angela, you're not going to try to do everything yourself, are you? You need time to talk to people and have fun yourself.

Angela: This time, I was smart. I've already hired two people to help us. One is going to cook on the grills and the other is going to help serve and clean up.

Gloria: What a great idea! Angela, let me know if there's anything I can do. I'd be happy to do anything you need.

Angela: Thanks, Gloria. If I think of anything, I'll call.

Page 124

The Big Picture: Gossip

B. Gossip. Listen to these people talk about their friends, family, and coworkers. Label each person in the pictures.

Conversation 1

A: Have you heard about Diana?

B: No. What happened?

A: Well, remember her engagement party?

B: Sure.

A: She's not engaged anymore.

B: No! I really liked Chris.

A: She's broken off the engagement. She met this new guy who moved into her apartment building and she's fallen in love with him.

B: And what about Chris?

A: She's given him back his ring.

B: Really? Do you have Chris's phone number?

Conversation 2

A: Have you seen Rosa lately?

B: Hmm-mm. I spoke to her yesterday.

A: She looks great, doesn't she?

B: Yes, she said her vacation was really relaxing.

A: She didn't take a vacation. She went to a clinic.

B: A clinic?

A: Yes, she had a face-lift. That's why she looks so good.

B: Let me know the name of that clinic! I'm going to make an appointment myself.

Conversation 3

A: Have you heard about Amy? She's in big trouble.

B: What happened this time?

A: She took her mom's car without her permission. And she had an accident on the way to the mall

B: Oh, no! Was she hurt?

A: No, she hit a mailbox. But, she's been grounded for a month. I've tried to call her three times, but her parents won't let me talk to her. They've taken away her cell phone.

Conversation 4

A: You've heard about Paul, haven't you?

B: No. What about Paul?

A: He's just been promoted.

B: Promoted?

A: Yup. To assistant sales manager.

B: You've got to be kidding! He's got the worst sales record in the company. He hasn't made a sale this month.

A: I know. But it helps when your cousin is the head of the sales department.

B: That explains it.

Conversation 5

A: You know Mary Johnson, don't you?

B: Yeah. We used to take the bus together.

A: Well, guess what?

B: What?

A: She's going out with a man twice her age!

B: Twice her age? Let's see. I guess Mary's about 35.

A: That's what I guess. And this guy, he must be about 70.

B: What's the attraction?

A: Money. I've heard that he has lots of it!

B: Well, I hope she's happy.

Conversation 6

A: Have you heard about Grandpa?

B: No. Is he OK?

A: Okay? Well, first he's a bought a new convertible.

B: A new convertible? He's 70!

A: He's 72. And he's dyed his hair red.

B: Red? No more gray for Grandpa!

A: And he left yesterday.

B: He left?

A: Yes, he's left on a cross-country trip!

B: Good for him!

Page 125

E. Surprise intonation. To show surprise and interest, a listener often repeats a few words of a speaker's conversation with question intonation. Listen and repeat the surprise intonation.

1. **A:** He bought a new convertible.   **B:** A new convertible?

2. **A:** He left yesterday.   **B:** He left?

3. **A:** He's just been promoted.   **B:** Promoted?

4. **A:** She's run off with a man twice her age.   **B:** Twice her age?

Listen and show surprise at statements 5–10.

5. They've moved to Alaska.

6. She bought a horse.

7. He's just won $50,000.

8. He's been fired.

9. She's expecting triplets.

10. She has fifty pairs of shoes.

Unit 9: Job Performance

Page 136

B. Listen again and circle the sentence you hear.

1. I've sold five cars

2. She's worked five hours.

3. They made 500 donuts.

4. She's walked five miles.

5. I helped 10 customers.

6. He planted five trees.

7. She's read 20 pages.

8. I've cleaned seven rooms.

9. He typed four reports.

10. I've checked in 50 passengers.

C. Listen to each sentence. Circle the letter of the sentence that shows the correct meaning.

1. The doctor saw all his patients for the day.
2. Benji has been ironing shirts for five hours.
3. The men have planted five trees so far.
4. The teacher has checked 30 papers.
5. Carlos has delivered 40 packages.
6. Mary called 100 people today.
7. Kathy worked at the hospital for fifty years.
8. Josh drives a truck between New York and Florida. He's driven 300 miles today so far.
9. Debbie was busy at the bank today. She handled over two hundred transactions.

Page 138

A. Read George's job description. Then, listen as he describes his job. Then, answer the questions.

My name is George Pappas and I am a bus driver for Metro Transit. I started here in 1998. Before that, I was a school bus driver. In the morning, the kids were tired and they were quiet, but on the way home, they were really excited and noisy. One day, I saw an ad in the newspaper for a city bus driver. I applied and was really lucky—I got a job offer the next week. I started here at $9.00 an hour. The company has a very clear salary policy. If a driver receives a good evaluation, he or she receives a fifty-cent pay raise a year. I've always received good evaluations, so I've always received my raise. If an employee has no accidents in five years, the pay will increase to $13.00. There is a top limit, so no one at this company makes more than $18.00 an hour. There's lots of opportunity for overtime, too. Most of us here work about ten hours a week overtime. Overtime pay is time and a half. And another thing . . . speeding tickets. The company is very strict about tickets. If you get a ticket, you have to pay for it. Also, the company fines you another $250. If you receive two or more speeding tickets in a year, you're fired. I've only received one ticket and I don't plan to get another one! I like this job and I want to keep it.

Page 140

The Big Picture: Performance Evaluations

B. Katie's evaluation. Listen as Mr. Davis evaluates Katie and check the appropriate boxes. He will focus on Katie's strengths and areas that need improvement. If Mr. Davis does not mention an area, you can check that she meets expectations. Then, answer the questions about her evaluation.

Mr. Davis: Katie, have you looked at your evaluation yet?

Katie: Yes, I have.

Mr. Davis: Let's go over some of these areas. You are always available to work, but you've arrived late several times. Since I've spoken to you about this, you have improved.

Katie: I've been trying. I was only late once last month.

Mr. Davis: You see that you also require improvement on showing initiative. Katie, when you don't have a customer, you stand and daydream. If I ask you to do something, you're always willing. But when you don't have customers, I expect you to polish the jewelry and the mirrors, put new paper in the cash register, restock the boxes, and do other things without being asked.

Katie: OK.

Mr. Davis: You are great with customers—friendly, respectful, complimentary. You enjoy sales and you are an effective salesperson. This is your number one strength.

Katie: Thank you. I really like to work with the customers.

Mr. Davis: Unfortunately, you have made several mistakes on your transactions, like entering the wrong price on the register and forgetting to enter in the sales price. You've overcharged some customers and they've complained. You've undercharged other customers and the store has lost money. You had several problems during our sale last week.

Katie: I know. When we're busy, I sometimes make mistakes.

Mr. Davis: I've decided to have Ms. Nickerson retrain you on our sales transactions procedures. Are you available next Saturday?

Katie: Yes.

Mr. Davis: Do you have any comments about your evaluation?

Katie: No. I like working here a lot. I don't understand why I've had problems with the transactions. I'll be more careful, you'll see.

Page 141

C. Amy's evaluation. Listen as Mr. Davis evaluates Amy and check the appropriate boxes. He will focus on Amy's strengths and areas that need improvement. If Mr. Davis does not mention an area, you can check that she meets expectations. Then, answer the questions about her evaluation.

Mr. Davis: Amy, have you looked over your performance evaluation?

Amy: Yes, I have.

Mr. Davis: Let's talk about several of these areas. Please notice that I checked *Requires Improvement* under *Appearance*. Do you know what that's about?

Amy: Yes, my nails.

Mr. Davis: You promised at your job interview that you would keep them shorter and paint them only one color.

Amy: I forgot. I really like them long.

Mr. Davis: Amy, people are looking at your nails, not our jewelry. It's distracting when your nails are striped or black with gold stars or whatever color or design you come in with each week. I'd like you to keep them shorter and one color.

Amy: OK.

Mr. Davis: Amy, you have an eye for color and design. You've shown some real initiative on our displays. You have some creative ideas for our jewelry displays and our counters have never looked so attractive. And you've done a wonderful job in our front window. Many of the customers have commented on how nice it looks. Have you ever thought of studying art or design?

Amy: Sometimes. It's my favorite part of the job.

Mr. Davis: You've been helpful with the customers and your sales are average. I think at times you could use more effective sales techniques. If a customer seems to like a necklace, be more complimentary. Say, "That looks really nice with your hair color," or "That would look perfect with a black evening dress."

Amy: I'll try.

Mr. Davis: Amy, you've had one serious problem—taking messages. When you answer the phone, you've taken the wrong information several times. For example, you've written down incorrect phone numbers and wrong addresses. This has caused problems because I haven't been able to return calls.

Amy: I'm not too good on the phone.

Mr. Davis: From now on, I want you to repeat everything back to the caller to double-check all the information. Do you have any comments on your evaluation?

Amy: No. I really enjoy working here.

Unit 10: Regrets and Possibilities

Page 149

B. Listen and complete.

1. I bought a used car. I should have bought a new one.
2. I didn't buy a new car. I shouldn't have bought a used one.
3. She didn't study for the test. She should have studied harder.
4. I registered for six courses. I shouldn't have registered for so many courses.
5. I left too late for the airport. I should have left earlier.
6. I didn't have a photo ID. I should have remembered to bring it.
7. Their car ran out of gas. They should have filled the tank.
8. He got a ticket for driving without a license. He shouldn't have driven without a license.

9. The electric company charged us a late fee. We should have sent the check on time.

10. She forgot to bring her homework. She shouldn't have forgotten it.

Page 152

A. Listen to a man calling 911 to report a problem in his apartment. Choose from the box below, and write the letter of the correct deduction on the space provided.

1. I came home and found my lock broken and my door open.
2. My stereo is missing.
3. The window's open, but I'm sure I locked it when I left.
4. My cat has been hiding under the bed, and he won't come out.
5. A steak is missing, and there are dirty dishes on the table.
6. My favorite suit is missing.
7. My large suitcase is missing and so are some of my shirts.
8. I found a pair of gloves on the floor.

Page 153

C. Pronunciation: Word Stress. Listen to the conversation and underline the stressed words.

A: <u>Hi</u>, Julia. <u>Why</u> didn't you <u>come</u> to my <u>party</u>? Everyone <u>missed</u> you.
B: <u>What</u> party?
A: I had a <u>party</u> last <u>Saturday</u>.
B: You should've <u>called</u> me.
A: I <u>did</u>. I left a <u>message</u> on your <u>machine</u>.
B: I <u>changed</u> my <u>number</u>. You could've <u>sent</u> an <u>invitation</u>.
A: I <u>did</u>. I <u>mailed</u> it <u>two weeks</u> ago.
B: You must've <u>sent</u> it to the <u>wrong address</u>. I <u>moved three weeks</u> ago.
A: You should've <u>told</u> me.
B: <u>Sorry</u>. Anyway, how was the <u>party</u>?
A: It was <u>fun</u>. You should've <u>been</u> there.

Page 156

The Big Picture: In the Counselor's Office

A. Mr. Dellaventura is the school counselor at Plains High School. Students come to see him when they have academic or personal problems. Sometimes the teachers send students to see him. Other times, the students come to see him on their own. Listen to Mr. Dellaventura counsel two students. Take notes in the spaces provided.

Conversation 1

Mr. D.: Come in, Amber. Have a seat. You look upset.
Amber: Well, you know I am the editor of the school newspaper.
Mr. D.: I know. The paper's been very good this year.
Amber: Thank you. I work very hard on it.
Mr. D.: Why did you come see me today?
Amber: The vice principal took away my job! I'm not the editor anymore! I need that job for my college applications! How am I going to get into college now?
Mr. D.: Hold on, hold on. Do you know why he did that?
Amber: I don't know. I'm the best writer on the staff!
Mr. D.: You must have some idea why he did that.
Amber: I guess he's punishing me.
Mr. D.: Punishing you? Why would he do that?
Amber: I think he's upset because I wrote a story that wasn't true about the football team.
Mr. D.: Now, Amber, why did you do that?
Amber: I was upset at my boyfriend. He's the captain of the football team. He had just broken up with me.
Mr. D.: You must have been very upset.
Amber: Yes, I was.
Mr. D.: So, do you think the vice principal should've punished you for printing incorrect information? The team must've been very upset, too.
Amber: I know. Yeah, I guess I shouldn't have done that. I shouldn't have used the paper to get back at him.
Mr. D.: It sounds like you're sorry. I'll talk to the vice principal. Maybe he'll just suspend you for one issue.
Amber: Thanks, Mr. D.

Conversation 2

Mr. D.: The last time we talked, Miguel, your classes were not going well.
Miguel: You can say that again. I was failing everything.
Mr. D.: We talked about the people you could've asked for help and the things you should've done to improve. Do you want to talk about that today?
Miguel: Yeah. I'm doing a little better. I got a C+ in math last semester.

Mr. D.: Your instructor must've been pleased.

Miguel: She was.

Mr. D.: Did you see a tutor?

Miguel: No, I didn't. I could've, but when I talked to my math instructor, she volunteered to give me some extra help. She also showed me a computer program in the learning center that could help me.

Mr. D.: Great. Now, how about your English class? Have your grades improved?

Miguel: Well, you know I can speak very easily, but writing's really hard for me.

Mr. D.: Do you go to the writing center for tutoring?

Miguel: I've been once.

Mr. D.: That's not enough, Miguel.

Miguel: I know, but I didn't like the tutor.

Mr. D.: Now, Miguel, there must've been another tutor who could've helped you.

Miguel: Yeah, I guess I'll go back and try again. By the way, I got the part-time job at the bookstore. Thanks for telling me about it.

Mr. D.: How's the job?

Miguel: Great! I have to work two nights a week and all day on Saturday. I get discounts on everything. It's easy. I help customers find books and other things.

Mr. D.: That's wonderful, Miguel.

Miguel: Thanks, Mr. D. I couldn't have gotten the job without your help.

Mr. D.: That's my job, Miguel. Now, go to the writing center.

Unit 11: Let's Get Organized

Page 167

B. Listen to Sergio talk about the things he wants to accomplish today. As you listen, write a to-do list for Sergio.

It's Saturday, and I don't work on Saturdays. I work Sundays, so I need to get a lot accomplished today. Let's see, I'm supposed to get an extra key for the house. My son lost his key and he needs to have one. I go to school and I have homework. I have about an hour's homework. And I promised to install the new DVD player. We bought the DVD player last week, but I haven't had time to connect it to the TV. My wife said she would take the kids to the video store and they would rent a movie for tonight. It's a nice day today, not too hot, a good day to wax the car. I haven't waxed it for about six months and it needs it. And let's see . . . My son—he's in fifth grade—needs to go to the library, so I'm going to drive him over there. He needs to find a few books about the planets for a class report. My daughter is on a soccer team. She's playing in the park today, so all of us are going to watch her at 2:00. And my wife's birthday is next week. I'd like a little time to shop for her. What should I buy her? Maybe a new watch?

Page 172

The Big Picture: The First Test

A. Diana started college last month. Her first math test is tomorrow. Diana is supposed to be studying for her test now. Listen to her telephone conversations.

[Phone ringing]

Diana: Hi, Susan.

Susan: Hi, Diana. What are you doing?

Diana: I'm supposed to be studying for my math test.

Susan: That's tomorrow, right?

Diana: Right. I'm not really worried. I understood everything in class.

Susan: Well, good luck. I can't talk now. I'm writing this English paper.

Diana: The one about cities and pollution?

Susan: Yeah. I'm in the middle of it. I'll call you tomorrow.

Diana: OK.

[Knock on door.]

Diana: Hi, Dad.

Dad: Hi, Diana. Studying for that math test?

Diana: I'm going to start in a few minutes.

Dad: You're great at math. You'll do well.

Diana: I hope so.

Dad: Remember to clean this room. How can you find anything in here?

Diana: Don't worry, Dad.

[Sound of Diana dialing. Phone ringing.]

Diana: Jacob? You at work?

Jacob: Uh-huh. I'm getting off in an hour. I can't come over tonight.

Diana: I won't see you?!

Jacob: No, I've got this science homework to finish. You know, that lab report. How's it going with your math?

Diana: I'm going to start to study in a few minutes.

Jacob: Why don't you go over to the math center at school? It's quiet there.

Diana: Maybe.

Jacob: Well, I'll see you tomorrow night. How about 8:00? After I get out of work?

Diana: That's good. Ciao.

Jacob: Bye.

[Sound of phone ringing]

Diana: Hi.

Alex: Diana, it's Alex.

Diana: Hi, Alex. Are you still at school?

Alex: Uh-huh. I'm here with Carlos and Mia. We're at the library now and we're studying for the math test tomorrow.

Why don't you come over here and study with us? This math is really difficult and it's helpful to work together.

Diana: I don't know. I think I'll study alone this time.

Alex: If you want to meet before class, we could go over a few of the problems.

Diana: OK. The test is at 10:00. Can we meet in the cafeteria at 9:00?

Alex: Sure. See you then.

[Sound of phone ringing.]

Diana: Hello.

Katie: Hi, Diane. It's me, Katie. I'm going to the mall. There's having a big sale on shoes at Gabby's. Wan't to come?

Diana: A shoe sale? You know, I need a pair of black boots.

Katie: I'm getting in my car now. I'll pick you up in ten minutes. OK?

Diana: I have a math test tomorrow. I really should study.

Katie: Don't worry. We won't stay that long. I'll see you in a few minutes.

Diana: Well, sure.

Unit 12: Becoming a Citizen

Page 180

A. **New citizens.** Listen to Marco and Luciana's story about becoming citizens of the United States.

Marco came to the United States in 1990 when he was 24. Ten years passed and during those 10 years, Marco leaned English, changed jobs four times, met Luciana, and got married. In 2000, life was still busy, but Marco and his wife began to think about becoming citizens. Their children had been born in the United States and were citizens already. Marco knew he had a good life and a good job. He was going to visit his native country from time to time, but he was not going to return there to live.

Marco and his wife obtained their naturalization papers from the INS (Immigration and Naturalization Service) and carefully completed the paperwork. They sent all the required documents and check(s) to their local INS Regional Service Center. They knew they would have to wait six months to a year to hear from the INS.

While waiting for their appointments, Marco and Luciana studied for their citizenship test. Ten months later, they received an appointment for their citizenship interview and English test. The immigration officer spoke to Marco in English and asked him a few questions about United States history. He also asked Marco to write a few sentences in English. Before having her interview, Luciana was very nervous because her English was not strong. The interviewer spoke slowly and asked her to name the president, the vice president, and the governor of the state. She had no problems with those questions or with writing three sentences in English.

Three months later, Marco and Luciana received their approval letters. At their swearing-in ceremony, one hundred men and women from thirty different countries recited the Oath of Allegiance to the United States together, and then, they signed the oath. They received a copy of a letter from the president of the United States, congratulating them and telling them about their rights and responsibilities as citizens.

Page 181

A. Listen to these sentences about Marco and Luciana. Fill in the gerund you hear.

1. Marco and Luciana discussed becoming citizens.
2. They delayed starting the process because Luciana's English was not strong.
3. Luciana regretted not beginning English classes earlier.
4. She began studying English at a local adult school.
5. A friend recommended enrolling in a citizenship class.
6. They didn't mind taking class one night a week.
7. Marco and Luciana enjoyed learning about U.S. history.
8. They practiced asking one another questions.
9. Luciana couldn't help feeling nervous before the test.

Page 187

B. Listen: Citizenship decisions. Listen to each of these immigrants speak about citizenship. Then, answer the questions. Many include a gerund or an infinitive.

A: My wife and I decided to come to the United States because of the opportunities here. Before coming, I was concerned about finding a job. I was lucky. I'm good at fixing things and I was able to find a job as a mechanic at a service station. My life is good here. I appreciate having a nice apartment and a car. I can afford to send my daughter to piano lessons. And we're able to take a vacation to the beach every summer. I'm thinking about becoming a citizen. My life is here, my family is here, my work is here. I'm not going back to my country. As a matter of fact, I want to sponsor my brother. I'm encouraging him to come here and work with me.

B: I've been living in the United States for 20 years. I'm from India and I love my country. I enjoy traveling back to visit my brother and sisters and their families. It's comfortable to walk around my hometown, speak my language, and see my old friends. I've been dreaming about retiring back in India. But now I'm not sure. My children are in the United States, and they plan on staying here. Part of my life is here, and part of my life is in India. I'm sure you know how I feel.

D. Listen to Martin talk about becoming a citizen. Then, complete the questions.

I came to the United States when I was only 20 years old. For me, it was easy to learn English and make friends. I was able to go to college and now I work in an accounting firm. At my office, people enjoy talking about politics and everything that is happening in the world. One of my friends encouraged me to become a citizen. He said I always had strong opinions about everything here. As a citizen, I'd be able to vote. It wasn't difficult to apply for citizenship. I became a citizen last summer, and I was able to vote for the first time in the November elections.

Page 188

The Big Picture: Running a Campaign

B. Listen and retell the story about the local political campaign.

Manuel: Hi. My name's Manuel. I've been a citizen for a few years now, but I never thought that I would get involved in politics. In fact, I've always avoided getting involved. I vote in the major elections, but sometimes I forget to vote in the city elections. Let me tell you what happened. A few years ago, a new neighbor moved in. His name is John. He's a nice guy and a great neighbor. He's married, and he has three children—a boy and two girls— and so do I. My family and his have become very friendly. We barbecue together in the summer. Our children play together, our wives enjoy spending time together, and our families like taking vacations together. John is an entrepreneur. He has a very successful bookstore and community computer center. He hires high school and college students for the computer center. He also has senior citizen volunteers to read to young children three times a week at the bookstore. He has a good business and he provides a wonderful service for our community.

Well, there's an empty seat on the City Council, and John has decided to run for the seat. At first, he complained about spending so much time campaigning and shaking hands, but now he's looking forward to giving interviews and meeting other people in town. My wife, Andrea, is good at organizing people, so she has a group of neighbors and other volunteers at our house almost every night. They've been talking about having a voter registration drive. It's important to get the vote of everyone that we can. So, they're thinking about setting up registration tables in front of the library, the high school, the mall, and the supermarkets. We're not worried about spending too much money because John knows many people who have insisted on donating services like vans to get people to the polls on election day, envelopes for mailings, and printing services for signs.

John's wife, Kathy, is anticipating doing a lot of work for the campaign. She quit working temporarily in order to support John's campaign. Kathy's in charge of getting volunteers to make phone calls to voters. She's reminding people to vote. Our children are interested in helping, too. They're making signs and stuffing envelopes.

And I surprised myself. I'm interested in helping John write his speeches. Back in my country, I was very involved in local politics, but until now, I've haven't been involved here. Now I'm enjoying helping John practice for next month's debate. I am pretending to be one of his opponents or one of the reporters who will be asking John the tough questions.

A campaign is a lot of work, but it's worthwhile, too.

Unit 13: Business and Industry

Page 201

A. Listen and write the questions. Then, look at the product map of a few Asian countries and write the answers to the questions.
1. Where are electronics manufactured?
2. Where is rice grown?
3. Which country is known for manufacturing automobiles?
4. What food products are grown in Thailand?
5. Where is clothing manufactured?
6. Where are coconuts exported from?
7. Where are financial services offered?
8. What minerals are found in China?

Page 204

The Big Picture: T-shirts—From the Field to Your Closet

A. Talk about the pictures. Then, listen and take notes on the pictures.
1. The top three cotton producers in the world are China, the United States, and India. China is the top cotton producer of the three.
2. In China, the cotton is picked by hand. Then, it is sent to a ginner where it is cleaned. The cleaned cotton is put into bales and the quality is decided.
3. The bales are sold to large plants or factories called spinners. At the spinners, the cotton is put on spools. The spools are put on knitting machines and the cotton is made into cotton fabric.
4. The cotton fabric is sent to a dye house. At the dye house, only 20 percent is dyed different colors. The remaining 80 percent is processed white.
5. The fabric is sent to a sewing plant. At the plant, patterns are cut. Then, the pieces are sewn by workers on a line. One worker sews the sleeves, another sews the neck, another does the shoulders, and the last one hems the bottom.
6. The T-shirts are folded and packaged. The T-shirts are sent to printers, where a logo is transferred or embroidered onto the t-shirt. At this stage, the T-shirt only costs about $3.
7. The finished T-shirts are shipped to warehouses. Because of many costs, including shipping, warehouse space, and inventory, the T-shirt price is increased.
8. The T-shirts are sold to a department store at an over 200 percent increase to $14. The store immediately doubles the price to $28. The store also has many costs, such as paying for sales help, insurance, and advertising. The T-shirt is marked and offered for sale for $28.
9. After two to three weeks, store customers have bought many of the shirts. Now, not all colors and sizes are available. The store advertises a 15 percent to 25 percent sale. After two more weeks, the price will be decreased again. Finally, after six weeks, any leftover T-shirts will be sent to discount stores. The price may be reduced to $14 or less.

Unit 14: Technology Today

Page 212

A. Listen to this information about inventions in the late twentieth century. After you listen, write the name of the inventor or company under each invention.

People have always seen problems and tried to invent a way to solve them. In the late twentieth century, single individuals continued to invent helpful devices and machines. Many of the inventions have become so complex that groups of researchers or companies work together to design and manufacture them.

The first anti-shoplifting tag was invented in 1965 by Arthur Minasy. These tags made it difficult for people to steal items from a store.

In the late 1960s, the Boeing Company began to develop plans for a jumbo jet to carry more than three hundred people. The first 747 was built in 1970.

The first video games were invented by Ralph Baer. These first games were very simple, not like the colorful realistic games of today. Baer is called the "Godfather of Video Games."

The artificial heart was designed by Robert Jarvick in 1978. It was developed to keep a patient alive while waiting for a heart transplant.

In 1980, a hepatitis B vaccine was developed by Baruch Blumberg. Hepatitis B is a disease that attacks the liver and is often fatal. Today, hepatitis B vaccines are required by most public schools and colleges.

Roller blades were designed by Scott Olson and his brother Brennan. Instead of having four wheels, positioned like the wheels on a car, the wheels were placed in a line. This is why roller blades are also called in-line skates.

NASA is the National Aeronautics and Space Administration. The first space shuttle was launched by NASA in 1981. It orbited the globe in less than two hours.

Many engineers and researchers were involved in the invention of the personal computer. The first personal computers were manufactured by IBM in 1981.

The first minivan was designed and built by Chrysler Corporation in 1983. The minivan was designed to be a family car and was an immediate success.

The laptop computer was invented by Sir Clive Sinclair in 1987. Today, laptop computers are slowly replacing desktop computers in popularity.

The digital camera is another invention that involved many people and ideas. One of the first easy-to-use digital camera was introduced by Apple Computer in 1994.

The disposable cell phone was invented by Randi Altschul in 1999. Do you have this new invention?

Page 219

B. Listen to Hui-Fen describe school in Taiwan. Then, answer the questions.

I am from Taiwan. I was born in Taiwan in 1963 and raised in the capital, that's Taipei. I attended public school. Most students in Taiwan are educated in public school. School in Taiwan is very strict and we had to follow many rules. First, we were required to wear a uniform. The girls wore a blue skirt and white blouse and the boys wore blue pants and a white shirt. I couldn't have long hair. Girls had to keep their hair above their shoulders. And the boys could only have hair one inch long. Very short!

We studied very hard. We went to school from 9:00 to 4:30 and we were assigned about three hours of homework. If we didn't do our homework, we were punished. Maybe the teacher hit our hands with a stick or we had to stand with a book on our head. We were given exams in the middle of the year and at the end of the year.

Boys and girls studied in separate classes. The only time we were together was for after school clubs and activities. Boys and girls were not allowed to date in high school. We were not allowed to call one another on the phone, either. Students began to date in college.

In Taiwan, our native language is Taiwanese. It's a spoken language, not a written language. When we begin school, we are expected to study, talk, and learn in Chinese, which is a new language for us. This is very hard for the students, especially when they begin school. Also, when we are in middle school, English is taught as a foreign language. By the time we finish high school, we can speak Taiwanese, Chinese, and English.

Vacations in Taiwan are similar to the United States. School is closed for two months in the summer and we have a one-month winter vacation in January or February, around the time of the Chinese New Year.

Page 220

The Big Picture: Shopping

A. Look at the pictures and listen to a short history of some of the inventions and ideas that have made shopping easier.

For many years, shopping was a simple process. A person went into a small local store, bought an item, and paid in cash. Another popular way of shopping was to buy merchandise from a traveling salesman. Many people lived far from the city, so salesmen traveled around the country by horse and wagon, showing the customers their merchandise.

In 1872, a traveling salesman named Aaron Montgomery Ward, had an idea to help his customers see more of his merchandise. Ward decided to print a catalog with pictures of the items that his company sold. The customers could look through the catalog and order the items they wanted. The first mail-order catalog was printed in 1872 and became an immediate success. Catalogs are still a very popular way to shop.

Before 1884, clerks kept money in the store in a drawer or cash box. When a customer bought a product, the clerk wrote a receipt by hand. In 1884, the first cash register was invented by James Ritty. People could receive an immediate printed receipt.

In the 1900s, stores were becoming larger, especially grocery stores. Customers were buying more items at one time. The owner of one of these grocery stores, Sylvan Goldman, had an idea. He put two baskets and wheels on a folding chair and the first shopping cart was invented. Goldman formed a company to design larger and better shopping carts.

Up until this time, people paid for their purchases by cash or check. In 1950, the first credit card was issued. At first, credit cards were used by business travelers for restaurant and hotel bills. By the 1960s, many companies were offering these cards. People did not need to carry so much cash. They could buy items and pay later.

Another idea that was developing at this time was the idea of a bar code. At the time, stock clerks had to put a price on every item. The clerk rang up each item on the cash register, punching in the price of each item by hand. Store owners, especially the owners of large supermarkets, asked about a method of automatically reading information about products during checkout. Several inventors worked on the idea, but there was not a standard on how to identify each item. The Uniform Pricing Code, known as the U.P.C., was invented in 1973. In 1974, the first U.P.C. scanner was installed in a supermarket in Ohio. It was no longer necessary to put the price on every individual food item. Now supermarket checkers simply scan each item and the price appears on the register.

In the 1990s, another form of shopping became popular, online shopping. The Internet offers an inexpensive way for companies to advertise their products to a worldwide audience. Customers can look at pictures of products, check prices, and place their orders over the Internet. This has made shopping fast and convenient. Customers are able to easily compare prices from several different companies.

Can you think of other inventions and ideas that have made shopping easier? Can you think of an invention that would help you with your shopping?

Unit 15: Country Music

Page 230

B. Listen: Country music. Listen to the history of country music. Then, circle *True* or *False*.

The people who first sang the country sound in the United States lived over a hundred years ago in the Appalachian Mountains. These people sang all the time—while they were working, while they were doing laundry, while they were at church, or while they were taking care of their babies. People used to sing to make the work go faster. The music that they sang was very simple.

The music, which is called country music, came from the British Isles: Scotland, Ireland, England, and Wales. The people who immigrated to the United States moved to a land that was similar to their homeland. These people brought their music with them.

Two instruments were common in country music bands. The five-string banjo, which came from Africa, became popular in country music in the 1920s. The fiddle, which had early roots in Nashville, was the main instrument in country music until the 1930s. The fiddler, who carried the melody of the songs, was usually the main performer in country music bands. Banjos and fiddles are still popular in country music today, but other instruments such as electric guitars and keyboards, are also used. Jimmy Rodgers and the Carter family, who first recorded in 1927, became the first superstars of country music.

Page 236

The Big Picture: Fan Fair

B. Listen to the history of the world's biggest country music festival. Take notes of dates, numbers, and places.

Like other types of music, country music has loyal fans. But, different from other types of music, country music fans have an opportunity to meet many of their favorite performers in person. Every June, approximately one hundred and twenty-five thousand country music fans go to Nashville, Tennessee, for Fan Fair.

Over 30 years ago, there was an annual country music disc-jockey, or DJ, convention in Nashville. Many country performers used to attend the convention to promote their projects. Fans would go to Nashville hoping to see their favorite performers. Eventually, so many fans began showing up in Nashville that the Country Music Association and the Grand Ole Opry decided to have a festival just for the fans at a different time. Fan Fair was born.

The first Fan Fair was held in April 1972, in Nashville for four days. Some of country music's biggest stars attended. Booths were set up so that fans could take pictures with their favorite singers and get autographs. There was live entertainment, and barbecue and beverages. About fifty thousand fans

attended. The first Fan Fair was so successful that planning began almost immediately for 1973. The date was changed to June, when the weather would be better. Over one hundred thousand fans attended the second Fan Fair.

Every year brought so many performers and fans to Fan Fair that, in 1982, it was moved to the Tennessee State Fairgrounds. Fan Fair stayed at the fairgrounds for another nineteen years.

One of the reasons that Fan Fair has stayed popular is because of the unexpected. In 1974, former Beatle Paul McCartney attended. In 1996, Garth Brooks, who made a surprise appearance, signed autographs for 23 hours. In 1992, more than six hundred reporters from Europe, Asia, and South America went to cover the appearance of a popular star, Billy Ray Cyrus, who had introduced a new country line dance. Movie and television stars and professional athletes have also visited Fan Fair. When a popular football star attended, even some of the country performers got in line for his autograph.

In 2001, Fan Fair returned to downtown Nashville as the World's Biggest Country Music Festival. But, the biggest crowd attended Fan Fair 2002. Over one hundred and twenty-five thousand fans attended to see some of the 445 performers.

As you can imagine, fans who want to attend Fan Fair must plan ahead. They can buy tickets online or by telephone as early as seven months ahead of time. The ticket packages include four days of live performances. Every year there are new surprises and activities for the fans, which keep them coming back year after year.

Irregular Verbs

Simple form	Simple past	Past participle	Simple form	Simple past	Past participle
be	was/were	been	lay	laid	laid
bear	bore	born	leave	left	left
become	became	become	lend	lent	lent
begin	began	begun	lose	lost	lost
blow	blew	blown	make	made	made
break	broke	broken	meet	met	met
bring	brought	brought	pay	paid	paid
build	built	built	prove	proved	proven
buy	bought	bought	put	put	put
catch	caught	caught	quit	quit	quit
choose	chose	chosen	read	read	read
come	came	come	ride	rode	ridden
cut	cut	cut	rise	rose	risen
dig	dug	dug	run	ran	run
do	did	done	say	said	said
drink	drank	drunk	see	saw	seen
drive	drove	driven	sell	sold	sold
eat	ate	eaten	send	sent	sent
fall	fell	fallen	set	set	set
feel	felt	felt	sew	sewed	sewn
fight	fought	fought	show	showed	shown
find	found	found	sing	sang	sung
fly	flew	flown	sit	sat	sat
forbid	forbade	forbidden	sleep	slept	slept
forget	forgot	forgotten	speak	spoke	spoken
get	got	got/gotten	spend	spent	spent
give	gave	given	split	split	split
go	went	gone	steal	stole	stolen
grow	grew	grown	stick	stuck	stuck
hang	hung	hung	sweep	swept	swept
have	had	had	take	took	taken
hear	heard	heard	teach	taught	taught
hit	hit	hit	tell	told	told
hold	held	held	think	thought	thought
hurt	hurt	hurt	understand	understood	understood
keep	kept	kept	wear	wore	worn
know	knew	known	win	won	won

Skills Index

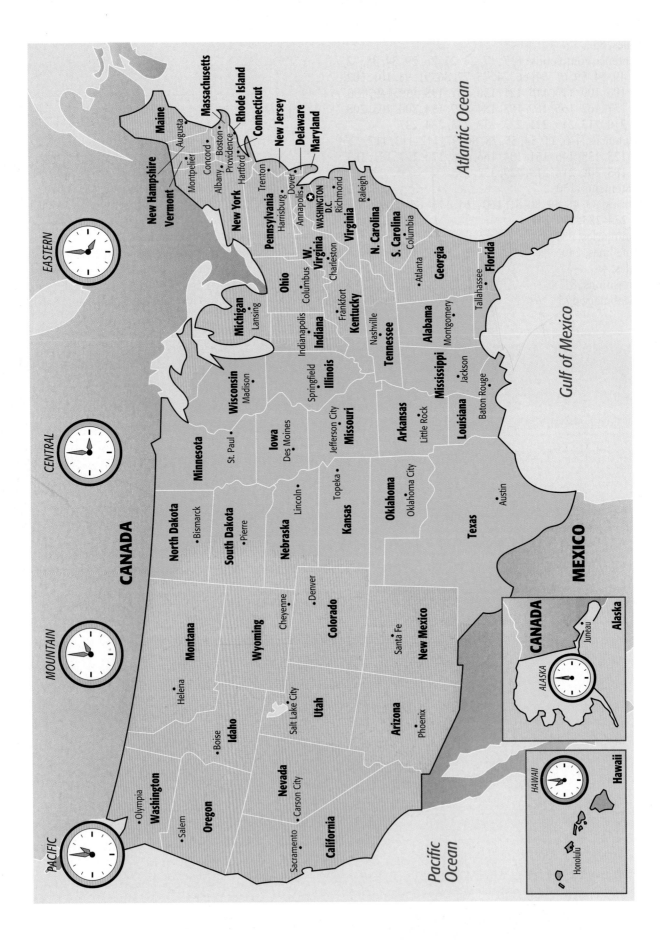